THE LIFE OF
SISTER MARIE
DE MANDAT-GRANCEY
AND
MARY'S HOUSE
IN EPHESUS

THE LIFE OF
SISTER MARIE
DE MANDAT-GRANCEY

AND

MARY'S HOUSE
IN EPHESUS

Reverend Carl G. Schulte, C.M.

TAN Books
Charlotte, North Carolina

Nihil Obstat: Reverend Matthew Bartulica
                 Censor Deputatus

Imprimatur: ✠Most Reverend Robert W. Finn
             Bishop of Kansas City-St. Joseph
             December 22, 2010

The Nihil Obstat and Imprimatur are a declaration that a book or pamphlet is considered to be free from doctrinal or moral error. It is not implied that those who granted the Nihil Obstat and Imprimatur agree with the contents, opinions, or statements expressed therein.

ISBN: 978-0-89555-870-1

Cover design by Tony Pro.

Cover image: *(top)* Sr. Marie de Mandat-Grancey, *(bottom)* the restored house of Mary in Ephesus.

Photographs courtesy of the de Mandat-Grancey Family, the Vincentian Community, and Erin von Uffel.

Printed and Bound in the United States of America.

TAN Books
Charlotte, North Carolina
2011

The Year 2010 marked the 350th Anniversary
Of the deaths of
Saint Louise de Marillac, March 15
and
Saint Vincent de Paul, September 27.

The Foundation of Sister Marie de Mandat-Grancey,
On the Feast of the Assumption of the Blessed Virgin Mary,
Gratefully gives to Sister Evelyne Franc,
The successor of Saint Louise,
*The Life of Sr. Marie de Mandat-Grancey and
Mary's House in Ephesus,*
The first published biography of
Servant of God Sister Marie de Mandat-Grancey, D.C.
Which the author dedicates to
Every Daughter of Charity in the World.

Contents

Foreword

TODAY we celebrate the feast of a young woman whose *fiat* opened her completely to God's will so that the Word could become flesh and dwell among us.

The Life of Sr. Marie de Mandat-Grancey and Mary's House in Ephesus is the story of another faith-filled woman in the Vincentian Family, Sister Marie de Mandat-Grancey, who lived in the post-French Revolution era. This Daughter of Charity embraced a life of service to find Christ, the Word Made Flesh, in those who were poor. During the first twenty-five years of her ministry, she responded to God's call by caring for the homebound, educating children, accompanying youth in their spiritual journey, and finding families for orphaned children.

In 1886, Sister Marie was sent to Smyrna, near Ephesus, Turkey, where she entered a world very different from her own. While serving in the hospital there, Sister Marie read and shared with her own Sisters and the local Vincentian priests *The Life of the Blessed Virgin,* which recorded the events of Mary's last years spent in Ephesus in a house built for her by St. John. Because of Sister Marie's great devotion to the Blessed Mother, she was determined to find this sacred spot.

Through collaboration with her Vincentian brothers, local Muslim guides, and the people of the area, Mary's house was found; but the discovery was just the beginning. Once rebuilt, Mary's House became a place where Muslims and Christians assembled in peace side by side as they came to honor Mary; pilgrims continue to journey there today. We are most grateful for the yes of Father Carl Schulte, C.M., whose research and writing opens the door to the world of Sister Marie de Mandat-Grancey and calls us to consider how our own *fiat* can make a difference to others, particularly to those who are poor.

Reverend G. Gregory Gay III, C.M.
Superior General
Congregazione Della Missione
Curia Generalizia
Feast of the Annunciation, 2011

Preface

THOSE of us who enjoy and value spiritual books, including devout history and biography, are not often accustomed to being intrigued or excited by our books. Such books may be important and edifying in many ways, but they are rarely exciting. *The Life of Sr. Marie de Mandat-Grancey and Mary's House in Ephesus* is an exception. I found its account of the discovery of the House of Mary outside of the ruins of Ephesus to be absolutely fascinating, and I'm sure many other readers will feel the same way.

This book deals with a small, seemingly insignificant structure, one that in the scheme of things should have little real importance. Yet, in reality, this little house may be among the most important structures from the ancient world that we know about, for it may be the little home in which the Blessed Mother lived on earth after the Ascension and before she was taken up into Heaven by her divine Son. It is interesting that initially the Vincentian experts who considered the prospect of looking for Mary's House dismissed the fact that her home could exist in Ephesus at all. Almost built into the side of the mountain near the ruins of Ephesus, it was a popular belief among the locals, but there was no hard evidence.

However, with the private revelations granted to Blessed Anne Catherine Emmerich, who was beatified in 2004, this began to change. This stigmatist and mystical nun had written a life of the

Virgin Mary. In it she described the house in which Mary lived exactly as she had seen it in her visions. Although few people paid much attention to this at the time, when people finally examined the area around what had come to be called "the House of Mary," as well as the house itself, and compared them with Blessed Anne Catherine's description of her visions, they were astonished to find that there was a startling similarity between the two. At that point Blessed Anne Catherine had certainly not been to Ephesus to see the area. In fact, very few people from Western Europe would have had the opportunity to see it. Even a number of people with scientific backgrounds were astonished at the accuracy of Blessed Anne Catherine's descriptions—not only of the foundations of this ancient building but also of the geography of the immediate area. This certainly gives much food for thought.

From the outset, however, there was one person, a Daughter of Charity of Saint Vincent de Paul, Sister Marie de Mandat-Grancey, who firmly believed that Ephesus was the final earthly home of Our Lady. In fact, from the moment Sister Marie read Blessed Anne Catherine's descriptions she became absolutely certain. When she was providentially assigned only a short distance from where the House of Mary stood, Sister Marie became convinced that the house would indeed be found.

Her original attempts to enlist the assistance of the local Vincentians met with little success, as they were opposed to the idea of searching for something based only on the descriptions of a mystic. Sister Marie, however, would not give up and ultimately convinced the Vincentians that her cause was worthwhile. The investigation began and eventually Vincentian Father Eugene Poulin became internationally recognized for arguing convincingly that the little house in Ephesus was, in fact, Mary's Home and the place from which she was assumed into Heaven. It was Sister Marie, through the help of her aristocratic family, who eventually obtained possession of Mary's House at Ephesus in order to preserve it for all mankind.

Popular interest in the House of Mary has grown over the years. There are now several replicas of it in various places around the world. Such unlikely places as Jamaica, Vermont; Buenos Aires, Argentina; Medjugorje, Bosnia-Herzegovina; Natividade, Brazil; and Eindhoven, The Netherlands, all currently have such replicas, and more in other places are being planned. People have become fascinated by the possibility of seeing the place in which the Blessed Mother lived and possibly ended her life on earth. (Although her life on earth ended, we must recall that we do not really know if it ended in death as we know it or not. Even when Pope Pius XII solemnly defined the doctrine of the Assumption of Our Lady, how her earthly life ended was not defined. There is a long tradition that states that although Our Lady did not have to suffer natural death, she chose to imitate her Son. This, however, remains undefined by the Church; perhaps her days on earth ended in a different way, a way unique and befitting the Mother of God. Instead of saying that Mary died we simply say that she fell asleep. In the Christian East, the holy day we call the Assumption is called the Dormition—the falling asleep of Mary.) Earlier tradition said that Mary's earthly life came to an end in Jerusalem, which seems to make much sense. In Jerusalem you can still see the alleged tomb of Mary, in which it is said that she was laid before her Assumption into Heaven. Which is really right? We cannot know, but Father Schulte makes a fascinating and convincing case that Mary lived in Ephesus. In fact, the whole book is an absolutely fascinating study. Not only those who are devoted to the Blessed Virgin Mary but those who are interested in early Christian history will find it very rewarding.

Archbishop Giuseppe Bernardini, OFM Cap, the retired archbishop of Izmir (ancient Smyrna) has lent his support to studies on the House of Mary at Ephesus and to the life of Sister Marie, as have other clergy and laity. This book will give a great many readers the opportunity to grow. It gives an experience that involves adventure, history, archeology, and insight into possible mystical happenings. And most importantly, it fulfills Sister Marie's lifelong dream—it brings us a little closer to our Blessed Mother.

Reverend Benedict Groeschel, CFR

Worldwide replicas of Mary's House.

Author's Preface

EACH generation has the privilege of building on the Body of Christ. Sister Marie gives us a very brief account of her inspired contributions in her pre-teen years just prior to receiving her First Holy Communion. You will find them at the beginning of several chapters in this book. They are the product of her young and faith-filled heart along with the teaching accorded to her by her mother, father, grandfather, and selected tutors. Some of Sister Marie's other teachers were indeed saints.

Two teachers who contributed greatly to her lifelong commitment to Christ are Saint Vincent de Paul and Saint Louise de Marillac, even though they preceded her by a couple of hundred years. They left a way of life for her to follow. Father Vincent had acquired a great reputation and respect that attracted the attention of most everyone who came into his sphere of activity; king or archbishop, banker or pauper. Through his prayer life he was able to find Jesus Christ in the poor, the sick, the lonely, the hungry, and even in the forgotten. This insight derived from prayer changed Saint Vincent's entire lifestyle and approach to work. He was always ready to serve whomever God did send. Finding the depth of his spirituality most inviting, people said of him, "Father Vincent is always Father Vincent." He was simple in his approach and he said of himself, "My gospel is simplicity."

It was this direct simplicity that Saint Vincent employed in guiding people. He responded with utmost generosity to a bishop's request that he give spiritual guidance to a young woman in need of someone who was both kind and challenging. We know her today as Saint Louise de Marillac. The two of them—Saint Vincent and Saint Louise—eventually became the Founders of the Daughters of Charity, a newly formed type of religious life. Its membership was the first in Church history to live outside a monastery. They dressed like girls who lived in the country. They worked among the poor. They carried soup pots to the homes of the sick. They also became the fastest growing community of religious women in an extremely short period of time.

Saint Vincent and Saint Louise were God-sent and treasured teachers to Sister Marie and although they were not physically present to her, their conferences and directives were available for study and discussion by the new postulants. These first Daughters were absorbed into the spirit that existed among them and they were tempered by the conferences given by Saint Vincent himself. Copies were made of the conferences so they could be preserved and passed among the membership. As the Daughters absorbed the spirit of them, they in turn became teachers to the next group of recruits. That practice continues to this day.

An unknown member of the Daughters of Charity, a person who resided at Rue du Bac a few years ahead of her, also became a memorable teacher of Sister Marie. No one was told who she was. The lesson she taught came through the Director of the Daughters of Charity. The Archbishop of Paris had been told about this particular sister, saying that the Virgin Mary had appeared to a Daughter of Charity in the chapel of their motherhouse on Rue du Bac. The Blessed Virgin had appeared in the same chapel where Sister Marie now prayed. Sister Marie received the news, and with the other sisters, she also received a new medal designed according to the revelation given to this unnamed Daughter of Charity. Today of course we know this Daughter of Charity as none other than Saint Catherine Labouré. The medal, which came to be known as the Miraculous Medal, was a pictorial remembrance of the Immaculate Conception of the Virgin Mary made at the request of Mother Mary herself. In the same apparition, the Blessed Virgin Mary also requested that Saint Catherine's spiritual director form the Children of Mary. Sister Marie would take this lesson to prayer and to heart. The Daughters of Charity had been given a special gift to share with the world. With this, Sister Marie's love for Our Lady deepened as did her commitment to the Children of Mary whom she continued to serve with great devotion for the rest of her life. As you will learn in the coming pages, a half-century later, the Blessed Mother bestows upon Sister Marie de Mandat-Grancey, another member of the Daughters of Charity, the great privilege of uncovering the Blessed Virgin's last home on earth, which she occupied prior to her Dormition and Assumption into Heaven.

The spirit that was given to these earliest Daughters was one of simplicity. They were God's servants. What they were supposed to do as good Daughters was voiced by Saint Vincent himself during his last illness. A young Sister Jeanne was being sent on her first visit to the poor. She was asked to visit Father Vincent for his blessing and advice. He rose from his last sick bed and came to visit her and this is what he said:

> You will find that charity is a heavy burden to carry, greater than the kettle of soup and the basket of bread. But you must keep your gentleness and your smile. Giving soup and bread isn't all. That the rich can do. You are the little servant of the poor, the maid of charity, always

smiling and in good humor. They are your masters, terribly sensitive and exacting as you will see; but the uglier and the dirtier they are, the more unjust and bitter, the more you must give them of your love. It is only because of your love, only your love, that the poor will forgive you the bread you give them.

Reverend Carl Schulte, C.M.

Acknowledgments

The Life of Sr. Marie de Mandat-Grancey and Mary's House in Ephesus appears because of the extraordinary assistance of two persons: Erin von Uffel and Lorraine Fusaro. One day Sister Connie Boulch, a Franciscan Sister, handed me a prayer card, saying she had received it from Mother Thérese, a newly arrived Benedictine Sister of Ephesus. She was told that I occasionally made mention in a homily of something said or done by Saint Vincent de Paul or one of the Daughters of Charity. The prayer card she was giving me had a picture of Mary's Home with Sister Marie de Mandat-Grancey on it with a prayer seeking the beatification of the Sister Marie. I was stunned. For twelve years I had served as the Provincial Director of the Daughters of Charity of the Mater Dei (Mother of God) Province in Evansville, Indiana, and I had never heard anyone mention Sister Marie's name. Phone calls to several Daughters of Charity around the United States told me that I would have great difficulty finding anyone who knew of her. Mary's Home and Sister Marie were unknown to any of us, it seemed. I ordered one hundred more cards for distribution among the Daughters from two provinces who were to gather for a meeting. The cards vanished in five minutes.

Shortly after that a phone call from Erin von Uffel came, thanking me for interest shown in Sister Marie and promising more information about her was on its way. Erin, I soon learned, was a Promoter of the Cause for Beatification of Sister Marie. That was followed by a plea for assistance, particularly in publication. I offered to secure help for her from a Daughter of Charity or a Vincentian Father. After finding no assistance for Erin's needs, she pleaded for my help. I assured her I was old, unskilled, and retired. She did not hear me and came back with a plea; I felt compassion for her and submitted an agreement if she would introduce me to this unfamiliar sister. This Sister Marie had a wonderful life that should be made known in the Church.

Erin was most exact in fulfilling her pledge of seeking information for me to use. I soon learned she was a busy wife and mother of five grown boys in universities and high schools, and she was a ready speaker on Sister Marie at religious gatherings. Living in New York this refined lady was supporting me in Missouri by her daily prayers and occasional phone calls. Bit by bit we had a collection of materials, pamphlets, and a couple of books pertinent to the subject of Sister Marie and Mary's Home.

When the time came for me to make another revision of the text, she told her dear friend, Lorraine Fusaro, of my need for physical assistance as I was approaching eighty-nine years of age. Lorraine is a wife and the mother of six children and has a deep appreciation for her own spiritual life and that of her family. Both of these active Catholic women have fallen in love with Sister Marie. To them, I am indebted.

As this literary work was progressing one person after another came with assistance. Among them were Baron Jacques de Mandat-Grancey, the great-nephew of Sister Marie, with assistance on family matters; Sister Evelyne Franc, the Superioress General of the Daughters of Charity, and her secretary, Sister Ana Marie Olmeda; the late Vincentian archivist, Father Paul Henzmann, together with Father Hugh O'Donnell, helped with community information. Canonical law aid was given by Father Michael Joyce, C.M. Ephesus archival texts were made available through the Quatman family of the American Society of Ephesus. For translations, aid was given by Jannic and George Driscoll; Father Robert Cameron; Sister Judith Mausser, Daughter of Charity; Cathy Hershey; and Frances Bouton. Readings were made by the Franciscan Sisters Josephine Boyles and Dorothy Brownsberger. I express thanks to Sister Mary Beth Kubera, Daughter of Charity, for her editing assistance and to Sister Margaret John Kelly, Daughter of Charity; also to M. J. Cornelius, secretary of the Vincentian Parish Mission Center, Independence, Missouri, and Gabriele Koontz for supplying my daily household needs. I owe special gratitude to Sister Catherine Madigan, Daughter of Charity, who to measure the understanding of the text with young people outside the United States, shared with three classes of her postulants in Nairobi, Kenya, the texts as they were being developed. Thanks also to Frank Chau and Eric Strianese of F. Chau & Associates, LLC, who assisted with obtaining the copyright, and Paulette Kardos who assisted in providing us with documents.

It is with heartfelt gratitude that I thank the Vincentian confreres with whom I have lived during the time of developing *The Life of Sr. Marie de Mandat-Grancey and Mary's House in Ephesus*—particularly my local Superior, Father Richard Gielow, C.M., who has been most supportive in this work; his twin brother, Father Robert Gielow, as well as Father Thomas Cawley and Father Michael Mulhearn. Nor can I forget Father Richard O'Brien, who during this period of time was missioned to Saint Mary of the Barrens, Perryville, Missouri; and Father Frank Crowley, who helped with the establishment of the parish mission program and then bade us farewell as he went on his last mission to Heaven.

Introduction

DURING the last agonizing moments of His life while hanging on the Cross, Jesus said to His Mother, "Woman, there is your son," and to John, His disciple, "There is your Mother." The care of His Mother was the last gift Jesus gave us during His lifetime. In reflecting upon the wonderment of who Jesus is and what He gave us, Saint John summed it up in this simple evaluation: "God is Love." From then until now, this mystery has been repeatedly pondered as witnessed by Pope Benedict XVI's first encyclical: GOD IS LOVE.

Saint Vincent de Paul pondered it, too. It impelled him, along with a friendly nudge from Saint Louise de Marillac, to found the Company of the Daughters of Charity. These sisters would do what Jesus did by serving Him in others. They were not to live in a monastery but to live and labor among the needy. They were to find and serve Jesus in the person who was sick or suffering, hungry or thirsty, lonely or imprisoned, wounded or dying. It was to such a spirituality that Adele Louise Marie de Mandat-Grancey was called by God. She was called to do the Corporal Works of Mercy.

Adele Louise had no serious difficulty putting aside her nobility, when she became known as Sister Marie de Mandat-Grancey. She felt secure in her choice, believing that the grace which impelled her to become a Daughter of Charity was the same force which beckoned the Wise Men to go to Bethlehem "seeking Him who was born King of the Jews." She, too, came with open heart to serve Christ. During her first thirty years as a Daughter, she served Christ in healthcare, social services, and academic works. She met Him in the youth when she directed her first Children of Mary group. She felt His guiding hand in her administrative duties in school, orphanage, and sick room.

When Sister Marie was nearing fifty years of age, she felt like one of the Magi who was guided by the star, as she traveled east into a Muslim country to serve Jesus in the sick and suffering. There she manifested her trusting dependence upon divine guidance. It was in Turkey, while living and working in Smyrna, near Ephesus, that she was given the singular privilege of recovering the site of Mary's last home prior to her Assumption. Then Sister Marie had the privilege of rebuilding it as a Marian shrine. With utmost humility she fulfilled this honorable duty with the same self-effacing attitude that accompanied all her past apostolic activities. Each of them had been Christ-oriented.

THE LIFE OF
SISTER MARIE
DE MANDAT-GRANCEY

AND

MARY'S HOUSE
IN EPHESUS

Chapter One
A Noble Heritage

THIS is to introduce to you Sister Marie's mother, the Countess of Grancey, by way of a letter she penned to her father. Just then she had made one of the most important decisions in her life, agreeing with the choice made by her twenty-year-old daughter to enter religious life. Read it. You will see that she is a rather astute woman, a mother who knows her daughter very well. And then read it again and feel the pain she endured in the making of that agreement.

What made her decision so difficult was the fact that when a young lady entered the Daughters of Charity in that era, she never returned to her family home. The separation was permanent. Fortunately for Adele Louise Marie, the Countess had a deep spirituality, and she knew her daughter quite well. They both had strong convictions. Her letter was undated, but it was probably written on May 28, 1857.

Marie has written to you, dear Father, at the time she was leaving the house to go to the rue de Vaugirard. I hastened the departure so painful for all, to spare her any additional anguish, and I was right, I believe, at least it was the viewpoint of the Superior to whom she is entrusted. I visited her yesterday. She was very red, very over-excited. She had neither slept nor eaten. She was wearing the big white apron with a big bunch of keys and a big rosary. She had gotten up at 4:00 a.m., heard Mass at 6:00, swept the refectory, set the table, worked at the pharmacy, marked two shirts and spoken with two postulants her age who have been there for a few weeks. She will soon go to classes, starting with the last one and then will accompany the sisters on their visits to the poor and the sick. In short she will become initiated to the life of dedication, abnegation and hardships, because the Sisters of St. Vincent are not exempted of these. I am convinced her calling is sincere and will only strengthen itself over time. If God asks me for her I will give her to Him wholeheartedly, and that will be a handsome present, because with her fervor for goodness, her self control and her intelligence, she can serve Him gloriously and usefully. There are seventeen sisters in the house and the Superior is an angelical creature of great capability. She has always been in the house and is very good at building on callings. Her heart did not harden in that position with the Daughters of Charity, and she was as moved as I was the day before yesterday. Not only does she allow me, but she wishes me to see Marie every day, at the time I want. This might delay my departure a bit, and as you say so well, my return to Grancey alone with Leontine will be quite sad, despite the fact that Leontine will be more adorable than ever. . . .

Adele Louise Marie de Mandat-Grancey was born into one of the more distinguished noble families of France who lived and worked for the Church and the Country. The recorded nobility of Jeanne-Louise-Eugenie-Rachel de Cordouse wedded to Galliot-Marie-Francois-Ernest de Mandat, Comte and Comtesse of Grancey stretches back into the fourteenth century. In 1361, Eudes, the sire of Grancey, with his wife Mahner de Moyers, and their son Eudes, Sire of Pierpont, founded a Collegiate Chapel in Grancey, dedicated under the patronage of Saint John the Evangelist. It is adorned with a lovely stained-glass window, a gift of the children to their parents on the occasion of their Golden Wedding Anniversary. The window is a pictorial history of the family from 1361 to 1880. It reads:

> In the Year of our Lord 1880, on May 18, in honor of the 50th anniversary of the marriage of Galliot-Marie-Francois-Ernest de Mandat, Count of Grancey and Jeanne-Louise-Laurel-Eugenie-Rachel de Cordouse, their children and their children-in-law offered to their parents this monument of recognition toward God, and toward those of their ancestory remembered among the venerables and the saints, and of the particular cult that they adopted to Saint Gaul, their special protector.
>
> In 1361 Eudes, sire of de Grancey, Mahner de Moyers, his wife, and their son, Eudes, Sire of Pierpont, founded at de Grancey . . . this chapel of Saint John, which, over the years, has had its structure inspected and remained intact.
>
> We read their motto which is placed under the Coat of Arms: BY THE SWORD AND WORD . . ."[1]

Generation after generation added to their reputation for their fidelity to Church and Country, gaining fame and wealth. It was into this noble family that Adele Marie was born on September 13, 1837, and on the following day, the Feast of the Triumph of the Cross, with the permission of the local bishop, she received the Sacrament of Baptism. A full ceremony of prayers was delivered the following Sunday with a celebration of the family. From that time on she was addressed as Marie.

On the Coat of Arms memorial the list of notable relatives grew longer: Saint Gaul, the patron of the family; the dearly beloved Venerable Raingarde, who was deeply appreciated and recognized for her sanctity; and her beloved son, Peter the Venerable. Peter answered God's call and having joined the Monks at Cluny was chosen by them at the age of 30 to be their Abbot. So well did he defend his faith that he is recognized in history with that title of Venerable. As the Ottoman Empire was building rather rapidly, he was the first to have the Koran translated into Latin, thus enabling him to cite authoritative texts from their sacred book when he was involved in religious debates.

Sr. Marie's maternal grandparents.

POPE CLEMENT VI AND POPE GREGORY XI

The Family Coat of Arms also includes two Rosettes with the faces of two Avignon popes related to the Grancey Family through their mother. The Avignon Papacy was the period from 1309 to 1378 during which seven popes resided in Avignon (modern-day France). The conflict between the Papacy and the French crown brought forth such strife between Pope Boniface VIII and King Philip IV of France that finally in 1305 a Frenchman was elected pope. Not wanting to move to Rome, he decided to remain in France, and in 1309 moved his court to the papal enclave at Avignon, and there it remained for the next six popes, who, too, were all French. The two Avignon popes of the Grancey Family pictured in the stained-glass window are Pope Clement VI (1334-1342) and Pope Gregory XI (1370-1378).

Stain glass in family Collegiate Church of St. John, depicting the saints and Popes in the family heritage

Although Pope Clement VI had a lengthy list of critics both in Rome and in France it is interesting to note, that he took control of Smyrna during one of the Crusades. So many generations later the same family would be chosen once more for an important historic role to play in Smyrna. The first family member, Pope Clement VI, in Smyrna excluded Muslims; the second family member, Sister Marie, established a Shrine that is open to Muslims.

Pope Gregory XI, on the other hand, was a man of sound principle. He is best remembered for ending the Avignon papacies and for his Bull on the heresies of Wycliff of May 31, 1376.[2] Shortly following his election, Pope Gregory was soon subjected to the full force of Saint Bridget of Sweden's and Saint Catherine of Siena's exhortations to return the papacy to Rome. With the apparent fulfillment of Saint Bridget's admonition in the death of his predecessor, the Pope strove from the beginning of his pontificate to induce the clerical members of the Avignon curia to transfer back to Rome. But he provoked opposition, not only in the curia itself, but at the French court.[3] The mystics' prayers and words, some of which were very harsh, only added to the friction. They insisted that Gregory bring Saint Peter's Chair back to Rome. He agreed and despite the opposition, held firmly to this purpose.

Pope Gregory XI started his journey back to Rome on September 13, 1376, a date that will have significance for the family in 1837 with the birth of Adele Louise Marie de Mandat-Grancey.[4] With his arrival on January 17, 1377 came an interdict that was ignored by Florentines who fought on the streets of northern Italy, making the streets flow with blood. Eventually in 1378 a congress was arranged in Sarzana, Italy, where a peace agreement was signed. However, it had laid such a heavy toll on Pope Gregory XI that he died without enjoying the fruit of his labor. It is interesting to note that the two most important dates in the reign of Pope Gregory XI happen to be the day Sister Marie was born and the day Sister Marie died.

FAMILY LIFE

Marie was the fifth of the six de Mandat-Grancey children: Antonin, Charles, Christine, Leontine, Adele Marie, and Edmond. When the children reached maturity, following the custom, the men entered military service: Antonin joined the Navy, but during the Franco-Prussian War he transferred to the Army and died in the last days of the war at the head of his regiment; Charles served as an officer in the Army; and Edmond became a Naval Officer. Among the girls, Christine was a Lady in Waiting for the Queen of Belgium, Leontine had an early death, and Marie became a Daughter of Charity.

Left: Sr. Marie at the age of 5. *Right:* Her brothers Antonin and Charles.

The education of the noble de Grancey children in their multi-storied, spacious castle began at a very early age. Numbers of visitors changed most frequently, some staying for a day, many for a week. The importance of the family became evident to the children by the fact that their parents were frequently consulted by these visitors. The Baroness Eugenie seemed not only involved in public concerns but took special interest in giving personal instruction when it came to talk about the dedication of one or another in their prayer life. She often spoke about her favorite relatives, the Venerable Raingarde, and her son, Peter the Venerable. The children, with ever-changing people in the castle, seemed to enjoy their visitors and the change of pace that accompanied their presence.

The grandeur of the de Mandat-Grancey castle, with its lovely architecture, rated it as the finest in the Burgundy Province. The family living quarters were on the second floor. The painted portraits of ancestors hung on the walls of the library and along the corridors. Support staff tending the family lived in separate quarters. Some dwelt outside the castle in one or another of the several ground buildings, giving the estate the appearance of a thriving village. The family's collegiate church, which still stands today in silent splendor, provided a sacred space for prayer and worship.

In this rather opulent setting Marie de Mandat-Grancey received her earliest education at the hands of her mother and a number of tutors. She learned the history of her noble ancestors as she walked past their paintings and heard their histories retold. In the hearing of their accomplishments and the manner in which they lived, she was being instructed on how she was expected to live. She learned that she had a place in history as surely as they had. It was here, too, within the castle that family stories were retold and her mother expanded their religious instructions. Responsibility was a burden which each of them was to fulfill. The de Mandat-Grancey family was always concerned about the assistance they felt obliged to give to those who were dependent upon them for employment and livelihood. They committed themselves to caring especially for the sick and infirm among them.

Skillful tutors were hired to instruct the girls in writing, penmanship, drawing, painting, embroidery, and other needlecrafts. For both boys and girls, there were other extracurricular classes for dancing, recreational games, and etiquette. The de Mandat-Grancey children learned early in life that each of them was expected to learn not only how to ride a horse, but also how to care for it. More than that, they were to be recognized for their horsemanship. With dignity and poise they were to compete in races and win. The children enjoyed telling each other their accomplishments, and throughout the Province they gained fame.

During the course of the year the family made trips to Paris, taking up residence in their city home. While there they attended selected academies for specialized studies. Various churches were frequented to broaden their spiritual formation, and museums were visited to expand their education as royal citizens. Life in the city contributed much to their cultural perfection. One chapel the Countess chose for family prayer was at 140 rue du Bac, the residence of the Daughters of Charity. This chapel had become extremely popular a few short years before Marie was born. Our Lady had appeared there to one of the novice sisters and asked her to have a medal struck honoring the Immaculate Conception. People claimed the medal had special powers and called it the Miraculous Medal. Great reverence was manifested there. The community chapel was open to the public and daily received people from all parts of France and many other countries, as well. Despite the crowds that filled the chapel, people said it was a place of prayer—quiet and reverential. The Countess had a fervent devotion to the Blessed Mother and encouraged her children to put trust in Mary as their spiritual Mother.

Sr. Marie's parents: Jeanne-Louise-Laurel-Eugenie-Rachel de Cordouse and Galliot-Marie-Francois-Ernest de Mandat, count of Grancey.

Above: The Collegiate Chapel on the de Mandat-Grancey Estate in Burgundy. *Below left:* Chateau de Grancey in Burgundy, France, Sr. Marie's childhood home. *Below right:* The de Mandat-Grancey's Paris home.

Chapter Two
Religious Vocation

"Grant me, I implore you, my God, a vocation to the religious life, because I feel I would never have the strength to resist the temptations that I would be exposed to in the world. Give me the grace, O my God, to completely detach myself from the things here below and to aspire only to heaven. O Holy Virgin, my good patroness, intercede for me before God so that He will answer my prayer, because then I would have the most sure way of coming to Him and of being eternally happy. Amen."[1]

WHEN and where the thought of joining the Daughters of Charity came to Marie de Mandat-Grancey, we do not know. The Daughters of Charity were not like the nuns of famous orders such as the Augustinians, the Benedictines, the Franciscans, the Dominicans, or the Carmelites. The Daughters were different. They lived and worked outside the monasteries. Their religious habit was different. It was a French-blue heavy, commodious working garment with a heavy apron of the same material. Their head was covered with a large white cornette.[2] Their habit was based upon the dress of a country girl from one of the French Provinces. Because these sisters were doing corporal works of mercy, they were recognized and wanted in most all the dioceses of France. Quite naturally, they were soon wanted in other countries, too. Prior to the French Revolution, they were the fastest growing community of sisters. They were well known in Burgundy, where the de Mandat-Grancey Family lived. Their motherhouse was in Paris on the rue du Bac. Marie undoubtedly met them in both Burgundy and Paris. It was the charity of Jesus Christ lived by the Daughters that imbued her with the desire to become one of them.

The historical time in which she made her decision was a period in which the Church had just begun to operate rather freely again after the "Great Revolution." It was a time of widespread poverty and political turmoil; a time of hope and a time of despair. And the grace of God touched Marie. She believed God was calling her to help people in need. She believed she was needed. She wanted to contribute. She knew she had to give up living among the nobility, and she believed it was important for her to abandon it. She chose the Daughters of Charity because they were spiritual-minded women who worked with the people—the poorest and the neediest of people.

Who were the Daughters of Charity? They were founded in 1633 after Saint Louise de Marillac had been urging her spiritual director, Saint Vincent de Paul, that there was a need of them. They both knew the call was to work outside a monastery with the poor and needy people. It was a bold move within the Church because up until then religious-minded women had been confined to live a prayerful life within a cloister, behind the protective walls of a monastery. The Daughter of Charity would be schooled to contemplate Christ in service to the poor. She was to learn that she could leave Christ in prayer to serve Him in the poor person, just as a mother would leave other deeds to tend to her sick child. She was never to abandon Jesus Christ but to serve Him in the sick or the needy and then return to formal prayer. It was leaving God in one work to serve Him in another. That meant she had to leave convent walls. The plan, as lived, was approved by the Archbishop of Paris, and it opened the door to great numbers of women who wanted to serve Jesus Christ in need.

Left: St. Vincent de Paul, Founder of the Daughters of Charity. *Right:* St. Louise de Marillac, co-foundress of the Daughters of Charity.

During the French Revolution, the Daughters of Charity kept working, publicly professing their faith in word and deed. The revolutionary government turned against all religious organizations. Because the Daughters of Charity refused to take the oath of allegiance to the state against religion, several of them were imprisoned and guillotined as though they were troublemaking citizens. When the revolutionists dispersed their community, the Superioress General of the Daughters of Charity gave them permission to dispense with their religious habits in order to continue their good works of charity.

After Napoleon had overextended his armies into the furthest parts of Europe and had named his mother as the head of all female religious communities, he invited the Daughters of Charity to reassemble that they might nurse and tend his wounded officers and soldiers. They responded as though it were an invitation from God. However, their numbers were fewer and their funds were so short that they could not afford to buy materials to make their religious habits. For a considerable time people did not recognize them by their dress, but by their charity. They looked as poor and shoddy as those they served. But these were the Daughters of Charity. They came once again to serve the Poor.

After the Revolution, the Archbishop of Paris installed the Daughters of Charity on the estate of the Countess of Lavalliere on the rue du Bac. During the times of Marie's stays in their Parisian home, civic life was not always street-safe, being troubled with numerous political frays. But this did not deter Marie. She knew that in this place, in this time, her Lord had called her . . . and she would answer.

The chapel of the Daughters of Charity at Rue de Bac where the Blessed Virgin appeared to St. Catherine Labouré in 1830.

Chapter Three

Initial Formation

"My God, I ask of you but one thing, that is to love you with all my heart, because in truly loving you, I will think often of you, I will keep your commandments, and I will merit by that to love you for all eternity."[1]

WHEN Marie announced to her family that she desired to enter the Company of the Daughters of Charity, there was a mixture of acceptance and shock. Prior to the Revolution the Daughters had gained national prestige. The family greatly appreciated the Daughters and their work. That Marie wanted to become one of them brought the family together for discussion. To some it was not a surprise; they were expecting it. Not so for Antonin, her eldest brother, who was opposed. We know not the reason, but it caused a rift among them. It could have been the complete change that Marie would have to make in her own life. It might have been the kind of work which nobility was unaccustomed to. She might be exposing herself to all types of infection. More likely, it was the fact that, as she expressed in the note she wrote her grandfather, she would be making a complete separation from her family, not just then but for the rest of her life. Following the family discussion, Antonin withdrew his objection. Marie's note was likely written on May 26, 1857. It reads:

Dear Grandfather,

The time has come for me to proceed with a plan I have been forming for a long time and what Mother must have talked about with you. Maybe you have already guessed what my decision was. Far too often my conduct did not match my desire, nor what I hoped would be my vocation. Often, I am afraid, I failed in my duty as a granddaughter, and today, more than ever I need to ask for your forgiveness. Please forget, dear Grandfather, all you ever had to blame me for. Forgive the pain I might have ever caused you, and do not refuse to give me your blessing in this important step.

Do I need to ask you, dear Grandfather, to help me with your prayers in the days to come? Tonight I will have left my paternal home, maybe forever. I do consider myself happy to offer God the sacrifice that He appears to be asking of me in this moment, but I do have a broken heart when I see the regrets I have left behind me, regrets I only well know I deserve.

Goodbye, dear Grandfather. It is not necessary, I hope, to ask you to believe that even in my absence the affection I have for you will always stay the same. A thousand affectionate kisses from your respectful granddaughter.

Marie

Marie de Mandat-Grancey entered the Daughters of Charity as a postulant in the Parish of Saint Sulpice, Paris, France, at the age of twenty years. Her life of nobility closed. A whole new world opened to her. She was now one of seventeen young postulants. Her mother noticed the strain placed on her that first day in community life.

This excerpt from an undated letter written by Sister Marie's mother to her own father attests to that:

> Marie has written to you, dear Father, at the time she was leaving the house to go to the rue de Vaugirard. I hastened the departure so painful for all, to spare her any additional anguish, and I was right, I believe, at least it was the viewpoint of the Superior to whom she is entrusted. I visited her yesterday. She was very red, very over-excited. She had neither slept nor eaten. She was wearing the big white apron with a big bunch of keys and a big rosary. She had gotten up at 4:00 a.m., heard Mass at 6:00, swept the refectory, set the table, worked at the pharmacy, marked two shirts and spoken with two postulants her age who have been there for a few weeks. She will soon go to classes, starting with the last one and then will accompany the sisters on their visits to the poor and the sick. In short she will become initiated to the life of dedication, abnegation and hardships, because the Sisters of Saint Vincent are not exempted of these. I am convinced her calling is sincere and will only strengthen itself over time. If God asks me for her I will give her to Him wholeheartedly, and that will be a handsome present, because with her fervor for goodness, her self control and her intelligence, she can serve Him gloriously and usefully. There are seventeen sisters in the house and the Superior is an angelical creature of great capability. She has always been in the house and is very good at building on callings. Her heart did not harden in that position with the Daughters of Charity, and she was as moved as I was the day before yesterday. Not only does

she allow me, but she wishes me to see Marie every day, at the time I want. This might delay my departure a bit, and as you say so well, my return to Grancey alone with Leontine will be quite sad, despite the fact that Leontine will be more adorable than ever. . . .

The time of *postulatum* is the transitioning period for an applicant to pass from the secular life to religious life. Marie's life changed from being served to serving. Within the short time of two months Marie sent another letter to her grandfather, dated June 26, giving every indication that she had adapted exceptionally well to her new state of life.

Dear Grandfather,

You must wonder why I have not yet thanked you for your very thoughtful gift. Because I did not write sooner than this, you must have considered I did not have the time. Oh, when the basket arrived, addressed to Sister Marie—novice—who is still mademoiselle and a postulant, I would have loved to throw my arms around you and say, "Thank you. Thank you for thinking of me." Since I was not able to say it to you then, I do so today, even though I am tardy in saying it.

I feel quite certain that you directed the packing of these beautiful red currants that arrived here in perfect condition. It was so well done, but dear Grandfather, I would have much preferred to receive them in less fresh condition and have you spend a few moments jotting me one of your fine lines of greeting. And so, dear Grandfather, please, do drop me a line. It may not seem like a gift that you would be sending but I would find it so.

Remember just one of your good letters, as you did send in the past, would make me happier than any gift you deem necessary to send.

It is now two months to this day and hour that I wrote to you with a broken heart and eyes filled with tears. Today, it is not the same. I cannot tell you how much I congratulate myself on what I did. Everything makes me feel that I am here where God wants me, and I fear nothing in the future.

It is true that my not-so-generous nature wanted to refuse the sacrifice that I was called to do, and I can assure you that as a result, one has to suffer cruelly, but God does not refuse His grace to those who, at the bottom of their heart, wish only what He wishes, as I have now myself experienced so well. He knows how to alleviate the burdens that seem most crushing.

Have you had, like me, news of our English friends and do you know that the future naval officer [she is referring here to Edmond, born June 28, 1842] has shown that he is the son of his mother, even to the point of getting seasick?

I hope that this would have consoled mother for the little success that the youngster had in the last part of his exams in Naval School until next year, which would give him more time to mature before being sent far away in spite of all the progress that he seems to have made these past couple years. I am still somewhat mistrustful regarding his pride to not fear a little for a success more premature than that of my brothers.

I rejoice to see again our travelers, during their passage here, although visits now give me as much pain as pleasure. I am hungry for news from our dear Antonin. Do you know that he received very badly the first mention of my project and do you know that in the letter I received from him since I am here, he expressed to me all sorts of regrets about that fact and that a ship had not brought him any letter from you? Did he ever tell you, as he has told me, all the happiness that you give by writing to him? Goodbye, dear Grandfather. I do hope that the week will not pass without giving me some sign of life. To incite you to do it, remember that I am no longer there to learn of your letters to mother and have not a vocation of being a good correspondent. Do write to me, I beg you. Goodbye again, my dear Grandfather. I give you a big hug with all my strength and from the bottom of my heart and assure you of the lively and respected tenderness of your completely devoted granddaughter.

Marie

On May 27, 1857, Marie de Mandat-Grancey entered the *Postulatum*. The year passed rapidly. Like other Daughters of Charity who successfully completed their preparatory period for religious service, we find little about her in those early days of her formation in community life. With her early rising, she found sufficient time for prayer to seek divine assistance for all the many new demands the active apostolate placed upon her. Within the year she successfully completed that introductory program in the Parish of Saint Sulpice. On May 21, 1858, she was transferred to the Motherhouse of the Daughters of Charity on rue du Bac to enter the Seminary (novitiate) to be known henceforth as Sister Marie de Mandat-Grancey.

The second step in the Community life of the Daughters of Charity was directed by a Sister well trained in the charism of Saint Vincent de Paul and Saint Louise de Marillac. Much of the time in the Seminary was spent in establishing a strong personal prayer life as recommended by the founders. The Seminary sisters were being taught to become active contemplatives—serving Jesus Christ in the Poor. It was in the Poor that Saint Vincent had found Jesus Christ. Saint Louise, under the guidance of Saint Vincent, followed that same pursuit. However, since Louise served so many suffering poor persons, she saw in them the Crucified Christ. For Him she had a special devotion: Saint Louise placed on the Community seal around the crucifix the words: *The Charity of Jesus Christ Crucified urges us.*

Sr. Marie de Mandat-Grancey in the habit of the Daughters of Charity.

Along with her prayer life, Sister Marie was sent with an older member of the Daughters of Charity to visit the sick and the poor. She was instructed to greet those who were poor with a smile and to serve them as she was serving Jesus Christ. She was to offer with them a prayer to Jesus, a prayer of love and gratitude for His gifts and a plea to assist the person being aided. She was learning to contemplate Jesus in her suffering patient.

Life on the streets of Paris during the time of Sister Marie's Seminary formation was unpredictable at best. Political skirmishes were quite often threatening to the local residents in areas where political or economic conditions were unstable. Citizenry in Paris were known to bring their differences to the street. While in Paris, Sister Marie had the experience of going out with an older Daughter of Charity to visit the poor but only after having first checked with friendly neighbors to determine the best routes to reach those whom they sought to serve. Raucous factional outbursts, during the period in which Sister Marie was in the Seminary, were frequent and menacing. The clamor of mobs passing outside their walls was unnerving, leaving among the sisters the question of whether there would be an attempt to crash in their entrance door. Each time the presence of the mobs cast a pall of fright and fear over the sisters. Sister Marie, with brothers in military service, probably had the same concern that many Daughters of Charity had faced. Within the community of sisters there were family members on opposing sides. The sisters tried not to talk about sides, but to hold all of their family members in prayer.

Chapter Four
Apostolic Life

"Grant me, my God, that I may always accomplish your holy work which requires charity, that virtue which you love so much and of which you have given such touching examples."[1]

WHEN Sister Marie completed her Seminary formation in 1859, she was assigned to her first mission, the House of Mercy in Aire-sur-la-lys in northwestern part of France. It could not have been a more suitable place, situated in a safer, tidier part of the country on the border of Belgium. Sister Marie was ever so grateful to God for this, her first mission. The apostolic works were both plentiful and varied. Since she had professional training as a nurse, she was assigned to work in the pharmacy with additional duties in the dispensary. Like most of the Daughters of Charity, she quickly learned that these initial duties were just the beginning of her duties because there were other numerous deeds that would require her attention. For example, in two small nearby towns there were bedfast patients who were sorely in need of professional assistance. Sister Marie was asked to tend to their health care and any other matters that required help.

What thrilled Sister Marie the most was the fact that there were fifty-five young orphans in the House of Mercy who needed her loving care and attention. She would be allotted times for work and prayer with these youngsters. And there was more. There was another group of young girls, sixty of them, who were living with their families in Aire-sur-la-Lys. They came daily to the school and were enrolled in a special sewing program that would enable them to support themselves through needlework. That sewing program was hailed as one of the best and was attracting great attention. Sister Marie was most pleased to be asked to contribute to this program as time permitted. She would eventually broaden this program beyond sewing to include pattern making, color design, and special festive decorations. As a Daughter of Charity she easily pressed for a prayerful approach in the performance of their works. And the children, especially the girls in the sewing classes, recognized the care and love she had for them, and they responded positively.

This young Daughter who had just received her community training found that everything about this mission made it an ideal place and time for her. Community life was good. Her apostolic assignments were both plentiful and varied. She especially appreciated that fact that she could give attention to many young people who were in need. Pope Pius IX, already in the 23rd year of his reign, had been greatly stressing Marian devotions. For that Sister Marie was deeply grateful. In 1854, the Holy Father declared the Immaculate Conception as a dogma of Catholic belief. Young Sister Marie reflected on the love the Virgin Mary had for the Daughters of Charity, appearing to Saint Catherine Labouré and asking that she have a medal struck in honor of the Immaculate Conception. Sister Marie's heart, as always devoted to the Blessed Mother, stirred with a special new love and a secret hope that she be given the opportunity to share her love for Mary Immaculate in her works of charity with the young people.

Sister Marie was most conscious of the unforeseen opportunities given her to make known the power of God in the daily lives of those with whom she came in contact. She was already recognized as the Sister who always, publicly or privately, had a way of introducing—even to non-Catholics—the intercessory power of the Virgin Mary.

In 1865, Sister Marie had a special occasion to publicly proclaim the love and concern of Mary for a suffering people. An outbreak of cholera had broken out among the people. As soon as the alarm was sounded and it was confirmed that some deaths had occurred and were attributed to the disease, fear swept through the area. Sadly, the worst fears were realized. It soon became an epidemic.

The pastor, having talked with the health authorities, next spoke with the clergy, the sisters, and some leading members of the parish. Everyone sensed the need for public prayers. An evening Mass was scheduled on the next day with a procession honoring Mary, Our Lady Panetiere. The church was filled to overflowing. A great number of people had to wait outside during the Mass after which the procession began. First Sister Marie brought her Children of Mary Choir out of the church onto the public street. The Archbishop and the clergy followed with the cross-bearer and the acolytes to lead the group. Next came the people carrying lighted candles as the town's men led the prayers. These were closely followed now by the Children of Mary Choir and others who joined in along the way. All walked in procession honoring Mary in the hope of saving the city from plague and sure disaster.

Just moments before this scene unfolded, Sister Marie quietly stepped up to the Dean who was serving as the Master of Ceremonies for the Procession. She told him to have the cross-bearer and acolytes carrying candles make certain that they took a certain street. The Dean objected saying, "That's impossible. That adds some extra blocks and the route is already too long. It's too much for the men. The statue of Our Lady is too heavy. (The statue was made of heavy stone.) It takes twelve men to carry it and they will be worn out." To this Sister Marie replied, "That's of no importance, Mr. Dean. There is a Protestant woman on this street and she is to be converted. If you take this street, the Blessed Virgin will convert her." The good men of the town responded without complaint. The procession of prayer and song did pass by the woman's home. This woman had once been rather critical of Catholics. Although the very same morning she felt like she was in good health, by late afternoon she was gravely ill and death was approaching. She was so moved by the prayers and singing in honor of the Virgin Mary that she called out, "I want to be a Catholic." Someone tried to quiet her, but she kept saying, "I want to be a Catholic." One of the priests went over to talk to her. He heard her confession, blessed her, and she was baptized.[2]

There was quiet rejoicing that evening among the members of the Church. The people were so grateful to Sister Marie who seemed to have had foreknowledge of the status of the soul of this woman and the plans of God to convert her through Our Lady.

Sister Marie also reviewed what she had learned during her Seminary Year—that the Blessed Mother had told Saint Catherine Labouré that she wanted an association formed; the Children of Mary. She took that to prayer. She would need the assistance of the Virgin Mary herself to coordinate and implement Our Lady's desire as she tended to the task of working with two groups of youth for whose care she had just been given charge. Under Sister Marie's loving leadership the children, like flowers in Our Lady's garden, bloomed like never before. The association of the Children of Mary was vastly changed for the better due to Sister Marie's dedicated love and untiring charity. God had answered her prayers. Sister Marie was able to unite her love and devotion for Mary with her tenderness toward children. After all, these were Mary's children. This blessed combination of an ardent teacher abrim with love of

God and Mary, awakened in the youths a desire to fulfill the role she unfolded to each of them.

The response that Sister Marie received from the youths was most encouraging. The membership in the association of the Children of Mary developed so rapidly that more space was needed to care for all the activities. A new building was erected with the first floor being used for their games and shelter. The second floor was reserved for developing their spiritual growth; prayer services, retreat gatherings, personal or group instruction, business meetings, and the like.

The success of the program was overwhelming. Sister Marie had accomplished so much. In fact, the parents began complaining that the children had developed such a love of being with her that they were not spending enough time at home. She was surprised; and she was also pleased and comforted to hear that she had the support of her community for her work with the youth. She heard her local Superior reply to the complaints explaining that she understood; however, she exhorted the parents to be glad about the special care their children were receiving. She also encouraged the parents to strive to do at home for their children what Sister Marie was doing there.

Working with healthy and gifted children is somewhat easy. There were in the area, however, those who were not so blessed. Among them were the slow and weak, the lonely and the sickly children who needed Sister Marie's special care. Those afflicted with scurvy suffered the most. Running sores and noxious odors drove away most of their classmates. Sister Marie decided she needed to bring them into a group. She would arrive early each morning before class time. All her supplies and provisions were lined up in a row. She put aside the repulsion she felt at seeing their open sores and began washing and cleansing their poor ailing heads, removing the lice, and combing their matted hair. Finishing up, she handed these little ones fresh, clean clothing in exchange for the soiled ones she collected. It took time, but she relieved them of that terrible affliction which separated them from their classmates. The unity of the Children of Mary had begun.

Chapter Five

Marie Takes Her Vows

"My God, you have done so much good for me, how
can I not have for you the love of a child for her father.
Put charity more strongly in my heart and preserve it
there always, O my God."[1]

EVERY Daughter must take vows between five and seven years
from the time of her entrance into the community. For Sister
Marie this was not a problem; in fact, it was an event that she was
joyously awaiting. It was not the vows that made her a Daughter of
Charity. She became a Daughter when she entered the Seminary.
Her vows would be a committed expression of giving herself to
God in service to the poor in a life that was codified with regards
to material goods, people, and behavior. The details were expressed
in her rules. Her vows would be a spiritual and legal bond with the
community that was recognized by ecclesiastical law. Benefits,
especially spiritual enrichment, would flow from that bond.

In the course of her preparation for vows, Sister Marie reviewed
the vision and the writings of Saint Vincent and Saint Louise along
with other works from various community leaders. Her study also
included the Church legislation that touched upon the life and work
of the Sisters.

By the time Sister Marie was studying for vows she could appreciate how greatly the cause of women in the Church had grown.

She herself was trained in nursing and made the choice to serve God with this training and these gifts in the community of the Daughters of Charity. With them she could live a life consecrated to Christ with service to the destitute and the infirm. It had its own spirit, so clearly expressed in its rules. As the Daughters of Charity lived those rules, they captivated the attention of even those who had harbored thoughts of destroying the Church. She thought about that again as she studied the vows. Even Napoleon realized that the country needed the Daughters. Sister Marie believed she was being asked to vow her life to God for the care and service of the poor. She prayed that she might have the same kind of humility the Virgin Mary had when she said, "I am the maidservant of the Lord."

When a Daughter of Charity makes vows for the first time the date is selected by the Community. After a brief retreat she proclaims her vows aloud before the members of her local mission. Thenceforth, she will say them in silence during the Mass on the Feast of the Annunciation. Every year she must ask permission to offer vows. If she chooses not to renew vows, she must depart the community. Every year on March 25, a Daughter of Charity is free to leave the Community, but the first time and every time thereafter that she makes vows it is with the intention of remaining in the Community.

The Daughters of Charity take four vows. The Vow of Service is central to the life of a Daughter of Charity, which is why it is listed as first among the vows. She was formed to contemplate Jesus Christ in the Poor. She comes to understand that any poor person may be in the ambit of her service. Service to those in need is to begin with a smile, a smile Saint Vincent says, for which the poor might forgive her the help she has given them. Each Mission of the Daughters of Charity has its own clientele with its particular need, or it may be tending several programs for the betterment of the people. This was manifested in Sister Marie's first mission.

Next is the Vow of Poverty, which allows her to retain personal funds and inheritances held by her or that may come to her. She exercises the Vow of Poverty by seeking permission to use the funds that are hers to benefit the Poor and for works of faith and charity.

The Vow of Chastity which she makes is akin to that of those made in other religious communities of women regarding celibacy and chastity. And the Vow of Obedience obliges her to observe the legislation found in their Constitutions and Statues; that is, the offices and the officers governing her life within the Community.

Sister Marie completed her study and secured permission to make vows in the presence of her local community on September 27, 1862, the Feast of the Death of Saint Vincent de Paul. For her it was a joyous celebration. However, for both her and her family there was sadness, too, because it was done without ceremony, and relatives were not invited to attend. That morning, like the previous mornings, she joyfully but quietly went to serve the people in her care. Sister Marie remained in Aire-sur-la-Lys for eight more years before the community asked her to serve elsewhere.

Chapter Six

Sister Servant

"Behold the handmaid of the Lord. Be it done to me
according to Thy word."

—Luke 1:38

IT WAS 1870. Sister Marie was given a new assignment. She was
asked to be the Sister Servant in an orphanage operated by the
Daughters of Charity in Le Pecq, a suburb of Paris. She had no
trouble saying "yes" to this new assignment. For her, it was another
call from God. To leave Aire-sur-la-Lys after a dozen joyous years
was not an easy task, however. This had been her first assignment,
and adjusting to the change of sites and works surfaced many
pleasant memories of understanding the call to serve Christ. She recalled her earliest visits to the sick, and the needed care she gave
to the youngsters. She watched with pleasure at how some of them
just seemed to blossom once their physical scars from scurvy were
cleansed and healed. And she was ever grateful to God when they
joined in all the activities of the Children of Mary. She would
always carry all of them in her heart.

As she was preparing to move, the peace and quiet in Aire-sur-
la-Lys was shattered by political upheavals. The talk of warfare was
loud and demanding, sounding worse now than when she was in
the Seminary. She, herself, was at peace and the sisters were more
visible than they were when she had joined the Community. As she

looked ahead she knew the duty of leadership given her would place a heavier burden upon her.Would she be able to travel safely and work in Le Pecq? Life seemed less tranquil there because of its proximity to Paris where turmoil always seemed to drift from other parts of the country. She allowed herself no time to reflect upon those thoughts, knowing quite well that war was about to break out again.

The orphanage to which she was reporting would play an important role in the history of Le Pecq. The Community wisely selected Sister Marie for its new Sister Servant. She had a wonderful record in health services, in youth activities, in music and liturgy assistance; and she had shown tremendous charity and community leadership. The Community had found her faithful and visionary. At this period in history, neither Church law nor the Common Rules of the Daughters had a time limitation for leadership service by its members. She was asked to serve as Sister Servant, and, of course, she took the matter to prayer. She knew God would supply all the support she would need.

Among the Daughters of Charity, the title "Sister Servant" has a particular and important meaning. A Sister Servant is charged with the responsibility of preserving the "primitive spirit" among the Daughters of Charity in her mission. The primitive spirit of a Daughter of Charity is to live out her life with the same dedication as did the very first Daughters, while striving to serve Jesus in the poor. Saint Vincent de Paul is the one who gave the local Superior that title. While giving a conference to a group of the early Daughters, he said, "I happened to be in a convent of nuns of the Annunciation Order, I think it was, and I noticed that their Superioresses were called *Ancelle,* which comes from the Latin word *ancilla,* which means handmaiden or servant. It is the title assumed by the Blessed Virgin when she told the angel she consented that the will of God should be fulfilled in her in the mystery of the Incarnation of His Son. This led me to think, my dear Sisters, that in the future, instead of calling Sister Superiors and Superioresses, we should employ the title, "Sister Servant." He asked, "What do you think?"[1] They agreed, and they all accepted it.

When Sister Marie arrived at the orphanage the Franco-Prussian War had broken out. Casualties in and around Paris were mounting. Fighting had extended into the Le Pecq area. She knew that the Sisters would be called upon for assistance to war victims. One of the first items of news she had when she came into the orphanage was that a sizeable number of orphans had just been deposited, doubling the population under the care of the Daughters. There was little time for welcoming Sister Marie because she was immediately engaged in arranging the newly arrived children for placement within the home. It seemed like nothing that anyone might say had any effect upon these little ones. They were totally alone within a friendly crowd, devoid of any appreciation for human consolation. All contact with their loved ones had been brutally and abruptly severed; mother, father, brother, sister, home . . . it was all gone. This is where Sister Marie stepped up and became a figure that gently yet effectively penetrated that thick wall of vacancy. She showed the traits of a truly caring, loving mother.

Little by little she was making progress in those first few days when someone came to the orphanage door and called for her presence. She entered the foyer and, at first, could only stare at the man who announced that he had just brought another group of orphans. In that one moment, the number of orphans tripled. He said this was the latest group of boys and girls who had just learned their mothers as well as their fathers had been killed in the recent attack by enemy soldiers. Sister Marie simply directed the man to bring the children in. With arms outstretched she beckoned the little ones to come in. In her arms and her heart, they would find comfort. She called to dedicated co-workers, who were as yet practically strangers to her. She gave them a nod of gratitude for their devoted care and concern. In the coming days as she talked with the sisters she taught them to concentrate on these new young individuals, their hearts and their souls, not on the question of where they were going to lodge or how to feed them. Sister Marie simply entreated the Sisters to extend their arms to welcome them.

Once the bedlam had begun to dissipate, she gathered the Daughters and thanked them for being kind, gentle, caring mothers to the poor children who had lost everything. As the Sisters were settling the newly arrived children into their new home, Sister Marie was developing plans to send the Daughters into all parts of the city to beg for help. She instructed the Sisters that they should recognize that everyone was going through a difficult period, but they should emphasize to the townspeople that they were speaking on behalf of children who belonged to Le Pecq and that the Daughters were helping both the town and the orphaned children. Having called them together, she directed them to prepare an appeal, giving them the example and instruction to go out as individual beggars, never afraid to speak to anyone on the streets on behalf of these children. She gave them the words to say.

They went out in twos in different directions to meet as many people as they could. The sisters said that they were in need of the help of the townspeople to save their own dear children who had just lost their mothers and their fathers. The Daughters explained to the people that they would lovingly take care of their children, but could not do it alone. The sisters stated with simplicity and candor the fact that they needed help with clothing, beds, bedding, food, and anything else that the children might need. The sisters accepted all donations with abundant gratitude, knowing that the times were very hard for everyone but always reminding the donors that for these orphaned children it was the worst of times.

This proper attitude and the care of these children were the primary concerns of Sister Marie. She emphasized these concerns when she instructed the sisters to declare "These are your Children." The response from the people was good, especially realizing that they, too, were suffering because of the war. There had to be shortages of every kind: food, clothing, school supplies, and medicines. Sadly, along with these shortages many also suffered the loss of family and friends. However, this did not keep the local residents from helping the sisters with what charity they could.

It is quite reasonable to consider that one such response to Sister Marie's requests for help might have come from a source close to her heart. While we have no written evidence to support this possibility, it does seem plausible to believe that the de Mandat-Grancey Family would have been among the many unlisted donors to help these children. We know the family had a long-standing reputation for support of its religious and moral beliefs, that the family was most generous in its charities; and, that there was also a proud concern for Sister Marie and her various works. Now that her assignment was near Paris, where the family often spent several months each year, one has to expect that in such a terrible need for material assistance they would have been one of the great anonymous donors. If they were, Sister Marie never sought praise for the family nor herself.

Approximately four years after the arrival of Sister Marie in Le Pecq, one of the officers of the Formation Team in Paris asked if she would accept a Sister Rosalie who had completed her Seminary stay. She was told that there was a concern for her. She had the desire to be a Daughter of Charity, but it seemed that she was physically unfit because of severe physical pains which afflicted her from doing some of the heavy works expected of a Daughter. She had spent an excessive amount of time resting in bed while others were out working on their assignments. She still had four more years before she must take vows or be dismissed. The Sisters in Paris were asking Sister Marie to evaluate Sister Rosalie's vocation.

Sister Marie graciously accepted the challenge and began by setting up a schedule for Sister Rosalie with a massage, exercises, and work periods. In doing so, she became Sister Rosalie's therapist, counselor, and spiritual aide. Sister Rosalie soon began to show signs of improvement, and her pain abated. After a full report was given on her to the Sisters in Paris, Sister Marie was told to prepare Sister Rosalie for her first vows at the proper time. From this chapter in the life of Sister Rosalie there grew a strong personal and friendly relationship which the two enjoyed for many, many years to come, indeed for the rest of Sister Marie's life.

Life in Le Pecq moved on rather smoothly. There Sister Marie held the office of Sister Servant for twenty years. It was well known among the community members that Sister Marie had an excellent education. She was well read and kept abreast of the latest developments and publications in the Church. In 1880, the private revelations given to Anne Catherine Emmerich were published. Since they were of a spiritual background, Sister Marie immediately secured a copy for her own personal enrichment and shared it with her community members. Talk of *The Passion of Our Lord Jesus Christ* and Emmerich's private revelations on the life and death (Dormition) of Mary abounded in Europe at the time. The books became a topic for Sister Marie's prayer, reflection, and conversation in the convent as she encouraged her sisters to greater confidence in Mary, her patroness. The love she had for the Blessed Virgin continued to grow.

In these years as Sister Servant in Le Pecq, Sister Marie had many reasons for thanking God for favors received. During the last period of time that she was in Le Pecq the Holy Father, Pope Leo XIII, showed his appreciation for the Blessed Virgin Mary. In his writings, quoting Saint Thomas Aquinas, he referred to the Virgin Mary as Co-Redemptrix and Mediatrix of all Grace. Pope Leo XIII was so impressed by the gratitude of the Family of Saint Vincent de Paul for his writings and teachings about Our Lady, that he arranged for them a special Office and Mass in honor of Our Lady of the Miraculous Medal.

Sister Marie's care extended beyond the religious needs of her community while in Le Pecq. Over the years Sister Marie had worked with the civic officials, securing placement among the people of the city for many orphans. The program was so successful that these same officials came to an agreement with the officials of the Daughters of Charity in Paris that there was no longer a need for the Daughters to operate this orphanage. It could be closed! Mission accomplished! Sister Marie was now free and willing to go, ready to accept any post to which her superiors wished to send her. Little did she suspect what God had awaiting her. As we look back on her history, we can see that the Blessed Virgin Mary quietly, silently had prepared her for a very special role.

Chapter Seven
A Call for Help

SMYRNA . . .
Smyrna, which saw me born and which I loved so much,
In your ever blue sky, in your ever beautiful sea,
In your white minarets, raising toward the Eternal
The hearts of human beings, at the hour when all awakes,
Smyrna, which bears the name of a famous Amazon,
And which, in times long past, had a martyred bishop,
Could you, one day, give us hope,
In delivering from your flanks, your ancient cathedrals,
And your sacred tombs, the undeniable presence,
In order that, in these ungodly times unceasing struggles,
The Star of the East shines and again gives peace:
"To Men of Good Will."[1]

—Author Unknown

WITH the change in her mission assignments, Sister Marie was about to enter into a new world. She would, not immediately but in the near future, have another and totally different work added for her care. A brief review of historical events and people who helped set the scene she was to enter may be of some benefit.

In the last year of the 13th century, Ossman entered into warfare in Turkey and established his first great victory to begin the Ottoman Empire. A century and a half later, in 1453, Mehem II captured Constantinople. Constantine XI died in that battle and the

Byzantine Empire fell. In 1453 the name Constantinople was changed to Istanbul. The Ottoman Empire continued to expand, and by the 16th century it controlled much of Asia, all of Asia Minor, a goodly amount of southeastern Europe, and many of the Mediterranean port cities in Europe, Asia Minor, and Africa.

King Francis I (1494-1547) was quite anxious to have France recognized as a world power. To the shock of many world leaders he signed a trading agreement with Suleiman, the Magnificent, of the Ottoman Empire in the early 16th century. This gave him trading powers and supposedly safer sea travel.

In the mid-1800s the French Daughters of Charity, after two years of negotiations, signed an agreement to serve in the French Naval Hospital in Smyrna, Turkey. They were insistent that they needed a work that helped Catholics strengthen their faith and live exemplary lives; and so they earned the right to teach children in that hospital.

From the time of the treaty that Francis I signed with Suleiman, French nationals began to trickle into Istanbul itself. In the early 19th century Turkey had become part Asian and part European. The Crimean War (1853-1856), in which religious as well as political rights and claims were involved, greatly weakened the Ottoman Empire. Pope Leo XIII sought missionary assistance for the growing Church in Asia Minor. It was a natural request that the Vincentian Family of priests, brothers and sisters contribute to this need.

It was also a natural response for Sister Marie to respond to this papal request for assistance when the announcement was given her. She was a Daughter of Charity and she was a de Grancey, whose family members were French patriots as well as strong Catholics. She had brothers at that time who were military personnel and the family had a long-standing experience in foreign lands. Her health was good and she had both academic and nursing experience as well as her religious formation to offer. Sister Marie was delighted to respond to the requests for assistance from the Pope and the Daughters of Charity. And the Daughters were pleased because she also brought a rich administrative ability to an old French Hospital and school. Smyrna, Turkey, is home to one of the seven ancient churches that date back to Saint John, who mentions it in the first and second chapters of the Apocalypse (Apoc. 1:11; 2:8)! Sister Marie knew she was being truly blessed.

Sister Marie did not travel alone. It was customary for the Daughters of Charity to travel in twos. Her companion, of all people, was the sister who was sent to Le Pecq for health assistance, Sister Rosalie. And probably, at least one other Daughter was in the group, Sister Jeanne, who lived and worked with Sister Marie in Aire-sur-la-Lys. We have written evidence that the three of them were in Smyrna. There may have been more on that same journey.

As they approached harbor in Smyrna, one can only imagine the thoughts that ran through their minds; new land, new people, new work, good friends and companions. But more especially—this was the land where Saint John and his companions entered just after the Resurrection of Jesus and the First Pentecost. Here he brought the Virgin Mary and Mary Magdalene and so many others during a time of persecution in Israel.

What prayers of thanksgiving went up to God for bringing them here! They would turn to Mary, His mother, their Mother. Saint Vincent and Saint Louise did much to bring them here. How blessed they were to be chosen to come to this holy place.

From the ship Sister Marie had her first glimpse of Smyrna. So much to see and learn as a new and different culture presented itself to them. They must respect the culture of the land they came to serve. A Christian touch would be essential as they treated all those they met with utmost dignity and sincerity. As she approached their new residence, Sister Marie's practical and keen eye caught a glimpse of a building in great need of attention. She knew it would be a challenge. Over the years the sea breezes left a salty residue on the buildings, causing damage. After a very brief survey of the buildings and land, Sister Marie felt most confident that she might be helpful here.

Although Sister Marie was not the administrator of the hospital, as a member of the Sisters' community she knew how to properly proceed to try to help. Any personal funds of Sister Marie spent on hospital improvement had to be asked of and approved by the local Sister Servant. There is no trace of any irregularity in this process on the part of Sister Marie or criticism by her Sister Servant. Following her walk-through visit of the hospital, Sister Marie took a critical view of needs and submitted them to her Sister Servant.

Upon Sister Marie's arrival, the hospital staff almost immediately showed its acceptance of her. They were rejoicing over the many improvements that had begun. Painters brightened rooms and corridors. Patients seemed much more cheerful by the brightened colors. There was an appreciative sense in the changes, and it was also noticed by the visitors. The medical staff rejoiced over the new look given their quarters, bringing with it a source of comfort in new furnishings. But for them the most wonderful part was the arrival of the latest and new medical equipment. The old Sacred Heart Hospital was beginning to look quite new and vibrant. Outdated equipment was gone. Doctors and nurses seemed more pleasant and joyous. There was a new spirit in the medical staff. Some of the personnel may have noticed that the changes began around the arrival date of Sister Marie, but few knew that they all occurred through the generosity of her gift of funds.

Within Smyrna there were several other religious orders. Word soon got around that the hospital may have changed looks but the poorest of all living quarters among the religious houses in Smyrna were the quarters of the Daughters of Charity in the old French Hospital. None of the funds of Sister Marie was used for that purpose.

Fewer French naval ships found it necessary to drop anchor in Smyrna around this time because by now the Ottoman Empire had lost much of its power. But even from those ships there always were a few sailors who made their way to the French hospital, ostensibly to bear greetings and carry a penned note or letter from a French naval officer whose sister was stationed in the hospital. Of course, Sister Marie would never let them depart without first enjoying a royal dinner.

As in so many institutions of the Daughters of Charity, it seemed that when a new sister was added, a new work also surfaced. Years before, when the naval station had been operative and busy, there was built on the land next to it an entirely new subdivision for the working class of Smyrna. This subdivision was still filled with the families of working class and their many children. Shortly after the arrival of Sister Marie, the Daughters of Charity were asked to care for their education. They gladly took the challenge. Sister Marie was hoping that her Children of Mary would help change the reputation of the city which had already become known for the rather sordid activities of its floating population.

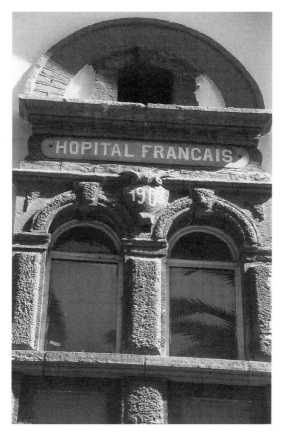

French Hospital in Smyrna where Sr. Marie as Superior lived and worked.

Chapter Eight

Sister Servant Anew

"My God, I understand now the purpose of prayer because without it we cannot obtain your grace. Forgive me the little fervor that I have shown up until now in praying to you, and give me the strength to correct all of my faults and to make a good and holy First Communion."[1]

IN 1890, Sister Marie was appointed Sister Servant of the Daughters of Charity and she held that position for twenty-five years until her death. With it she assumed many positions, such as Sister in Charge, school principal, and teacher of nursing, Director of the Children of Mary . . . and more to come. So great was her "enlightened and untiring, affectionate and maternal zeal for these dear youth of Smyrna,"[2] that her advice was sought in many areas. She was highly enthused to enter into this apostolate. To her it was akin to the earliest days of her missions. She was thrilled to be in a bright, cheery classroom once again, training girls in their new sewing shop. She enjoyed teaching so much because the students showed great eagerness to develop their talents. And then another need appeared.

The Holy Father, Pope Leo XIII, in 1891, had issued his Encyclical *Rerum Novarum,* on the rights and responsibilities of employees and employers. Numerous people, among them youthful girls, were coming to Smyrna with a hope to secure new employment. As she observed several Christian girls seemingly lost after finding no employment, Sister Marie determined that they must be given further assistance at this important time in their lives. From her own personal funds she had added to the hospital a separate pavilion, constructed and furnished for them, with all the protections a young woman might need. It was cheery, bright, and airy. Living together in a safe moral atmosphere they could bond and help one another. To them she extended the opportunity to enroll in the arts classes of the school in penmanship, printing, needlecraft, sewing, and other handicrafts, as well as training in domestic services. Of primary importance, however, was her work of Christian education.

> Her spirit of faith and her zeal also inspired all that she did for the hearts of the youth, living tabernacles, where it is necessary, at all costs, to maintain the presence of grace. If she wanted to group the young girls in a Christian workshop, instruct them, have them sing and act in plays, it was at the same time to give them good principles, elevate their souls, occupy their free time and distract them in an innocent way, sheltering them from the attraction and opportunity of dangerous pleasures. If she gave all her care to the Association of the Children of Mary, it was, without doubt, to honor the Virgin, but also to assure the progress, the perseverance and the salvation of these children.[3]

Once again, these children, like all the children before, loved Sister Marie. She filled a void in their life, and they were forever changed for it. They were known to write little spontaneous notes of gratitude. This particular note was written by one of the girls on behalf of all of them:

> We could well call her our Mother. She loved us, she, who despite her age, climbed up and down the stairs to

our workshop several times a day, without ever allowing herself to disturb us. . . .

She loved us, she who every Sunday night would gather us for class. With what goodness, what patience, what delicacy, she would humble herself and her wisdom, in order to put them at the service of our ignorance.

Indeed, she loved us, when in our small celebrations she seemed to be available to each one of us by the joy that she witnessed and the pleasure that we gave her, according to her, for learning something that would elevate us.[4]

And so, Sister Marie diligently continued to apply herself to the promotion of her beloved Children of Mary and delighted in the successes they had in their projects. Catholics were a minority in this Muslim-controlled country. Sister was marvelous in promoting the personal dignity of the children and took joy in developing ways of acknowledging and expanding it. People watched with wonder as the membership grew so rapidly, even into the hundreds. Her primary concern for the members was their spiritual growth. She called them to be models of Christian virtue within this Muslim country. Teenage years are often the most difficult years for good, honest relationships. Yet it was this age-group in Smyrna that heaped praise upon Sister Marie for all the good she had done for them.

With the election of Pope Pius X in 1903, extraordinary events occurred within the Church for its modernization. Among them was the introduction of the first Code of Canon Law, a special emphasis upon the Real Presence of Christ in the Eucharist, along with an injunction to pray the Mass. Two directives brought emphatic change and gave particular peace and joy to Sister Marie as it did to many in the Church at large: the first, a plea to learn and use Gregorian Chant in the liturgies; and secondly, one that had the most universal appeal, was the change of age for first communicants of the Holy Eucharist. The life of Sister Marie just brightened to its heights.

The announcement proclaimed that any child who had reached the age of reason, and had been given proper training, could seek permission to receive Holy Communion. Immediately the local community of Daughters of Charity began forming the school classes for readiness to receive First Communion in the next Easter Season. For Sister Marie, this meant that not only the children had to be catechized and prepared, but that the parents and the congregation must be readied for it, as well. She involved the parents seeking their help and encouraging their cooperation not only with the upcoming First Holy Communion preparation, but also with all her future work with their children.

The Daughters were immediately given assignments to prepare this great celebration that would occur several months from the announcement. Sister Marie herself would strive to have a choir fully prepared, and playing her harmonium as accompaniment, she taught the children to sing special hymns and to begin simple Gregorian chant. She also applied her skills in needlecraft and design to make a new altar front with Eucharistic symbols.

Sister Marie was so very blessed by God with many and varied talents, and she used each one of these gifts in her service of God. Everything Sister Marie did, she did for God; for His Son, Jesus Christ; for His Holy Catholic Church; for His Mother, Mary. Zeal for beauty in the house of God consumed her. One of her Sisters in the Bulletin of the Children of Mary in Smyrna notes:

> Her faith gave to my sister de Grancey the love of beauty
> in worship and the zeal for decorating the house of God.

In the brilliant education she had received, she had successfully cultivated all the decorative arts. Her talents were to be exclusively devoted to religion. A musician, she would train the choirs and, to the extent that local circumstances would allow, her repertoire would comprise only serious motets, from good and beautiful music, and religious canticles worthy of name. A painter, she would decorate banners, chasubles for the canons and vases for the altar. Deft at needle-work, she would embroider with infinite patience and, with a composite art all her own, vestments, copes, canopies, and altar frontals. She loved to weave all the traditional, pious emblems, as well as beautiful texts taken from Holy Scripture.[5]

French college of the Sacred Heart in Smyrna.

All these God-given talents Sister Marie used to serve God and the ones He sent her. In this happy new endeavor of preparing for this First Holy Communion, she had great confidence in her youthful class of seamstresses. She ordered yards and yards of tulle to ensure that each girl making her First Holy Communion would have a proper and lovely veil. And with that, the neophyte seamstresses were also encouraged to complete the Communion dresses. For Sacred Heart Church, the First Communion Sunday would be one of its most joyous and memorable celebrations.

When Sister Marie was first assigned to this mission, little did she suspect that the Mother of God had a very special role for her, not just in Smyrna but also for the whole Church. Sister Marie knew that when Jesus was dying upon the Cross, as Saint John recounts, He looked to His Mother and said, "Woman, there is your son." In turn He said to the disciple, "There is your Mother." We are told that from that moment on, the disciple took Mary into his care. We know, too, from the Acts of the Apostles, that shortly after the Resurrection of Jesus, a persecution broke out in Jerusalem for those who followed "the Way." Between 17 and 49 A.D., no public record is known of the whereabouts of either Saint John or the Virgin Mary. There is a tradition, and it is entirely probable, that they had come to Ephesus, a city reputed to be the largest in the Roman Empire with its great financial center. The tradition maintains that this city had a mixture of cultures and peoples.

The New Testament Scriptures concern themselves primarily with Jesus Christ, not Mary. They give no information about Mary after the Pentecost following the Ascension of Jesus. There was a legend in Jerusalem that Mary died in Gethsemane. There was an even stronger tradition in Ephesus that she lived out her last years there, and that her Dormition occurred there.

In 431 A.D., an Ecumenical Council took place in Ephesus. The

Council met in the 2nd-century building called by the same name today, The Church of the Virgin Mary. Since the Council it is also referred to as the Council church. The aim of the Council was to solemnly pronounce Mary's divine motherhood. In the end it was pronounced as dogma that the Virgin Mary had given birth to Christ, the Son of God, and Mary's title of "Mother of God" (*Theotokos*) was proclaimed in grandeur. It is important to note that in the early days of Christianity a church was only dedicated to a person if he or she had died in that place. At the time of the Council, the existence of a church dedicated to Mary in Ephesus, and only in Ephesus, is compelling evidence that Mary was thought to have completed her earthly life there.

Add to this the discovery of what is believed to have been the last home of Mary, which does accord with the revelations given to Blessed Sister Anne Catherine Emmerich, this narrative follows the tradition of Ephesus, as does the choice today of most archaeologists and the Vatican authorities.

But of course, we know that our Sister Marie, who had read the private revelations given to Anne Catherine Emmerich years earlier while living in Le Pecq, was very keenly aware of how Divine Providence had placed her so close not only to Mary's House, but to her tomb and the holy place of her Assumption! Sister Marie held a special hope and prayer in her heart.

Sr. Marie contentedly doing some needlework. Much of her work catechizing and evangelizing was done while teaching sewing.

Chapter Nine

How God Works

"My God, preserve in my heart this virtue of hope that
you have placed there . . ."[1]

I T HAD been 49 years since Sister Marie had left home to join the
Daughters of Charity. She had completed two major mission
assignments. She truly believed that God had called her to serve what
is commonly termed the Mission at Gentes. In America we call it the
foreign missions. Just four years after her arrival in Smyrna, Turkey,
Sister Marie was appointed Sister Servant for the Daughters of Charity working in the French Hospital, Sacred Heart School, and the
Asylum which had been opened two years earlier. The Community
was flourishing. Nearby the male membership of the family, the
Vincentian Fathers, who were operating the Sacred Heart College,
were of great spiritual assistance to the Sisters. The strange and
wonderful unfolding of God's plan was demonstrated in the bond
between these two members of St. Vincent's family.

The following chapters concern Sister Marie, Father Eugene
Poulin, and Father Henry Jung: three very strong-minded people,
who, as Saint Vincent would say, were brought together in the plan
of Divine Providence.

Notice the distinction between their characters. First consider
Sister Marie, her religious fervor and her directness graced by her

sensitivity. As a noble person, she expected people to be as honest and direct with her as she was with God, the Blessed Virgin Mary, and the people God sent her, whether in community, in the classroom, or among friends.

Next note the clergy: both were well educated, brilliant in their fields, most direct. They stated things as they saw them and gave no room for fantasizing. Everything would follow accepted principles. Father Poulin was obedient in accepting his assignment. He would remain two years. He was certain that health would be an argument in favor of his return to France. He had also a stuttering problem which only worsened at times when he was determined that every syllable be pronounced correctly. Father Jung had been a soldier in the Franco-Prussian War. He was orderly, well seasoned, scholarly, and polite.

As these three worked together, there never seemed to be an argument. Their spiritual character allowed them to give each his due, and that turned into tremendous respect for each other, especially as their workload increased. They grew to heights of holiness and strength of faith, hope, and charity that most people would dearly desire. In these chapters, we will observe how Sister Marie approaches and fulfills her role, and how Father Poulin and Father Jung grew to sincerely appreciate her; how little by little they came to value her intuitive, determined character, and above all her steadfast persevering faith.

ANOTHER WAY GOD WORKS

"I'll send you the book," she [Sister Marie] said one day
and in conclusion, "Do promise me you'll read it."[2]

In religious communities it was a practice to have the reading of a book during mealtime. It is not surprising that Sister Marie, as

Sister Servant, asked Father Poulin, the Vincentian Superior, to rec-
ommend a good book for refectory reading. His reply was simple:
"Of course, Sister, I will have something for you tomorrow." The
incident went unnoticed, but Father Poulin recorded it in his journal. It began the series of events that led to the greatest archaeological discovery of the 19th century.

Father Poulin went to the library, mounted a ladder, and selected
some books from an upper shelf. He brought them to his room,
placed them on his desk for review, and found among them an old
octavo bound in sheepskin. He did not remember picking it up.
When he read the title page a flood of memories dating back twenty
years came rushing upon him.

In 1868-69, Father Poulin, then about twenty-five years of age,
was one of three young priests on the faculty of the major seminary
in Gregy, France. The Superior and rector of the seminary was the
distinguished and pious Father Denys, a Vincentian priest who had
served as rector of the Great Seminary of Carcassonne as well as
the Provincial Superior of the French Province. He greatly enjoyed
reading and studying the lives of mystics and frequently wanted to
share his thoughts on them during their recreation time. Inevitably
the three young Vincentian priests laughed and joked about them,
with Father Poulin being the one who most often led the derisive
remarks. Father Poulin wanted it known that he was not, nor ever
would be, partisan to the beliefs and practices of the many who
were chasing after the popular mystics.

As he glanced once more at the book, *The Suffering, Passion, and
Death of Jesus Christ* by Anne Catherine Emmerich, Father Poulin
still felt the same revulsion he had twenty years earlier. He quickly
shoved it aside with contempt. The next morning he gathered up
the unwanted books from his desk and brought them back to the
library.

That evening when he returned from classes, the same book was there on his desk. He was surprised, but thought that he must have forgotten to pick it up with the other books that morning. He would return it. The following evening the same book reappeared on his desk. He was quite certain that he had returned it to the library. So it happened two or three more times. Was someone pulling a joke on him? He wondered why it kept appearing on his desk, bothering him. It upset him so much that he felt angry. He picked it up and flung it into the farthest corner of the room. It fell with the pages open and broken in two. He felt better. It would no longer bother him.

The book lay on the floor for an entire week, and Father Poulin recorded in his journal that he took a childish glee in seeing it there. As he wrote of all these incidents, he also stated that he was asking pardon of any reader of the text because of the many details he was including. But, he said, it was necessary to understand how all this fits into the pattern of events that followed. He sincerely believed that he had to record them because he felt people are so often guided by events rather than the reverse. He considered this to be an act of Divine Providence.[3]

He noted that the book lay on the floor for an entire week. Strangely the houseman had never picked it up, nor did he even move it. And stranger still, Father Poulin did not let the tossed book bother him, although he found it quite strange, in fact very odd. One morning, about 6:00 a.m. he returned from morning prayer in the chapel and once again saw the book on the floor. At that moment he felt the blood pounding in his veins. He stopped and then thought that it is quite unreasonable to be upset with a book, at least with one like that, which he had never even read. In fact, he was completely unaware of its content. How could he condemn it? He took a deep breath while wondering about these things, and all at once he felt a change of mind within himself.

He thought that it really was ridiculous to condemn the book when he had not actually read it. All he needed to do was to take a step and he would reach the book. As he held the book he felt such a terrible aversion for it that he could not open it. His common sense urged him to open it, but he just stood there holding it for five or six minutes, just holding it, thinking about it. Once again he read the title, "The Suffering Passion." He said if it had just been "The Passion of Our Lord Jesus Christ," he would have easily turned the page. But the word "Suffering" was filled with mysticism, and it terrified him. Once again, he thought he should at least read something about this Anne Catherine Emmerich. Who was she? He could read that much at least and still not be obliged to read the entire book.

When he finally did open the book all he felt was fear. What if someone would see him reading it? He stood near the end of the table, ready to dash the book aside if anyone knocked on his door. He read the foreword and then the preface. After getting that much, he at last reached the note on Anne Catherine Emmerich. He kept looking for something stupid or odd. After all, Father Poulin was known to be a scholar of the classics. What he found, to his surprise, was something very simple, plain, and attractive. Father Poulin was still reading the note on Anne Catherine Emmerich when the 7:00 a.m. bell rang. He quietly put the book on the table, and he left for church.

At 8:00 a.m. he returned to his room, anxious to pick up the book and finish the note on Sister Anne Catherine Emmerich. He noted that his attitude had changed. He no longer needed to guard against getting caught reading the book. When he read the title page, he found that his revulsion toward mysticism was back again. He fought it, and this time it was such a momentary obstacle that it was easier to overcome. This time he was reading about the Passion of Our Lord. It was something he knew. Immersed in the account, he thought it had never been so well expressed anywhere except in the Gospels. He did not want to put the book down, and later upon finishing, he did not want to keep his delight to himself.

Eventually, when he went to recreation with his confreres, he had to blurt it out. The hoots and laughter from the younger priests were loud, but he would not let it bother him. One of the priests assured him that it was all girlish dreams and laughed him to scorn. Another said that if he read anything like that he would have to go to confession. The common criticism was that it was a waste of time to read such writings.

Left: Sister Anne Catherine Emmerich, the 19th century visionary who described Mary's House in Ephesus and the directions to it so accurately that her description was used by Sr. Marie, Fr. Poulin, and Fr. Jung when they decided to look for the house.

One evening while the bantering was still going on during recreation, either in late December or early January, an older priest named Father Dubulle approached him and said, "Father Superior, I too was like you. I did not believe any of the reports on Sister Anne Catherine Emmerich until I read her book." Father Poulin quickly interrupted him and said, "Oh, I don't believe it, but I do know that she does write in a simple, appealing style. It is very pious and still interesting." The elder priest asked Father Poulin if he had ever read Emmerich's book on the Life of the Blessed Virgin. He said no, that he had never read anything written by her before reading Emmerich's account of our Lord's Passion. When asked if he would read it, Father Poulin assured him he would be most pleased to do so. Father Dubulle excused himself and returned a few minutes later with a copy of it.

Shortly after that incident there was a noticeable change during recreation discussions. The priests went from talking about the Passion of Christ to the Virgin Mary and her life in Ephesus. Emmerich's account included detailed descriptions of the Blessed Virgin being brought to Ephesus and spending her remaining years there before her Assumption into Heaven. Emmerich described a house, Mary's House. A little stone home built just for her. The account was filled with details about the terrain, the landscape, the views that could be seen, and landmarks.

In the developing discussion of the priests there was a shift in tone. Something was different. One day someone said that they could settle the matter about the Blessed Virgin living in Ephesus once and for all by determining it for themselves. After all they were in Smyrna, a mere 75 kilometers from Ephesus. The brazen levity that colored their recreation periods lessened. With a serious approach to detail they began making plans to search for Mary's House in Ephesus during their summer vacation.

It was not a long time from those first days of ranting and teasing about the mysticism of Anne Catherine Emmerich before the Daughters of Charity learned that the Fathers were talking about Mary's House in Ephesus. A comforting smile came to Sister Marie. Her prayers were being answered. The Superior, Father Poulin, had moved to accepting some parts of the mystic. He also seemed more affable and relaxed. She had an ally.

There was also Father Henry Jung, chaplain for the French Hospital, a quieter man than Father Poulin. He had made a deep impression upon Sister Marie. For him there were special prayers, because she believed he was the man sent by God to do the work of finding Mary's House. This calm, judicious man carried a reputation of being a brilliant Scripture scholar, a Hebrew scholar, a teacher of the Jewish language, math and science, as well as a fine homilist. He was very orderly. It was a well-known fact that he had been a non-commissioned officer in the French army. He was also known in the archaeological circles for his work in that field. She judged him to be a gentle, kind, and resolute person. She believed he was the one she needed to trace down the location of Mary's House. She also knew he could be obstinate because he was a firm antagonist of mysticism. He would need many prayers. She began working on him, hoping to secure his agreement to work on the project of discovering Mary's House.

Father Jung, fortunately, had been assigned as chaplain to the Daughters of Charity. As Sister Servant, Sister Marie chose to serve breakfast to him following their morning Mass. She guided their conversation. In one of those morning talks about the Blessed Mother having lived in this area, she said, "Ephesus is not so far you know. We could at least check to see if Mary's House is truly there." When Father Jung fended off that suggestion, she hinted, then suggested, and finally pleaded with him to read about Mary's House in Emmerich's private revelations. Eventually she did get him to agree he would at least read it. He was most polite about it, but he said he would make no promises.

Within days, during an evening recreation of the priests, a bell sounded. A delivery man called for Father Jung. Everyone noticed the scowl Father made when he took the package. He knew what it was, and he tossed it aside. That evening when he entered his room, he disdainfully took the package and slowly tore open the wrapping. He did not want to hurt the feelings of Sister Marie, so he sat down to thumb through the book. He was very surprised when he began reading it. It was refreshing and relaxing. He turned to the next page and the next. The page turning never stopped until he finished reading the entire book at 4:00 a.m., the very hour the rest of the priests of the house were rising from sleep. During his night of reading, Father Jung had a complete change of heart.[4]

The change of heart for him meant that he found no reason to reject this writing. He had found no scriptural or theological errors in it. In fact, he thought some areas of the Scripture were more readily acceptable because they were so clearly expressed by her vision or her choice of expression. He wondered how a poor and uneducated young woman could write with such lucidity. Although he was not yet fully converted, he did confirm that the visions were true.

When he spoke about this to the other priests, they were surprised that now three faculty members expressed some belief in these revelations. Among them were their two best scholars, Father Jung and Father Poulin, who, if not giving full credence to the revelations, were accepting them as holding truth.

We do not have the exact date of change of heart for Father Jung, but we do have an earlier notable event that left a deep and different kind of impression upon him. This one came in February 1891, when Father Lobry, the Visitor[5] came to call on his Confreres at Sacred Heart College in Smyrna. The priests had told him about the conversations and arguments they were having during recreation periods on mysticism and Sister Anne Catherine Emmerich and her revelations; especially the possible prospect of the site of the House of the Virgin Mary being nearby in Ephesus.

Father Lobry, one of the major superiors of the Vincentian

Fathers, certainly knew all about the apparitions of Mary to Saint Catherine Labouré pertaining to the Immaculate Conception. Both he and they did accept them. The later apparitions of Mary to Saint Bernadette Soubirous at Lourdes and the Declaration of the Immaculate Conception were held in belief. He told the priests that recently he had been to Lourdes. There he saw miracles. He was ready to confirm the fact that they were miracles. He went on to say, "I don't believe . . ." but he stopped. The priests had just mentioned to him that evening their plans to hunt for Mary's House. Father Lobry reached into his pocket and handed a sum of fifty francs to Father Jung. He said to him, "Take them for your trip. See if you can find her House." This was a fine comfort and encouragement to both Father Jung and Father Poulin, who recorded this event in his journal. He reported to the other confrères that they now knew they had the backing of their superiors.

Fr. Poulin *(front)* and a Vincentian companion.

Fr. Jung standing in front of the north side of Mary's House.

CANTICLE ON THE MOUNTAIN

(sung to the *Lourdes Cantique* air)

What Gabriel said to you
in ancient times
is our Canticle now
Oh! Queen of Heaven.
Ave, Ave, Ave, Maria

On this hill guide our steps
O, Divine Mother
Don't leave us ever
Never leave us.
Ave, Ave, Ave Maria

Show us, O Mother,
The Holy Cross Way
On this earth
You saw us pray.
Ave, Ave, Ave Maria

Pilgrims in this life
We dearly hope one day
through Mary
for the Divine Place.
Ave, Ave, Ave Maria

—J.B. Heroguer,
August 23, 1891[4]

Chapter Ten
A Quest in Three Parts

B Y THE time Easter came and went the subjects of Mary's House and Sister Anne Catherine Emmerich were no longer popular topics during recreation time. Everyone on the faculty seemed to have a project that needed care. Father Jung was quiet and never mentioned Mary's House. In mid-July Father Poulin approached him and said he had to accompany Brother Verney to Constantinople for health care, and that he himself needed to see a doctor. Father Poulin took this opportunity to remind Father Jung of their plan made months earlier to go to Ephesus. He knew he himself could not go at this time, but he hoped the summer trek to Ephesus might still unfold as planned; Mary's House seemed to occupy his thoughts more and more as time went on.

There was a moment of silence, as often happened when the two old friends had a discussion. Time to think. Father Poulin wondered aloud if there would be an opportunity to do the research should they make the attempt. Father Jung responded, "Of course there would." Knowing where the conversation was headed, Father Jung queried, "Do you want me to go to Ephesus?" "Of course I do, my friend," said Father Poulin. Then came the answer that tells us exactly how Father Jung felt about the whole project: "Well, I will go, and I will dig up the whole mountain to be sure about this girl's

67

visions and prove that it is pure foolishness."[1] Although Father Jung had been impressed with the writing of this uneducated woman months before, he remained completely unconvinced. However, the whole affair troubled his mind and spirit enough to push him to decide that there was no option but to prove she was a fake.

And so in July Father Poulin found himself in Constantinople for health reasons. It fell to Father Jung to organize the trip. Since the priests had not given full credence to the revelations of Sister Anne Catherine Emmerich, there was only one purpose for setting out under a hot sun to search for Mary's House, built nineteen centuries earlier. That was to prove the writings were the figment of a loose mind. When the time for the expedition was approaching the faculty seemed to have lost much of its enthusiasm to begin the journey.

Father Jung now had little enthusiasm for this project, but just as he was trying to organize a worthy group, along came Father Benjamin Vervault, a Vincentian friend with whom he had done military service. He had arrived from the Island of Santorini for a few days of vacation. Since he, too, shared an interest in archaeology, he leaped at the offer to help get the trip started. Thomaso, a Persian servant who worked in the college, took charge of the baggage and Mr. Pelecas, a Greek railway agent and friend of Father Jung also joined the troupe. He was a great asset because of his business experience and great knowledge of the area. He was given the duty to secure the necessary legal information for the trip.

On Monday, July 27, 1891, the morning was already extremely hot and muggy, but the four men started out for Ephesus. As a scholar Father Jung wanted to learn from local businessmen the easiest route to Nightingale Mountain, where Mary's House had reputedly been erected. His inquiries came to naught, however, and local governmental employees gave them no useful information, nor did the police. Not even the railway agents could offer any assistance. The day's activity was not a total loss though, because it was in Ephesus that Mustapha, a black-skinned Turkish Muslim hunter joined them. He knew the mountain terrain quite well and carried a large hunting gun. His duty was to guide and protect them from brigands hiding out on the mountain. Additionally, they would shortly be joined by Andreas, a Turk who leased a small portion of land (actually in the area of Mary's House) on which he raised tobacco. With an historical knowledge of the area, he would prove to be a tremendous asset to the project both then and later.

Left: Andreas, the first Muslim caretaker of the House of Mary. *Right:* Mustapha, one of the guides on the expeditions to Mary's House.

Above: Thomaso, another guide on the expeditions to Mary's House. *Below:* Andreas (the first caretaker of Mary's house after it was recovered) and his family.

Sister Marie was filled with hope and anticipation as she realized her heart's desire to search for Mary's House was about to begin. She wished she could accompany the men, but knew that her prayers would have to go with them instead. Women religious of those times did not do such things. But this did not stop her from sending off the men with food and many good wishes for their safety, but most of all she promised her prayers for their safety and success!

The following day began for them at 4:30 a.m. These rather listless would-be archaeologists began a trek most challenging indeed. They were not hikers, and before long they became quite weary. Their intense concentration on following exactly the references in Sister Anne Catherine Emmerich's revelations was taking its toll as they tried to keep a careful eye on the overgrown path they had to tread. They also felt that they needed to be wary of the curious onlookers they passed as they marched along. All the while they were hoping to meet someone, anyone, who might know of a rest stop or an overnight lodging.

Before noon they came upon a monastery mentioned in the revelations. The entire membership, a Superior and a lone brother companion, came out to meet them. They enjoyed a tour of the monastery grounds, a very excellent and revitalizing meal, and good conversation. Father Jung took the occasion to steer the conversation to the Blessed Virgin Mary and simply asked, "Where do you think the Holy Virgin died?" Without a pause the Superior answered, "In Jerusalem." "Is that certain?" quizzed Father Jung. The response came, "I merely repeat what has been said. You are a learned person. You know better than I do." Good answer, Father Jung thought. That is contrary to Sister Catherine's claims.[2]

They were able to travel on and arrive at Scala Nova, where they could dine in a café about 6:00 or 7:00 p.m. Mustafa quickly arranged for a vehicle, which happened to be very old but did get them up a long slope, bringing them by 10:00 p.m. to Ayasoulouk, where, exhausted, they slept overnight.

The third day began at 6:00 a.m. Father Jung had awakened early, studied the narrative of Sister Emmerich, and made plans for the day. This was the day he hoped they would reach their goal. They spent three hours with compass in hand and trudged along the mountain path. Their muscles were sore; their feet ached, and their bodies were drenched with sweat. Fr. Jung called for a stop and drew Mustapha's attention to some trees near the top of the mountain, asking how they could best get there. He knew of no other way to get there except straight up this path.

It was then 9:00 a.m. and the sun was blistering hot. The old abandoned path was filled with thorns and brambles; it had deep ruts, making the climb most difficult. It seemed like they were scaling a cliff. They likened every step of it to climbing their Mount Calvary. Their clothes were sopping wet and sweat rolled into their eyes. They had to stop and wipe them at almost every step. Mr. Pelecas lay on the ground saying he could not move any further. He was lifted and shoved and was forced to put one foot in front of the other. They came upon a land shelf filled with tobacco plants and heard women's voices. Mr. Pelecas rushed toward them and collapsed as he said, "Water, water." They said they had none, but there was a spring about ten minutes further up.

The group followed Mr. Pelecas, who rose to his feet and scrambled toward the direction given them in the hope of finding the spring. He paid no attention to where he was going. One of them said that they were lost. Father Jung stopped and looked down the mountain and focused his gaze upon a clump of trees. They heard him say, "There has to be water there." They slid, they stumbled, and then rolled down the hill. Upon reaching the bottom they had to rise and climb yet again another hill. As they approached the trees they saw the spring, and an old hut near it, almost hidden. Dropping to the ground they drank deeply of the cool, refreshing water bubbling up from the spring. God was so good to them. They rested, drank some more, and then even more. It was so wonderful just to stretch and rest.

As they talked, they looked toward the old hut and noticed an elderly man standing in the doorway. A moment later it became clear that he was a friend of Mr. Pelecas. They had much to talk about with him. As they talked, they took in their surroundings with a keen eye to the archeological aspects of the setting. Father Jung decided that the hut had to be an old sanctuary.

Something was pricking at Father Jung's memory. He felt an odd sensation of anticipation. Then suddenly he remembered something he had read in the narrative of Sister Catherine. Taking in the surrounding scenery, he then focused on this artesian spring on the top of a mountain. He stood still, frozen in astonishment! Pausing to give his mind time to catch up to his senses, he finally . . . slowly . . . dared to ask himself with a heart full of wonder if they had just somehow actually stumbled upon the home of the Blessed Virgin Mary! It was overpowering! In haste he sent one of the men to the top of the mountain. He called to him, "What do you see?" The man said he could see Ephesus on the one side and Samos on the other side! It was all just exactly as she had related—and as he looked around the mountain he saw the terrace gardens, the old ruins, the stones, the trees, the spring. Sister Catherine's revelations were exact. Sister Marie's belief that it could be possible was fulfilled. On the blessed 29th day of July in 1891, Mary's House was found! Now he could believe! He must believe!

Father Jung kept the group together for another three days to help him record with precision every bit of what he judged had been recorded in the revelations. Then, for another two days, they scouted more of the mountain area. On that fifth evening they sat together while Father Jung asked many questions. Andreas told him the old chapel was called *Panaghia-Capouli*—The Door of the Holiest. For Father Jung that was confirmation enough of what they had discovered along the way—the place of pilgrimages for the Blessed Mother. Father Jung said that he had heard there was a big stone on which a cross was incised, on the hill behind Mary's House and that he would like to see it. This stone and others like it were known by the locals as the rocks marking the Stations of the Cross. These Stations were believed to have been carved by the holy hands of none other than the Mother of God as she wept, prayed, and relived the Passion and Crucifixion of her precious Son. Andreas led Father Jung to the stone, and as he looked at it, Father Jung asked if it was regarded as the cross for the last of the Stations. Andreas thought it had to be since there were no others found like it. He gave the stone to Father Jung but made him promise not to reveal to anyone that he had it.[3]

With journals full of information they said farewell to Andreas and then began the long trek home to tend to the many obligations of their vocations. (Father Vervault had left a day earlier.) The carriage was so crowded that they chose to walk, exhausting themselves by lugging their heavy bags. They were tired and sweaty but they did not exhibit any signs of disgruntlement. As Mr. Pelecas departed there was a friendly clap on his shoulder and words of joy as they separated. Thomaso, despite his swollen eyes from lack of sleep, seemed very alert. And Father Jung, with crumpled, damp clothes and weed fragments caught in his bushy beard showed no sign of hesitation as he headed directly back to the faculty residence. He had a mission that he wanted to fulfill, but it would have to wait until tomorrow. The Daughters of Charity were already retired, and so he must go home.

Father Poulin, however, had returned from Constantinople. As he had arrived in Smyrna, Father Vervault was leaving, so they had no opportunity to talk at length about the trip. All Father Vervault could do was to tell Father Poulin that he had a good visit and that Father Jung would certainly tell him all about the journey. Father Poulin was left to do nothing but wait and wonder.

There was a knock at the door, and the anxiety felt by Father Poulin was lifted as soon as he saw Father Jung. He recorded:

> I can see him coming into my room, in an usual mood, looking like a fox caught by a hen.
>
> "Well?" I [Father Poulin] asked him.
>
> "I think, Monsieur, we have found it," [replied Father Jung.]
>
> A loud laugh welcomed this opening. "Get along, with you, you comedian! Don't tell me fairy-stories!"
>
> "I assure you, we have found it."
>
> "What are you saying?"
>
> "The truth, sir."[4]

Both of them laughed. Father Poulin thought that he had to be playing a joke on him. But Father Jung reported, as incredible as it sounded, he was sure they had actually stumbled upon Mary's House. Unconvinced, Father Poulin simply said that, like Saint Thomas, he would not believe it until he saw for himself that Mary's House was actually there! To allay his doubt and prove the discovery to his wary friend, Father Jung willingly agreed to personally bring Father Poulin to the ruins of the House of Mary. "All right, my friend," he said, "I shall take you there myself and we shall see together whether or not it is really Mary's House."[5]

They would set a date before the Feast of the Assumption of the Blessed Virgin Mary to determine it. Until then this was about all they could think about, and yet they could not actually speak about it because it had to be held secret until it could be properly proclaimed. Oh, they did speak about one thing. They both agreed that first thing in the morning they must inform Sister Marie about this special gift of God to them all.

Sister Marie was certain when she opened the door to them the next morning that Father Jung had good news. And good news it was! Sister Anne Catherine Emmerich's writings no longer were an obstacle to him; in fact just the opposite was true. He believed. Humbly, joyfully, and graciously he was pouring out his debt of gratitude to her for pressing upon him the mission of discovering Mary's House. She stood in rapt attention, wide eyes glistening with gratitude. Her prayers were answered. Her hope was realized. Mary's House was just outside Ephesus, only a short journey from where she now stood. She never noticed how unkempt Father Jung might have looked to others after his grueling and arduous journey. She saw him as the priest who courageously responded to her pleas and whom God had rewarded with discovering this great treasure. Yet, this very same priest was standing there, with a heart filled with gratitude, telling her that it was she who was responsible for its discovery.

They sat there together with a few of the other Daughters of Charity as the story was retold. Sister Marie invited both Father Poulin and Father Jung into the chapel, and Father Jung asked that they all join in a prayer of thanksgiving to God and their Blessed Mother. He added to that a plea that God would bless them with the gift of prudence. They should keep the matter of the discovery quiet for the present time until they would have further evidence—rather, confirmation from God—that this was the Virgin Mary's last residence on earth, the holy place of her Assumption.

With that Father Jung gave the Daughters a blessing, and though weary in body, his spirit soared as he and a grinning Father Poulin went on down the street to return to the Vincentian residence.

THE SECOND EXPEDITION

Sister Marie spent the next two weeks in praise and thanksgiving to God for the gift He had given to them all and for the faith that had sustained her. Her faith and hope had been realized. Mary's House had been found. The enormity of this recovered treasure at times so filled her heart that all she could do was to look to Heaven with the words "Ave Maria" on her lips. Father Jung told Sister Marie that he and Father Poulin were planning a second expedition and the three of them began discussions about the prospects that could await them.

Sister Marie knew her dear friends were not outdoorsmen and certainly were unaccustomed to the rough-and-tumble lifestyle of hiking and climbing that they had been living the past month. She was concerned for their well-being and prayed to God for a way to assist them. Oh yes, of course her prayers would accompany the priests, but who on earth would see to their safety? It was then that God gave her an idea. Mr. Constantin Grollo! Why hadn't she thought of that before? Now here was a hardy, strong man of the land. In his capable hands the gardens of the hospital, the school, and the surrounding buildings had always remained not only tamed but beautiful. He was an excellent horticulturist, and she was certain that identifying the plants, the terrain, and the structures of the area around Mary's House would be of critical importance in both the search and the retelling of the story.

Not only was Mr. Grollo an expert gardener, but he also was a man who had spent most of his life outdoors doing the rough and difficult work of the land. He knew how to use a gun, and she would be sure he had one with him for their protection on this holy mission. And he was a gentle soul, ready and willing to take instruction. With his Greek background he also had the greatest devotion to *Theotokos,* the Mother of God. Yes! This was the man for the job! Sister Marie set about readying Mr. Grollo by explaining to him the amazing discovery that had been made and about the new journey he was about to take; a journey that would forever change the history of the story of the life of Our Lady. So grateful was Sister Marie for this idea, that before telling Father Jung and Father Poulin about her plan, she paused to take the time to visit the chapel and kneel and bow her head to thank God for allowing her, once again, to live her faith and be rewarded by her trust.

After an anxious ten days following the first expedition, Father Poulin made final plans for a private confirmatory trip to *Panaghia-Capouli* with Father Poulin. On Wednesday evening, August 12, 1891, they had a few hours of early sleep in the French Hospital near the train station because they did not want to travel a lengthy distance after midnight when they were awakened. As they headed out into the black darkness they noted it was very chilly, almost cold.

At 1:30 a.m. the three sojourners boarded a sort of freight train. There were no seats. Everyone, and there were several people who boarded with them, had to fend for himself—to sit on a carton, a box, or anything that served as a seat. Some stood, leaning against the wall of the car; others stretched out on the floor. Father Poulin and Father Jung had determined not to speak, even in French, about their destination lest someone might understand the purpose of their trip. They advised Constantin to do the same. It was a long, tedious trip, especially for Father Poulin. The train stopped at every little village. When it chugged to begin again, it revved up to what seemed to be the speed of an ox. Finally, at 7:30 a.m. they pulled into Aziziye and found a place that would sell them food and drink.

From this little rest stop Father Jung led them up a long slope, and then taking a path across a small valley, they detoured and walked and walked again until they came to the bottom of the mountain. As they stopped to take a short rest Constantin quickly supplied them with refreshments that Sister Marie had sent along with him. He also knew of and shared information about pilgrimages made by the locals, Greeks mostly, in honor of the Most Holy Virgin.

As they began the grueling climb up the mountain the sun was hot but bearable. Strangely, the ascent did not seem so terrible, despite the rocks and ruts they had to navigate around as they climbed. Perhaps it was easier, they recorded, because they had rested their legs and feet for six hours on the train and had been revitalized by the provisions sent by Sister Marie. There seemed to be some excitement in the air as they talked. They realized their adrenalin was running high because they had reached the big terrace next to the abandoned mine without fatigue. Ten minutes later Father Jung announced that they had come to *Panaghia-Capouli.*

As Father Jung looked at Father Poulin he saw that as they stood there, just peering quietly at the scene, his face and his attitude changed. His eyes widened as he looked all around at it. His mouth dropped open—he was totally captivated by it all: the mountain, the stones, the old crumbling house, the spring, the rocks. He who had read and reread several times the revelations of Sister Anne Catherine Emmerich was recalling each item in view. It was exactly as she had said. Later, Father Poulin would describe it all in his journal when he reached home. He stated simply: "Similarities *grosso grossomodo.*" He found it quite difficult to describe. He wrote: "I was astonished by the details, even on first sight, one after the other. They appeared suddenly, just as Sister Emmerich described. Truth suppressed conviction. There was nothing to say."[6] Father Poulin recounts in his journal the quick and excited back-and-forth conversation between the two priests as they called out to one another in joyful recognition of their surroundings:

"Here are the rocks behind the house."
"Here is the mountain above the rocks; from up there Ephesus can be seen."
"Here, we can see the sea in front of Samos, and the numerous hills of Samos."
"The terrace we crossed right now when coming past the mine is high and well-planted."
"Strange, more than strange . . ."[7]

It was all there just as Sister Anne Catherine Emmerich had said.

Meanwhile Constantin focused on the terrain and trails, being sure to keep his travelers safe and noting all markers and clues so they would know the exact way to eventually get back home. Sister Marie had made it clear that his job was to protect these priests at all costs and provide them with all the assistance and knowledge possible.

After they had evaluated the outside, Father Jung took Father Poulin inside Mary's House. It was a moment to treasure; to think that he was standing in the same house in which Mary had lived. Constantin, too, was filled with emotion. But wanting to be absolutely sure, Father Poulin had to bring out the book of Sister Catherine so that they could measure each revelation regarding the rooms within Mary's House. She said the house had two rooms, one in front of the other: the back room finished with a rounded back and a window on one side only. There was supposed to be an alcove.

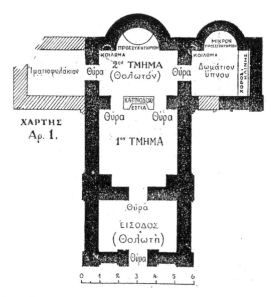

Floor plan of Mary's House in Ephesus. The left wing was too badly water damaged to be restored.

As the two priests compared the details of the rooms the discussion focused on the fireplace. One thought it should be in the corner of the room. The other said "no," and they went back to the book. One read as the other looked for evidence that agreed with it. The book said, "The house was divided by a hearth in the center. I saw fire in the center of the door." Father Jung stood in the center and Father Poulin, standing outside what would have been the narrow door, said it was indeed correct.

Next came the identification of an alcove. They looked around the crumbling remains and read the book over and over and over again, pacing, measuring. Yes, indeed, there was the place for the alcove! As they moved on, they had less fortune with the left side of the House. They walked around and around. On the bit of the wall jutting out of the wreckage they searched for a sign of a room. There was a sign of an arch, but that was all they could find and decided that for the moment they had to be content with that. They had even less fortune for the vestibule. There was found no evidence that a vestibule ever existed. Somewhat disappointed they looked at each other and talked it over. They decided that on this run not everything could be determined, but they had found more than enough evidence that *Panaghia-Capouli* did deserve their attention. In all likelihood the site had many hidden treasures waiting to be discovered.

Feeling very comfortable with the discoveries they had agreed upon, they went back to Ayasoulouk. From there, they continued on and took a path that Andreas had shown Father Jung on the first expedition while Constantin watched for their safety. He had become like their guardian, and they were very grateful for each moment he was in their company. He, too, had been struck by the awesomeness of finding Mary's House, and so his awareness and concentration on all their surroundings was heightened as they progressed on their journey. It seemed each new vista contained an unexpected surprise, and he wanted to remember it all to tell Sister Marie.

The three stayed on the current path for a while as it led them back toward the mountain. Father Jung kept looking about, seeming to search for something more, and was inspired to make a change in their route. He was looking for a particular and precious place that Sister Anne Catherine Emmerich had described in great detail, a place he thought where they might find the burial site of the Blessed Virgin Mary.

They approached a small plateau that attracted their attention. As Father Jung led them, all three stopped immediately and gazed in wonderment. The priests could be most grateful that Sister Marie had sent Constantin with them. With his knowledge and experience in gardening he quickly pointed out that underground water was keeping this place verdant. It was the most beautiful of all the sites they had seen that day. It had to be something special. While they were looking at all the wildflowers in bloom, Constantin, struck by the beauty of this spot, was naming each bloom and blossom as they all rejoiced in the beauty. God loved this place, he said. Could it possibly be the place of the Dormition and the Assumption of the Virgin Mary, the Mother of God?

Intrigued by the spectacular display of vibrant colors on this plateau, the priests hoped that it might be the site for which they were searching. Carefully they went over the entire plateau but they could find no evident trace of the tomb of the Virgin Mary. Although they found no concrete sign of their hope after going over the entire space, they made a mental note of this beautiful spot, recorded it in their journal, and with undeterred spirits knew they would continue the search for the tomb there.

Time had passed and the trio needed to continue their journey to Elias. They were carrying nothing with them, no extra food or sleeping gear. They would soon have to catch their train and head back home for some much-needed rest and nourishment. What they did carry, however, was a pack of challenging memories and many prayers and thoughts of thanks that assured them they had been graced. They would return, they knew, to render due respect for a site where their beloved Virgin Mary had lived and prayed and worked—and very probably from which she had been assumed into the glories of Heaven!

When they reached Smyrna it was 4:30 p.m., Friday, August 14, the Eve of the Assumption of the Virgin Mary. All three men paid a visit to Sister Marie, who had been waiting for them with a heart full of anticipation. Constantin, for his part, was invited to offer his thoughts, and he expressed his desire to go again to Mary's House. Sister Marie smiled with tender gratitude to him for his bravery, kindness, and service, which had been such a blessing to her friends. The extraordinary trio, Father Jung, Father Poulin, and Sister Marie, were finally able to sit and talk; and, Sister Marie's whole being drank in with fervor the lovely details that her friends patiently shared with her. The two priests thanked her profusely for the invaluable service of Constantin and above all for her loyal and constant prayerful assistance. She assured the priests that it was little enough she could do; her commitment to this holy endeavor was total. She was at God's disposal, His handmaid and theirs.

Their celebration of the feast of the Assumption was filled with wonder and praise. They knew God had singled them out for a special blessing.

THE THIRD EXPEDITION

There was exuberant joy in the celebration of this Feast of the Assumption by the Vincentian family in Smyrna. Sister Marie arranged for the Daughters of Charity and for many of the Vincentian Priests to come together for the sacred liturgy of the Mass honoring the Assumption of the Virgin Mary. For our remarkable trio, this Mass had an exceptional quality; gratitude and graces were flowing. Sister Marie had the members of the Children of Mary prepared to sing the Gregorian Chant for the *Kyrie,* the *Gloria,* the *Credo,* the *Sanctus,* and the *Agnus Dei.* The homily by Father Jung had a special note of appreciation for the Mother of God, as he invited all the members of the church to rededicate themselves to the service of their Mother Mary. Father Poulin's face was lit with joy. The Queen of Heaven surely did love this little congregation. As the *Salve Regina* was sung the accompaniment given it by Sister Marie on her harmonium had a triumphal air. Everyone rejoiced!

When the laity had dispersed after Mass, Sister Marie invited the Vincentian Fathers to join the Daughters already gathered in their reception room. Here coffee was served. Sister announced that Father Jung had something to say to them regarding Mary's House. He shared with the group that Sister Marie and Father Poulin had asked him to head the next necessary step in defining and leading a program to uncover and recover Mary's House and land. There was much that had to be done, but this was just the first step.

He explained that very soon they would have a week-long pilgrimage to *Panaghia-Capouli* composed of prayer and labor. There would be common prayer in the morning and evening, and their meals would be procured and prepared by Mr. Pelecas and Constantin, with the help of Andreas. Other members of the group would be Paul d'Andria, an engineer; Mr. Jules Borrel, the Director of the French Post Office; and Mr. Heroguer, a fine-arts man. The work would consist of attempting to identify as many of the items described in the book of Sister Anne Catherine Emmerich's revelations as possible. The cartography, as much as possible, would be done by Paul d'Andria and Jules Borrel. Each of the men had given his generous consent to be involved as much as needed with any work assigned. Mr. Heroguer, as record-keeper, would also contribute to their prayer life with his musical talent. They all gave every indication of being a joyous team, dedicated to the honor and glory of Mary Immaculate.

Before the meeting ended Sister Marie added her thanks and asked Father Poulin to give his blessing to the family of St. Vincent de Paul. She closed her eyes in silent prayer, asking every aid for the men whose works she would prayerfully and financially support. Her prayers rose to Heaven asking that this third expedition be a time of deep piety and devotion to Mary.

Father Jung scheduled the week-long trip to *Panaghia-Capouli* to begin on Wednesday, August 19, 1891. Thomaso, who suffered severe strain and could not come on this trip, was visited by Father Jung to help ease his disappointment. Andreas, along with his wife and daughter, rented that small tract of ground overlapping the property of Mary's House. He was already there and would be invited to participate in this important pilgrimage.

The men set out to measure every part of the mountain associated with *Panaghia-Capouli*. They recorded distances between various points, took pictures, and did several drawings for comparison. They found what they thought might have been a Station of the Cross on a high point of the ground, and they called it Calvary's Station.

Father Jung asked Andreas about the existence of a castle mentioned by Sister Catherine. After being assured there was no old castle, Father Jung repeated the question with a different lead, asking it again, maybe two, three, or four miles out. "There may be," Andreas said. "Are you talking about the Palaio Castro?" "The old Castle?" asked Father. "The Palaio Castle? Could be." Father Jung asked where it was, and Andreas answered, "Oh, it is about fifteen minutes from here. Between two terraces." When they got there and saw it, Father Jung was joyous. Sister Catherine was once again right. She had said that the remains of an old castle were about 12 kilometers from *Panaghia*.[8]

Back at *Panaghia,* the group was puzzled by another discovery. They found themselves on a lengthy terrace that had to have been made by human hands. It had a stone wall around it. Traces of a pathway were still evident. They cleared away debris from some partially covered stones that were standing on end. These had been set in circles and seemed to follow one after the other. Andreas did not know what they were, but he did know that they had been there a long time. Sister Anne Catherine Emmerich had stated that Mary had created the Stations of the Cross devotion. The more they studied these regularly placed circles of rocks, the more convinced they were that they had come upon the Stations of the Cross. Every doubt was removed when the path led to what was called Kara-Thalti, that high point of the ground more heavily decorative than the others: their Calvary Station.

The uncovering of any site had a great effect upon all the members of the group. Their bonding with one another deepened. Each day on the mountain they gathered for morning prayer, asking the guidance of God for a new day. They understood that what they were doing was being done with faith and piety. They never hesitated to share their feelings with one another; rejoicing over a discovery, disappointed if nothing was found that day. In the evening they gathered once more to praise God for what had transpired that day. Mr. Heroguer had a bent for music, and to honor Our Lady, he composed some verses to be sung to the air of the Lourdes hymn each evening.[9] They were a closely knit family missing only one: Sister Marie.

Their greatest act of worship, what they regarded as their most extraordinary privilege, was their participation in the celebration of the Sunday Mass on August 23, 1891—a day all of them would remember! They tidied up a spot in the house where once the altar had been installed. Andreas had taken three old wooden shelves and made of them a rather shaky altar. Mr. Heroguer took the place of choirmaster. The wife and daughters of Andreas were able to join the group for Mass. Father Henry Jung had the most honorable office of all: he was the celebrant of the first Latin Mass in Mary's Home after the lapse of so many, many centuries. Also among the participants in this sacred liturgy were, of course, Mr. Jules Borrel, Paul d'Andria, and Constantin.

Standing near this altar in Mary's House was such a great privilege. There is no recorded statement on their emotions. It had to be overwhelming. A profound silence followed the *Ite Missa Est*.[10] The

Mass was over, but they stayed in prayer for several moments longer, each one offering personal thanks to God for this extraordinary celebration honoring God and the Virgin Mary, and no doubt also offering thanks to God for Sister Marie and her faith, which began the whole beautiful story.

Following the Mass their conversation was lively and joyous. Included in this little congregation was a group of Orthodox Greeks who had come for their annual visit to *Panaghia-Capouli* and who felt very privileged to observe this Mass. They begged Father Jung to remain through August 27, when they would celebrate their Feast of the Assumption of Mary. Unfortunately Father Jung was obligated to return to Smyrna as the Vincentian priests were going to begin their retreat on the 26th day of August.

There was one great difficulty. According to the revelation, Mary's Home was supposed to be octagonal, but from their tracings the back looked as though it was round, and yet it seemed to have some angles. We know now what it took them to learn over a period of three more years with considerable excavation. About a yard deeper they were to find flat at that depth of ground a perfectly formed black octagon upon which the original structure had been built. It was just as Sister Anne Catherine Emmerich had said.

On Monday, the 24th, they began winding up their work. They assured themselves that they had made photo and drawing copies of almost everything they found. They had noted the terrain and horticulture with the help of Constantin. They checked it all once again, and departed for home on the 25th. Later, in 1896, and under the name of the Vincentian Fathers, they published their findings in their book entitled, *Panaghia, or the Home of the Blessed Virgin Mary Near Ephesus.*

In Smyrna Sister Marie was anxiously awaiting their return. As she listened to the recitals of each of them, her heart beat more rapidly with joy. They relived with her their precious moments of discovery, and with eyes glistening she listened with gratitude to God for allowing her to be a part of this moment of history. Tears of joy, though not seen by many, filled the bright and beautiful eyes of Sister Marie.

Sister Marie received a full report of everything, just as she had with the two previous visits. As they talked they realized that they had come upon one of the great prizes of archaeology. They had made three separate trips up the mountain. Many people saw them and did not recognize them as ordinary pilgrims such as their own people were. People would be talking. They had carried photography equipment with them. They had an armed guard each time they went. They could not be going up there the next time with pick axes and shovels without raising many questions. Who owned the land? They would need his approval to work on it. The more they conferred about it, the more they realized they needed lawful permission to work on the site. Eventually, it came to the point when one of them said that they really needed ownership of the site. And only God would know whom to ask.

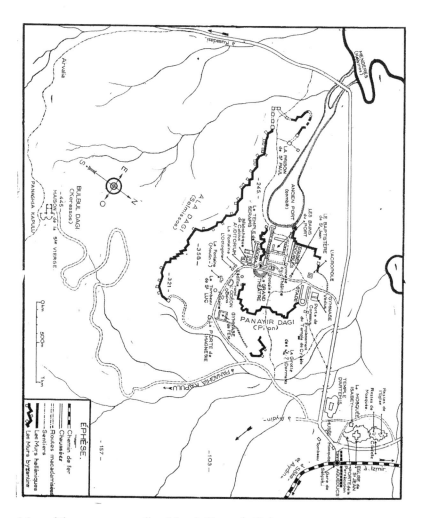

Map of the area surrounding Mary's House in Ephesus.

Above: The ruins of the Basilica of St. John the Evangelist, in Ephesus.

Below: Floor plan of the Basilica of St. John the Evangelist.

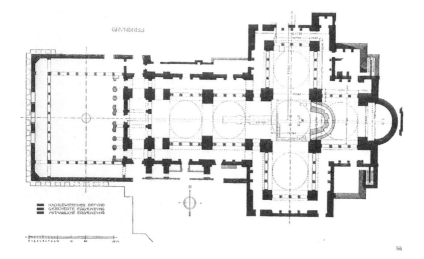

Above: A model of what the Basilica of St. John the Evangelist originally would have looked like.

Below: The ruins of the famous Celsus Library in Ephesus.

Above: Mary's House as it was first seen by Frs. Jung and Poulin in 1891.

Left: Entrance to Mary's House as found on the first expedition, July 29., 1891.

Above: South side of Mary's House as discovered in 1891. *Below left:* A sketch of the interior of the House of Mary as seen on the first expedition. *Below right:* An actual photograph of the same.

Above: A priest stands on the terrace in front of Mary's House which looks out over the sea of Ephesus. *Below:* Tomb of St. Luke in Ephesus.

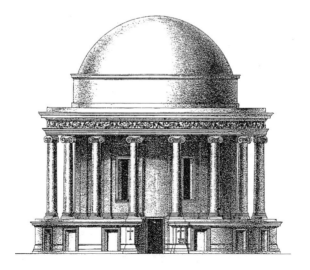

Chapter Eleven

The Purchase of *Panaghia-Capouli*

SISTER MARIE was the one who first thought about the possibility of finding Mary's Home. She was the one who prayed that the Home and the site of Mary's Dormition and Assumption would be found. She urged the priests to read the revelations of Sister Anne Catherine Emmerich. She helped organize the search trips, furnished the protection guards, paid the expenses, and as always, her participation was the least publicly known.

While the discussion plans ensued, Sister Marie listened. Once she knew that Mary's House could be identified, she knew that it was her personal obligation to secure the ownership of it for the Catholic Church. She had already written to Father Antoine Fiat, the Superior General of the Congregation of the Mission, her major superior in spiritual matters. She gave him an account of what they had discovered, and she requested permission to purchase from her own personal funds a portion of Nightingale Mountain in Turkey, on which Mary's House had been built. Father Fiat's response, granting that permission, was dated October 21, 1891. He wrote: "I am not accustomed to opposing the sisters in the employment of their personal fortune, whenever it concerns a good work. So, if you can, buy it." She knew he was in favor of it. She said a prayer of thanks and for the moment told no one about it except her Blessed Mother.

On Wednesday, January 27, 1892, Father Poulin went by train with Father Jung to Ephesus. They brought along a local professional businessman, a Mr. Binson, to handle the legal matters. As they took their places on the train, they were eager to spend this time in private discussion about their business of the day. They were terribly disappointed when a man wearing a fez[1] opened the door and took the last seat in the compartment. They saw in each other's faces the very same disconsolate reaction that each of them felt. However, Mr. Binson knew well the business etiquette in Turkey. After they had greeted each other, he politely offered the man a cigarette and inquired how far he was traveling. It so happened he was going to Scala Nova, the same city of their destination, but they never told him that.

When Mr. Binson inquired about any news of the day, the gentleman mentioned that in Scala Nova a huge scandal was rocking the city. He seemed most anxious to reveal all the details of the case, because it brought one of the famous families of the city—that of the Bey[2] of Avaria—to court. He said the Bey, a very likeable person, and his family were very wealthy and owned much of Nightingale Mountain. He had a nephew, who was most personable, but a gambler and a great spendthrift. He owed money to several people and sought the Bey's financial assistance. Being a kind man, the Bey loaned him a very large sum of money, but its repayment was long, long overdue. The young nephew kept dodging payments to the Bey. The Bey, however, did know that the nephew still held a deed to a portion of the mountain next to his. In the conversation Mr. Binson discovered that the particular portion of the land owned by the nephew was the property on which *Panaghia-Capouli* was located.

The priests were stunned. Mr. Binson glanced at them and they all kept quiet. Not one of them wanted to reveal to the man their shared understanding that, although they at first considered it a great inconvenience to sacrifice their travel discussion time, they now understood they were beneficiaries of the Divine Providence of God. Arriving in Scala Nova they graciously bade the man good-bye. They turned and walked directly to the Bey's home. God certainly had directed their journey. They also knew that Sister Marie was surely praying for them.

It was late morning when the Bey most politely invited the two priests and the well-groomed businessman into his home. Custom demanded that they should spend the next hour in pleasant talk. He held up a staying hand. He would be most honored to have them dine with him today, he said, because Divine Providence must have known they were coming. A friend had just brought him, an hour earlier, a large fish. He told the chef to prepare it for him and these fine gentlemen. Right now, he insisted, they must relax from their trip and after that they would have time to talk. Business matters could wait until after their meal. They felt most comfortable with this polite, sensitive man.

After the dinner they learned that the Bey could not possibly sell the property right then, but if they could return in two weeks, he would then be pleased to sell it to them. The date was set for February 11, and the priests felt very good about it because it was the Feast of Our Lady of Lourdes. On that day, however, when they came back, he said he was still unable to sell it. Would they please come back after one more week? On that occasion Mr. Binson returned alone because the priests had classes to teach. Again it was disappointing, because the Bey said that he truly wanted to sell it to them, but the mortgage held against the nephew could not yet allow it to be sold. They would have to be patient.

While all those attempts to secure the land continued, Sister Marie was also doing her own work; as usual, this work was critically important but quiet and behind the scenes. On February 27, 1892, she went to the Smyrna branch of the Lyonnais Bank and deposited a check for 45,000 francs. It was placed in an account set aside for the purchase of the property in question. With that task completed, she increased her fervent prayer and continued what she had become quite good at—waiting.

Although it was late January of 1892 when the two priests and Mr. Binson began negotiations for the purchase of *Panaghia-Capouli,* and one month later when Sister Marie deposited in the bank the funds for its purchase, the matter dragged on and on. It was not until October 20 that they learned the transactions were finally begun. The good news finally came by telegram, which read, "November 14, 5:40 pm to Poulin, College, Propaganda, Smyrna, Scala Nova, 623, Congratulations. Business complete. Binson." The very few words of the text belied the enormity of the message. Father Jung, Father Poulin, and Sister Marie rejoiced in this announcement as welcome news indeed. Mary's House was safely in their care.

Father Poulin asked Sister Marie, "In whose name should the property be listed? Do you want it in the name of the Superior General? The Visitor of the Vincentian Fathers? The Superior of Sacred Heart? Under whose name will we buy it?" She said, "Mine." He said, "Very well, my Sister. It will be registered in your name." They knew she meant it and also that she understood all that this would mean for her in the future. Not knowing of her forward thinking and faith, the priests conferred with each other their belief that she would somehow secure the funds. It was then that she told them she had already deposited the funds to cover the cost. It was also clear that she understood that she would be responsible not only for the purchase of *Panaghia-Capouli* but also for its maintenance, the continued excavations necessary to uncover it, the construction of roads and buildings, the improvements to be made on the property, the planting of trees, salaries for workmen, taxation, and so forth. Those who were present and heard some of these remarks also recall that she said, "Make use of me while I am here. After my death I will not be able to help you."

But of course, how could the very humble Sister Marie have ever imagined that her help would continue in service to Our Lady long, long after her death?

Chapter Twelve

Reactions

PURCHASING land in Turkey at this period of time was not an easy matter. First, buying a portion of a mountain seemed improbable. Sister Marie was a woman attempting to transact a business venture in a man's world. She was a Catholic in a Muslim country. Moreover, she was no ordinary citizen but a religious Sister. The group talked about it and agreed that if any woman could do it, Sister Marie could. She was well known in the city. She had an established reputation for business administration in both the hospital and the school. She was well loved by the town's folk who benefitted from the health care her hospital so charitably supplied. And the families of children in her school were all most familiar with her loving ways and kind guidance. The priests, also, knew she would have the help of the Virgin Mary.

When news of the purchase of *Panaghia-Capouli* by the French Catholics became public, the Greeks were upset. They claimed to have been developing a plan to finance their own buying of that property but in time accepted the turn of events and considered themselves outsmarted. The Turks, however, were indignant that this Christian group procured the land they were planning to buy. Some even hurled threats against the Catholics. The Bey himself and his associates were maltreated because, of course, they were blamed for having allowed this to happen. Petitions were sent to the

Sultan with the hopes that the contract given to Sister Marie could be broken. In the end, however, Sister Marie, with the help of prayer and the efforts of her Church and legal associates through it all, remained owner of *Panaghia-Capouli*.

Panaghia-Capouli. It did not look much like a valuable sale, overgrown with weeds, crumbling walls, and little to nothing in the ways of usable trails. But it had been and should still be recognized as the place of Mary's last home while on earth. For Sister Marie it was the most precious of all properties on earth, a holy treasure: what had once been the home of the Blessed Mother was now legally her very precious property, entrusted to her by God to hold until it was rejuvenated. So grateful and joyful was she that it was as if the prayers of her heart which sang loud and strong to Heaven could be heard by more than just the angels . . . *O dear Mother, we must now prepare your House for your children who will come streaming here from all over the whole world to visit and pray at your altar.* Her great devotion to the Blessed Mother and the Children of Mary helped her to understand that all God's children were also the children of Mary. She knew they all would want to come and see for themselves the home in which Mary had lived. After all, so many children of God loved Mary: not only Catholics but even Muslims, the Orthodox, and more.

But this was Turkey, 1892. Unfortunately she was not allowed to make any improvements because everything was held in abeyance by the government of Turkey. Bureaucratic details tested her mettle as well as that of her devout team members. She did manage to fund the construction of a small building, under the direction of Father Jung, to house Andreas, his wife, and daughter. Sister Marie decided that he who had been so respectful and helpful with the historical background during the expeditionary visits would be the best choice for the first caretaker of Mary's House.

Despite all the wearisome troubles in the legal handling of the property, the emotions of Sister Marie were quite high and steady as ever: joy, satisfaction, hope, expectation, gratitude, thanks, and now and then, a bit of frustration. Her emotions hardly fluctuated with the processes she had to endure. The reality of it all, the ability to reach her goal of making the House of Mary beautiful once again, she knew, must wait until the government would allow it. Ah . . . waiting . . . well, that was something at which she was becoming an expert!

Chapter Thirteen

Archiepiscopal Reaction

THE BAN to keep secret the fact that they had discovered Mary's Home had lost its force. Their trips up the mountain brought curious inquiries. The mixture of men of varied nationalities drew questions. They were not pilgrims, nor were they vacationers. They were serious, and they obviously had a goal in mind. It was also clear that they were determined to secure the house because they brought along armed guards for protection. Since they were of a mixture of backgrounds and they carried photographic equipment with them the onlookers began to wonder if they were spying for the French government? Or for the Greeks? What was their purpose? They needed to be watched.

There were other reasons rumors were beginning to circulate about the men who came out of Smyrna. Sister Anne Catherine Emmerich had stirred up the interest in many others besides Sister Marie de Mandat-Grancey. For example, it was a known fact that ten years earlier the Abbé Gouyet of Paris, after reading the revelations of Sister Anne Catherine Emmerich, had come to Smyrna in 1881. He had visited Archbishop Timoni, who assigned a young man to accompany the Abbé on a trip up the mountain. (The young guide, by the way, later became a priest.) The Abbé had written of the success he had in locating the House of Mary. That report was not favorably received in Rome. Nothing more was reported about the discovery, and the Roman Catholic shrine of Mary's Assumption near Jerusalem continued to celebrate the event as having taken place in Jerusalem. All interest in the claims by Abbé Gouyet quietly ceased.

Another incident, not so publicly known, but already spoken about, came from Father Poulin, who said that the Vincentian Provincial Superior in Aydin, Father Lobry,[1] had communicated a discovery made by his friend, the popular Father Philippe, Superior of the Mechitaristes. Father Philippe had announced that he had done some research for Mary's House at the request of a woman in Germany. He claimed to have found it and reported it. (What he actually saw was the old monastery at the base of the mountain.) But the news was out that people had heard of Mary's House in Ephesus and had done some research looking for it.

Sister Marie was aware of these claims. She also knew that she now owned the crumbled remains of Mary's House and all the land on which it had been erected. Realizing that the property truly belonged to the Church, she repeatedly suggested to Father Poulin that they give Archbishop Timoni a full account of what they discovered. Fr. Poulin kept delaying it, saying, according to the practice of Saint Vincent de Paul, they would await the time assigned by Divine Providence. He assured Sister Marie that the Lord would let them know when it was time to do so. He finally decided three months after their third visit to Mary's House that the time had arrived.

He wanted to make a low-key presentation of it to the Archbishop. On the 29th day of November 1892, Father Poulin called upon Archbishop Timoni, requesting his presence for his annual appearance in a celebration held by the college. Once that was settled, Father Poulin made a quick mention of the discovery that the

Vincentian priests had made at *Panaghia-Capouli.* The Archbishop seemed stunned. He immediately took charge of the conversation with great excitement.

Archbishop Timoni was keenly aware of the immensity of the matter about which he had just been told. He had long lived with the legend which held that the last several years of the life of the Blessed Virgin Mary were spent in Ephesus, that it was there she underwent her Dormition and Assumption into Heaven. If her home was discovered, it would bring glory to the Church of Ephesus and to the Church as a whole.

This news from Father Poulin filled him with new enthusiasm. When he learned that the Vincentians planned to go up the mountain the next day, on the 30th, a holiday in the college, the Archbishop said he would join them. Father Poulin was taken by surprise, because one just does not bring an Archbishop up a rugged mountain path, climbing, and struggling as they had been doing. Father Poulin wanted to show him proper respect, especially before the local citizens. The Archbishop fended off each attempt to change his mind. Finally, Father Poulin capitulated saying, "All right, Archbishop, but you must come as the Archbishop." They both knew what this meant. This would be an official Church visit to the site, and the Archbishop would bring with him a group of officials to record the event. These records would later be submitted to the Archbishop for his review and finally shared with the Church in Rome. He agreed.

When Father Poulin returned home and related that news to the confreres, there was a loud cheer and applause. They were now going to receive official public recognition for their work and the site. Prayers of thanksgiving were said. The official date of the visitation was set for December 1, 1892.

Late that afternoon a special visit was made by the priests to tell

Sister Marie what had transpired that day. Father Poulin was so excited. Sister Marie, for her part, wore her biggest and brightest smile. God was blessing their efforts once again, and she knew the Blessed Mother's long-kept secret would not be a secret for much longer.

On Thursday, December 1, 1892, at 7:30 a.m., the group left the train station of Smyrna for Ayasoulouk, where they had horses awaiting them for the trip up the mountain. In order to impress the local citizenry of Greeks and Turks they arranged a special parade of dignity for their Archbishop with a well-groomed horse with decorative rein and bridle. It bore the episcopal colors with the initials of the Archbishop in bold relief, and Mustapha tended him. Along with the Archbishop's horse in full regalia, there were horses for each of the official travelers and priests. It was quite a sight; a parade of the finest Turkish horses, known for their grace and beauty, extravagantly tacked and fitted, upon which rode these men of God, looking stately and purposeful in their clerical garb.

They started out to climb the mountain, a grand parade indeed. As they moved along, Father Poulin answered inquiries from the Archbishop concerning the directions of the road, where it would lead, the direction of the mountain, the distance to Ephesus, and other such items—data for the official episcopal report that would be compared with the revelations of Sister Anne Catherine Emmerich. The matter of the Way of the Cross, although a matter of certainty in their hearts, was not yet sufficiently proved to them for official submission, so it was not added to the report for identification at this time. The official report follows.

Chapter Fourteen
Record of Evidence

W E, Andre Polycarpe Timoni, Archbishop of Smyrna, and Apostolic Vicar of Asia-Minor As Well as the Undersigned Certify and Attest That Which Follows.

Recent research, undertaken in accordance with the indications of Sister Anne Catherine Emmerich, has seriously drawn the attention of the nation for some six months toward an area close to Ephesus and called *Panaghia-Capouli* (Door of the Virgin). We wanted to verify for ourselves the exactitude of the report that was given us. To this end, on Thursday, December 1, 1892, we were transported to said area of *Panaghia-Capouli*. There we found the ruins, well enough preserved, of an old house or chapel whose construction according to a competent archaeologist dates from the first century of our era and which, as much for the location as for the interior plan, corresponds clearly and entirely to that which Catherine Emmerich said in her revelation regarding the house of the Holy Virgin at Ephesus.

I. REGARDING THE LOCATION

The visionary says: approximately three or three and a half leagues from Ephesus—to the left of the route coming from Jerusalem—on a mountain to which one arrives by narrow paths

111

which are south of Ephesus—and from the summit of which one sees Ephesus on one side, the sea on the other and the sea even closer than Ephesus (*Life of the Holy Virgin,* the 6th Edition, Casterman, 1898, pages 461, 462, 474).

All of these details are rigorously exact.

It took us three hours to climb from Ephesus to the house and two hours to descend. It is, indeed, to the left of the route when coming from Jerusalem. It is indeed, on a mountain and from the summit of this mountain, one effectively sees on one side Ephesus and on the other side the sea and the sea even closer than Ephesus.

The visionary says further, that behind the house, quite close, there are high rocks, —that in the surrounding there was a castle inhabited by a dethroned prince, friend of St. John—that toward the summit of the mountain was located a high terrace well planted (Ibid., pages 461, 462).

Twelve meters behind the house there are rocks rising abruptly that measure 40 to 50 meters in height. Fifteen to twenty minutes away are the ruins in large blocks of an old rectangular building that one may suppose is the castle. The terrace still exists; today it is a tobacco field.

Finally, the visionary speaks of a small wood located not far from the house and of a stream, unusually winding that could be seen between the mountain and Ephesus (pages 462, 466).

Five minutes away from the house we encounter a small valley filled with small trees and bushes, a little further, down below and to the left, a cluster of trees. Is it the remainder of the small wood? We can neither confirm nor deny it. The stream is no more, but at one time it certainly existed, as it is clear from first, the 5 or 6 torrents which still run through the part of the plain identified by Catherine Emmerich; secondly, from authors, in particular, Mr. G. Weber, who informs even after Strabon of two streams running into one another and which he names one Marnas and the other Selinus.

II. Regarding the House Itself

Catherine Emmerich says the house is in stone and that it is comprised of two rooms, one in front and one in the back (pages 462, 463).

The house is indeed in stone and of the same construction as the gymnasium at Ephesus.

The two rooms exist, one in front and the other in back, behind the first. These two rooms today are preceded by a vestibule, but it is easy to observe this vestibule, although from the same century as the remainder, has been added afterwards. It is not linked with the main structure, but only juxtaposed.

Catherine Emmerich said that the house ended with a platform, and the ceiling of the second room formed an arch (pages 462, 463).

The ceiling of the roof has completely disappeared, so nothing can be said about it. The roof of the second room also disappeared, but on the two lateral walls, the beginning of an arch is perfectly visible.

The visionary said that the back room ended with a semi-circle and that the rear of that room was the oratory of the Virgin Mary (page 463).

Indeed, the rear of that room ends with a large niche that forms a second protrusion outside and which permits an altar to be installed inside.

The visionary said that the windows were placed at a consider-able height and that the second room was darker than the front room (pages 462, 463).

There is no trace of windows in the walls, except at two and a half meters above ground.

It is easy to understand why the back room was darker than the front room. The back room could only receive light through a single and very narrow window at the rear of the room and situated at more than three meters above ground.

Catherine Emmerich said: the second room is separated from the first by the fireplace, which is located between the two rooms, and by the doors of light material, which hang on either side of the fireplace (pages 462, 463).

The fireplace and doors disappeared more probably when the apostles transformed (according to Catherine Emmerich, page 507) the humble house into a chapel, but two protrusions of the walls, on the right and on the left, exactly between the two rooms, show clearly still today the place where the fireplace and the doors must have been located.

The visionary said: On the right of the oratory, the door led to the bedchamber of the Virgin Mary—across from and on the left of the oratory was another room for Mary's clothes and furniture (page 465).

The doors, which gave access from the oratory to the two rooms of which Catherine Emmerich speaks, are walled in, but quite apparent. The room on the left, with Mary's clothes, is buried in the ground; nothing can be said about it for the moment. The room on the right, that is, the bedchamber of the Virgin Mary, is in ruins, but everything can be identified. One can clearly see the niche against which was placed the bedroom, the rear where the plank was, and the oratory close to the couch (page 492).

The visionary said that the couch of the Virgin Mary, placed against the wall, was one and a half feet high and its length and width were very ordinary (page 465).

At the back of the bedroom, at 45 centimeters of soil, there is in the wall, a protrusion that seems to have been put there expressly to serve as a support for the Virgin Mary's couch.

The visionary said finally that a curtain going from one room to the other formed the oratory located between the two rooms.

This is evident from a cursory look at the place.

CONCLUSION

Having grounds, on the one hand, given the homage paid to the trustworthiness and to the virtue of Catherine Emmerich by her contemporaries and superiors, to think that her revelations merit at least some belief,

Observing, on the other hand, book in hand and with our own eyes, the perfect conformity that exists regarding the place and the house itself, between the ruins, which we have visited, and the description given by the visionary relative to the house of the Virgin Mary at Ephesus,

Knowing also that local traditions, consulted once more very particularly and recently on this matter, affirm in the most positive manner that the Virgin Mary had lived in three different places in the area surrounding Ephesus and lately in *Panaghia-Capouli* where she would have died and would have had her tomb,

We are strongly inclined to believe that the ruins of *Panaghia-Capouli* are effectively the remains of the house of the Virgin Mary and we pray that this good Mother help us to shed full light on a question that interests so highly the Church of Smyrna first and then the whole Catholic world.

Seal of the Archdiocese

A. P. Timoni, Archbishop of Smyrna
M. Varthaliti, Canon, Chancellor of the Archdiocese
D. Eugene Hambar, Canon of the Basilica of St. John

Abbot Octave Mirzan, Priest of the Basilica of St. John
J. Vasseur, p. d. l. m.
H. Jung, p. d. l. m.
J. Borrel, Director of the French Postal Service at
    Smyrna
Giuseppe Morroni, Choir Master
E. Poulin, Superior of the French School,
    (LaPropaganda) at Smyrna
Paul d'Andria, Engineer
Gaspar Dumond, p. d. l. m.,[1] Copyist

This official visit unexpectedly came at a most opportune time for Father Eugene Poulin. Like so many other incidents in the discovery of Mary's Home, it had not been planned. However, it gave the undertaking official recognition. Unlike the earlier citing by Abbé Gouyet, this one seemed designed by God. It needed the inspiration and faith of Sister Marie de Mandat-Grancey with her noble character, knowing that she was called by God, not only to serve Jesus Christ in the poor, but for directing the program of recovering the last residence of the Virgin Mother of God before her Assumption into Heaven. Her name does not appear on the Record of Evidence, just as her name does not appear in most all the works in which she was involved. The people of her time knew her worth: *She was a Daughter of Charity* and out of their love for her they called her the *Mother of Panaya*[2] or as Father Poulin referred to her in his diary; *Panaghia's Mother.*[3] She completely emptied herself, like a good mother. What she had, she gave to the poor. What she did was a service to the Children of Mary for love of Mary and her Son, Jesus Christ. And so she was known as *mother.*

The Record of Evidence gave ecclesiastical legitimacy to the archaeological work that the men did during the next several years.

What had occurred on *Panaghia-Capouli* was approved by the Catholic Archdiocese of Smyrna. It also gave official recognition to the revelations of Sister Anne Catherine Emmerich. This brought special joy and comfort to Sister Marie and the Daughters of Charity who assisted in the beautification of the Home and grounds of Mary. Most of all it was an official Record of Evidence that was sent to Rome. Shortly after the Record was shown to Pope Leo XIII, the indulgences attached to the shrine of Mary in Jerusalem were removed.

Chapter Fifteen

Safe at Last

DECEMBER 1, 1892—Memorable day. It has been just two years and a month since the time that Sister Marie went public to uncover, verify, and recover for the Church Mary's Home. It all began with prayer and has been, up to this moment, sustained by her prayers. First, after being led by the Holy Spirit to select them, Sister Marie needed the conversion of Father Poulin and then Father Jung that led them to believe in Sister Anne Catherine Emmerich's revelations. She still marveled over the manner in which Mr. Binson and the two priests learned of the ownership of *Panaghia-Capouli.* She was also most grateful that her father was so gracious in aiding her with the ownership of the property. She could now rejoice in the fact that the Archbishop of Smyrna gave his official approval to recognizing the fact that Mary's House was found in his Archdiocese. She was truly happy that this official act did not proclaim her name in connection with this prestigious declaration. Her smiles and the sweet consolations of her accomplishment would be shared with the Blessed Mother alone.

The Archbishop may have been excited and joyous over hearing that Mary's House had been discovered, but his next responses had to be *where is it?* and *who owns it?* Certainly he was quite pleasantly surprised to learn that Father Jung discovered it and Sister Marie owned it. Father Poulin, seriously striving to be most urbane, wore a joyous smile across his face. He and Father Jung both had imposed silence on making public any and every aspect of their discoveries. They felt such relief that now with the Record of Evidence, the news could be proclaimed!

For Sister Marie, that was fine, but if she had found tension in the past couple of months, she was about to learn what the word truly meant. While various groups were shocked that they could not claim even a part of its ownership, there were some who were going to try every personal, religious, or political tactic as they attempted to budge her out of her title. The title, of course, meant nothing to her. She knew that the heavenly treasure of Mary's House was never hers to possess. As always, Sister Marie was acting in total obedience to the Constitutions and Statutes of the Daughters of Charity.[1] She was only at the service of Our Lady to see to it that her House was found and then to protect her House so as to pass it on as soon as possible to the Church. In fact, her dream was to place Mary's House into the hands of her beloved family of St. Vincent so they might share it with the whole world.[2] One day this dream would come true, *not exactly* as she had planned but in God's way and in God's time.[3] For now, though, a decision had to be made, and quickly too, as many parties were in the wings waiting for our trio to make the slightest little mistake or misstep so they could rush in, stake their claim, and take possession of *Panaghia-Capouli.* Sister Marie knew the law. And since Turkish law (both then and now) does not recognize religious orders of any faith and therefore prohibits them from owning property, and since Sister Marie was the person providing the funds, in prudence she must immediately put the deed to *Panaghia-Capouli* in her name. Mary's House was safe at last. For the moment her heart could rest . . . but not for long! God still had much work for Sister Marie to do.

Chapter Sixteen
Quietly Arriving

FATHER JUNG was a brilliant scholar; he was also quite a businessman and administrator, polite and encouraging and tough when he had to be. He did receive government permission for the construction of a road—not for vehicles but for donkeys—enabling him to bring tools and other equipment to the site of Mary's House. It became a strenuous, massive construction job over precipitous, craggy mountain terrain. There were also neighborhood problems. The Bey owned property through which the road must be dug. The Bey eventually gave permission to cross his property, after learning it would enhance its value, provided that a second special road would be built from the mountain to Aravia, the town in which the Bey resided. It was a necessary added expense. To add to the general difficulty of the whole situation, native officials who did not appreciate a foreigner owning this part of the mountain made matters worse by having the local police make frequent unannounced visits to ensure that no unapproved work was being done. Periodically, during the next few years, official government inspectors also appeared with the hope of finding cause to bring the new owner to court. The prayers and the respectful treatment accorded these officials won out.

The new road did, however, add another entrance to *Panaghia-Capouli*. It was well understood and duly appreciated with the deepest gratitude of Father Jung that none of these plans or projects could have been begun, or had any hope of being accomplished, without the sustaining prayer, encouragement, and financial support of Sister Marie. It was she who, as Father Poulin explains in his journal, bore all the expenses of "repairing roads, construction of buildings, maintenance of the chapel, amelioration of the property, planting of trees, annual expenses for excavations, etc., etc. She has done this with endless generosity and good will."[1]

Father Jung had twenty-seven men working with picks and shovels on the main project, and then he had to add another ten or twelve for the Bey's road. On occasion the number reached one hundred. To save time and travel, the men stayed the whole while in three very large tents. A horseman delivered the daily fare for the workers.

It was a most impressive scene to have all these men working with shovels and pickaxes, hand-grading a passable road over that long, treacherous mountainside. One day they stopped and removed their hats when they saw Sister Marie from the Sacred Heart School, Sister Therese from the French Hospital, Father Poulin, Mr. and Mrs. Borrel, and Mr. and Mrs. Dumont approaching. It was quite a scene: the women shaded by white umbrellas under the beating sun while riding their donkeys, and tended by herdsmen. This was a day to be recorded: It was December 12, 1892, the day on which Sister Marie made her first visit to *Panaghia-Capouli*. She had prayed for what had seemed endless days for this moment, and now she could stand inside the old house that had once been occupied by the Virgin Mary, her dearest Mother. Her heart swelled. Sometimes in life, very infrequently, there are moments when a soul is showered in consolations and believes with every fiber of her being that God has smiled upon her. It's a moment of transfiguration; a moment on the mountain with God. This was one such moment for Sister Marie; on Nightingale Hill inside the little dwelling-place of the Mother of God. There were tears of joy and gratitude and reparation and love.

Sister Marie was able to spend a few hours in prayer in the house, as it was, without most of the roof. She made mental notes, striving to impress upon her mind what the House must have looked

Above: Sr. Marie and a few of the other Daughters of Charity travelling to the House of Mary. *Below:* Sr. Marie prays in front of the Blessed Sacrament in the House of Mary.

like in its original beauty. She had memorized what Sister Catherine had written about it. Before departing, she had to see the stone background, the terraces, and the Stations of the Cross. She would carry back with her these images in her heart and mind and spend sweet moments speaking with her Blessed Mother all about them. The day before Sister Marie visited *Panaghia-Capouli,* Father Jung had faced a possible threat. He had just arrived and it was Sunday morning, and the men talked about taking off for a visit to one of the nearby towns. He knew that if they went, they would not return; and so he soon made a public announcement. The adroit Father Jung said, "My friends, today we will have a feast in your honor. Here are two kids; roast them and we will have a good dinner and wine. You will drink to my health. If you don't drink, I will give you four metals." No one went down the mountain. It was a great feast, rowdy and loud. There was the daring game of "dancing with dagger," and no one got hurt.

In the following year, for the Feast of the Assumption, August 15, 1893, all the Daughters of Charity in Smyrna joined the public pilgrimage. Several of the Daughters with white parasols were riding donkeys, while others took turns trudging along with the animal tenders up that new and very uneven mountain road. The workmen stopped their labors, removed their caps, and stood respectfully watching and nodding to them as they passed. It was for all a precious and memorable moment. The number of pilgrims was very impressive: men, women, children . . . all of them with the Sisters and the clergy. There was Mass, Rosary, and each group made contributions of prayer. There was special singing of favorite hymns. The seeds of this project she had planted so long ago, and to which Sister Marie had devoted so much of her heart, mind, and soul had truly blossomed into this beautiful pinnacle of worship and praise.

That afternoon, in a joyous, restful hour, the sisters offered their prayers before the sagging altar in the ruins of Mary's Home, knowing that Mary once prayed there as they were then doing. Emotions were very high. Sister Marie had tears of joy in her heart as well as on her face. As she looked around and saw the rubble strewn about, her heart ached. This was Mary's House, now so broken down. It surely needed all the efforts she could put into refurbishing it as best she could.

When Sister Marie prayed in the dilapidated House, she found herself in the most intimate union with Mary. It was here that Mary had spent so many hours reliving life with her Son from the moment of the Annunciation to His Ascension. Some fervent hours were spent with His youth and His apostolic life. There were pain-filled prayers, too, spent once again with the horrors of His Passion and Death, but they always came back to the joy of the Resurrection. With the visits from the Apostles right there in *Panaghia-Capouli,* her prayer centered upon the continuing work of her Son in the world.

Sister Marie recalled that the Way of the Holy Cross was laid out on the grounds by the plan of Mary, who, when she lived in Jerusalem, went back and walked over that Way of the Cross and measured the steps from one Station to another. When St. John had brought her to this mountain, according to the revelations, she laid out a path for the Stations of the Cross, the distance of which corresponded to Christ's original ascent to Calvary, and walked and prayed these Stations every day.[2] When the Apostles came to visit singly or in groups, she would always take them with her on that prayerful journey of the Cross. They would sit for a talk and she would listen to their reports on their efforts to spread the Word of her Son in the various parts of the world. They came back, some of them annually, all of them on special occasions. They spoke gratefully of the strength given them on that Pentecost Day when all of them received the gifts of the Holy Ghost. As she stayed there in prayer, Sister Marie knew that she had the help of Mary and the Apostles to rebuild and restore the site that St. John had given to Mary and the Church for that time and for our time.

While they were on the mountain, Sister Marie did not spend all her time in prayer. Being a true administrator she began making notes on what must be brought on the next trip for the needs of the archaeological workers. She was already thinking of the needs the public would have when the Home would be opened for their visits.

The roadwork was done by a collection of Turks, Greeks, Montenegrans, Kurds, Albanians, and a few others. The learned and jovial Father Jung held together this mixture of nationalities even during a couple of disturbing incidents. On one occasion he had just returned home from *Panaghia-Capouli,* when he learned by letter on the evening of December 23, that his intervention was needed to prevent a strike. All the next day he traveled through heavy rain, first by train, then by horse, and finally by foot. The storm was so bad that people questioned his sanity for sloshing through such a downpour, but he kept walking because it was Christmas Eve and he was determined to be in Mary's House for this holy day to pray for this special intention. When he finally reached Mary's Home, he changed clothing, donned his cassock, put on his vestments, and began Christmas midnight Mass.

The altar was makeshift. The room had a bed on which the candles burned. Three crew members were attendants of the Mass. The two dogs, kept outdoors, made an attempt to get indoors. They climbed on the roof and poked holes in it, and the rain came dripping down upon the altar, making it difficult to keep it out of the chalice. Christmas seemed more realistic with the ox and three horses looking on. There was also a little hearth fire. The sky was totally dark, but to Father Jung there was a light that shone. He felt it. This was the first Christmas midnight Mass in Mary's Home since . . . he did not know for how long. He felt certain that Mary was with him in prayer, as surely as she had been in Bethlehem. He did say a prayer for Sister Marie, who was his light, his guiding star, for she had directed his thought to coming here. It was she who enabled him to overcome his unbelief and give him this first Christmas Mass in *Panaghia-Capouli*. All of this! It had to be shared and told to her. He owed her this joy.

Chapter Seventeen

Her Mother's Daughter

IT WAS in 1893, when Sister Marie, with her motherly desire to care for her sisters, spoke about the need for a chalet that could be built to house sisters or guests overnight. With the chalet there would be sufficient space to store tools and equipment for the dig, which looked as if it might go on for some years. There is a letter dated March 2, 1894, to her brother Charles, expressing some of her feelings. She wrote, "I had the honor five years ago to buy *Panaghia-Capouli,* after prolonged negotiations, but without having acquired the right to break ground to build anything greater than an ugly structure. Before being authorized by His Majesty, the Sultan, to erect anything else, I began to think that I would be *'ad patres'* [dead, with my anscestors]."

However, as time went on, some building efforts were made, very important ones. They were protective edifices over much of the uncovered remains of Mary's Home. The archaeologists were extremely careful not to dismantle parts of the Home. The original structures had to be preserved insofar as it was possible. Debris that collected over these ruins during the past several centuries had to be removed. The necessary materials for constructing these protective roofs and panels, made of wood and glass, had to be ported by pack animals up the mountain and then professionally erected. All of this was done, and done well, under the direction of Father Jung.

As an aristocratic young lady, Sister Marie knew manners and courtesies; she was quite comfortable around the wealthy, the highly educated and the finely polished people of the day. Most of all she was very prayerful, never alluding to the fact of her nobility nor to the favors the Daughters of Charity received from Mary through the Miraculous Medal. She was just another Daughter of Charity totally committed to the service of God's children. She was also truly compassionate toward the needs and the sufferings of people around her. She was known for her tender motherly qualities. Early in life she observed and assisted her mother, the Countess, in preparations for entertaining officials of Church and State. She gained further lessons of etiquette; especially in meeting and serving the poor while in training in the Seminary at rue du Bac. She learned to meet and treat crowds of people coming to the Shrine of Mary who sought help, spiritually or physically. Sister Marie certainly knew why she had been missioned to Smyrna; why she had become, as Father Poulin notes in his journal, *Panaghia*'s Mother. It seemed her whole life had been a preparation for what her Mother now needed from her. Her Mother needed her service, her *fiat,* for a mission the magnitude of which this Daughter could only imagine; and this Daughter would not fail her.

Chapter Eighteen

Excavations

"Forgetting that, without her, they would have been able to accomplish nothing, one word from a letter [written by Sister Marie] paints the entire picture: 'I have only the merit of my poor crowns [coins].' "[1]

A S OTHER workers joined the force at *Panaghia-Capouli,* they soon learned the immensity of the program. Every fragment had to be treated with care and appreciation. The work was tedious but most rewarding in the discovery of treasures uncovered. The House, so ancient and fragile, had to be protected as the project progressed. Tools and other necessary equipment were treated with respect and had to be safely stored. A workhouse with living conditions was a necessity. Donkeys were needed to transport all the equipment. Food, and sometimes people, had to be carefully handled over the several-mile stretch of treacherous terrain. Thankfully, a better road was being provided. The workers and the animals needed food and water. Father Poulin, who in his priestly life served as procurator in early assignments, was in charge of such matters. It was he who gave Sister Marie the long lists of necessities. She also helped with the plans. She carefully checked the items needed and generously provided the funds. Not much more could be done until the government, over a prolonged period of time, gave approval to continue the works.[2]

In July 1894, to ready the excavation of the House, the workmen decided to level the ground behind it. This would enable them to erect a building for the storage of their equipment and also provide a place where the Sisters would have overnight lodging. In their absence, the workers or visitors made use of it. In the preparatory grading work they immediately stumbled upon two tombs. The heads of the skeletons were facing Mary's House. They judged the tombs dated back to the fourth century. Many funeral and burial objects were also found. Among them were civic medals, funeral lamps, and even a terracotta mold for making images of Eucharistic hosts bearing symbols of wheat and grapes. It was obvious that a Christian service had been associated with Mary's House.

A sketch done of the Christian tombs found during the excavations behind the House of Mary.

After finding this cache, they had real hopes that they would stumble upon the tomb of the Blessed Virgin Mary. The four hired workmen were eager to search various spots on the mountain, trusting that they would come upon the prized tomb as narrated by Sister Anne Catherine Emmerich. Despite their mighty efforts, Mary's tomb was not found. Two of their men died during this period of work.

It was on August 23, while digging five feet deeper behind the chapel of Mary's House that they found the most startling surprise since the project was started. There was a turn or a bend in the foundation indicating that it was part of an octagonal frame. The puzzlement over why their findings regarding the foundation shape did not coincide with the description in the revelations of Sister Anne Catherine Emmerich was now a moot point. What they had just found coincided perfectly with the description given by Sister Anne Catherine Emmerich. There was no longer any question. They were certain that they had come upon the base of Mary's House.

Excavations and rebuilding around Panaghia Capouli.

When they dug through the floor, they came upon the greatest find of all. It was a cache of black, broken marble pieces. At first they did not understand what it was. After studying it, they concluded that it had to be pieces from the fireplace in the middle of Mary's Home. To think that the Blessed Mother herself had at one time rested and kept warm there, cooked food there, and gazed into the little flames emanating from this fireplace as she recalled the life, death, and resurrection of her Son was enough to give them all pause to think and wonder. It was a holy moment. This was the hearth of Mary's Home; the heart of the House. While they treated with great respect the various finds in Mary's House, these newly uncovered pieces seemed to be the most precious of all. The workers gently and prayerfully handled them, and in so doing they were receiving favors, even miracles, just as Mary at rue du Bac had given miracles to people who sought them.

The workers were so deeply moved by what was happening with their finds and the progress made on the project, they decided to stay with this digging rather than start on the projects they had earlier planned. They erected a large sprawling building with windows to protect the treasure they had uncovered, and with the hopes of uncovering more. It was not until 1903, a wait of ten years, that they finally got around to erecting the building they first planned as a shelter for the Sisters.

The long, winding, newly built mountain road was serving its purpose. *Panaghia-Capouli* was getting good publicity. Pilgrims, as well as other archaeologists, were motivated to come and investigate. Another discovery was made by Sister Marie. She had seen in the area some rocks with Jewish engravings. The priest scholars translated them: they were markers for the Stations of the Cross. Sister Anne Catherine Emmerich had said that Mary, while staying in Gethsemane, had measured the distances between the Stations her Son had made. Here in Ephesus she established her own Stations of the Cross on this Nightingale Mountain and made that sorrowful, pain-filled walk every day. Local pilgrims said that for centuries their own people came to pray the same Stations that the Virgin Mary had walked and prayed and sometimes wept. With as much love and care as she could muster, Sister Marie roamed the mountain site to pick up those stones and replace them in their proper setting. The first time she walked and prayed those Stations was so memorable; a deeply intimate spiritual journey shared between Sister Marie and her Mother. She united herself completely with her Mother Mary in prayer and tears and gratitude.

In the archives there is a page of a handwritten letter from Sister Marie mentioning the fact that the Blessed Mother prayed the Stations of the Cross. The year of the letter is not recorded, but it is very revealing. It reads:

> As you know, it was on August 13th last year that the Holy Virgin Mary appeared with a black veil. Indeed, the Carmelites told me that since then they are accustomed to celebrate the death of the Holy Virgin Mary on that date. They believe that she died on the 13th and was laid

Sr. Marie, Fr. Jung and a woman companion pray the Stations of the Cross found behind the House of Mary.

to rest in her grave the same day. She arose on the 15th like her divine Son on the third day. As far as the black veil is concerned [the words are missing] . . . Father Lobry was reading for the thousandth time [word unreadable]. Then, the other day on the mountain he saw that it was with a black veil that the Virgin Mary went for the last time to pray the Way of the Cross. Black veil again when she went to St. Elizabeth.[3]

During those intervening years Sister Marie continued her duties as Sister Servant of the Daughters of Charity, Director of the nursing school, and Director of the Children of Mary. Along with these offices, there were the legal duties associated with *Panaghia-Capouli* that needed tending. As the work progressed, the added needs for overseeing the development of the entire site had to be addressed. She had practically memorized Sister Anne Catherine Emmerich's revelations pertinent to Mary's life in Ephesus. She ordered young olive trees and shrubbery to be planted near the Home. The grounds had to be kept neat and attractive. Out in the yard in front of the chapel Sister Marie placed a metal statue of Our Lady of Grace, her arms outstretched in welcome, a sign of the graces she dispenses upon people who ask for them of her. That statue marks her Immaculate Conception. Sister Marie, in accord with her attentiveness to remaining humble, makes no reference to the fact that this was the model that was given to a member of her community, the Daughters of Charity. She always placed emphasis on the grace of the moment, neither on herself nor on anyone associated with her.

The number of pilgrims steadily increased. A petition box and a guest book were added. Muslims outnumbered other visitors in those early years. Their comments were most edifying. People were praising Mary as often as they were pleading for her assistance. Among the numerous pilgrims were archaeologists, museum directors, professors, and representatives from fields of science and history. What was surprising was the fact that they came from almost every country of Europe as well as Africa, Asia, and later, the Americas. The guest book had one name of particular interest that brought special joy to Sister Marie. Her nephew, Baron Antoine de Mandat-Grancey came, and they had a wonderful family visit together.

Left: The statue of the Blessed Virgin which Sr. Marie placed on the path leading to Mary's House, resembling Our Lady of Grace from her Mother House, the Miraculous Medal Shrine in Paris. *Right:* The statue of Our Lady of Ephesus errected in 1991 by the American Society of Ephesus to commemorate the finding of Mary's House in 1891.

Sister Marie was about to celebrate her 70th birthday and her 50th anniversary as a Daughter of Charity when military fighting broke out in Turkey. That put a further strain upon her; she was still in charge of her religious community and the hospital. Governmental demands were affecting her work at *Panaghia-Capouli*. It was quite obvious that the Ottoman Empire had spread around the Mediterranean Sea, into the Balkan Countries and Russia. Throughout the vast Persian Empire there were signs of serious political deterioration. Government regulations were rapidly increasing as turmoil spread throughout parts of Asia and Europe. The 1908 Revolution added more to her work with strict regulations levied on *Panaghia-Capouli*. These disruptions to her regular duties caused by a government in turmoil were only a prelude to the problems she would meet with the eruption of World War I in the Balkans.

In her youthful days Sister Marie had to work through the unexpected changes in France caused by the Great Revolution. Next she saw the Crimean War come on the world stage, followed by the Uprisings of the Communards that weighed heavily upon her people. On top of that she had vivid memories of the Franco-Prussian War. Now as war clouds were darkening over Turkey, people visiting Mary's House were asking the help of her prayers. She knelt with them, and looking about, she saw the varied groups of religious persuasions. All seemed to become edified as Sister prayed the *Ave Maria*.

Here in *Panaghia-Capouli* there was still peace in troubled times. Sister Marie took the occasion to speak with these visiting groups, asking them to kneel and beg for Mary's intercession to keep peace among all their countries. She reminded them that this was Mary's Home and Mary had brought them here to pray for peace, and not just worldly peace, but true peace, which is possible only through Mary's Son.

Remnants of the stones from the Stations of the Cross built by Our Lady

Above: A closer view of the south side of the House of Mary. The boarded up wall covers the original opening to the room where Mary stored her linens and extra furniture for guests. This room was too badly damaged by water to be restored. *Below:* The north side of the House of Mary prior to restoration. A temporary roof was constructed to keep out the rain.

Above: Fr. Jung views the south side of Mary's House. *Below:* J.G. Borrel looks at one of the olive trees in front of Mary's House.

Above: A closer view of the front of Mary's House as seen on the first expedition. *Below:* The approach to Mary's House from the North.

Above: Fr. Jung *(center)* with two other Lazarist priests. *Below:* Stones from Our Lady's fireplace which were uncovered during the excavation of Panaghia Capouli. They were given to Sr. Marie as a memento.

Chapter Nineteen
Children of Mary

"I am not a priest and cannot bless them, but all the heart of a mother can ask of God for her children, I ask of Him and will never cease to ask Him."[1]

THE Shrine was a special place where Sister Marie held close to her heart in prayer the Children of Mary, that precious apostolic work which she regarded as a special priority from her first days as a Daughter of Charity. She worked zealously with a sound missionary thrust to instill in the Children of Mary a determination to live the Catholic Faith. She prayed for their innocence, their fidelity, and their zeal to be good Catholics. She reminded them that being true Children of Mary meant that they were striving to live the life of model Catholics. Sister Marie told them that it was not she, but the Virgin Mary herself, who called them to be her Children. The Blessed Mother was their Guiding Light, and God had given each one this very special gift.

Sister emphasized, too, that by their exemplary Catholic life they diffused this light of Mary and were a light to others, having a great impact on them, especially upon their own personal families, even though their families might not tell them so. Sister Marie would never know him, but Pope John Paul II also was profoundly touched by the great effect that youth around the world had made on him. He realized they could impress the world as lay missioners, who were sent by Mary. He was joyous and he praised the youth who came for his public Masses. He called all Marian Youth Groups together and invited them to prayer. He asked them to accept the motto of his pontificate as their own: *Totus Tuus, Maria!* Totally yours, Mary! Their numbers have continued to increase with the scholarly leadership of Pope Benedict XVI, as both Pope and youth celebrate the truths of our faith and love of Mary, our Mother.

Father John Mary Aladel, confessor to Saint Catherine Labouré, had no desire in 1830 to start a youth organization, but Mary did indeed get her request fulfilled. From its origins, Mary entrusted the Association of the Children of Mary to the care of the spiritual family of Saint Vincent in the persons of Saint Catherine Labouré and Father John Mary Aladel. This fact makes implicit the adherence of the Vincentian charism. This charism is so clearly seen in the life of Sister Marie, who lived it with great zeal, in all humility, and with abundant charity.

From that first group, so long ago nurtured along the way by people like Sister Marie, it has grown into one of the great international organizations in the world, as they quietly, prayerfully, zealously work for a change in moral behavior. And because of Sister Marie the Children of Mary have a special place to call "home"; a place to pray for peace and conversion; a place to gather at our Mother's knee to learn of Her Son: Mary's House.

The Marian Youth Movement is alive and well in our times! In the United States, as in other countries, it seeks:

1. to follow Christ, Evangelizer and Servant of the Poor, with deep faith;
2. to live, praying and following Mary simply, humbly, according to the *Magnificat;*

3. to strengthen a missionary spirit through service to
the poor and the abandoned;
4. to strive to be responsive, collaborating with paro-
chial and diocesan activities.

The Vincentian Marian Youth, like those formed among other
religious orders and communities, is now international too. They
are strongly mission-oriented, often found in high schools, col-
leges, and universities. They spread their message according to the
needs of the country in which they are living, studying, or working.
They seek their own apostolic works and are not assigned them;
however, the community does affirm their works. All of them are
dedicated to improving the living conditions of the poor.

These days the Internet is a popular tool for keeping in touch
with others in the Vincentian family and spreading the Word of
God throughout the world. This was not available to Sister Marie.
She relied completely on the inspirations of the Holy Spirit under
the obedience of her spiritual director to guide her path. In this
way we see that Sister Marie believed that the Blessed Mother,
under the aegis of the Holy Spirit, had chosen her for this apostolic work.

Sister Marie would be very pleased to see that her beloved Children of Mary in the Marian Movement are doing their best to follow her recommendations to honor the Blessed Mother and her
Son, Jesus Christ our Lord. "Two days before her death, she
charged the assistant directress with transmitting to the Children
of Mary her last recommendations: 'They should be closely united
to one another, loyal and devoted to the Association, they should
always be courageous Christians, devoted within the family, exemplary outside the family and they should avoid all that could
adversely affect their faith or their dignity.' "

Sister Marie did all she could to give to the Children of Mary the precious treasure of Mary's House. All God's children are also children of Mary. The doors to Mary's House are open for all of God's children and for a very important reason: hope for peace and conversion to Christ. Although the Mother's children struggle to live in peace with one another, we are united in our love for Mary (Meryem[2]), and our Mother's prayers for us are our hope for peace in this world, and for the restoration of all things in Christ.

Chapter Twenty
Conflicts

"The tradition, according to which the Very Holy Virgin died at Ephesus was accepted by Pope Benedict XIV, who, in his Treatise of the Holy Mysteries on Holy Friday, comments in this manner the words *'accepit eam in sua.'* St. John leaving for Ephesus took Mary; and it is from there that the Blessed Mother was assumed into heaven."[1]

ALONG with the political problems affecting Mary's Home were the scholarly conflicts over the validity of the claims given to *Panaghia-Capouli*. The news of that find was made by Father Jung and companions, but it was announced to the world by Father Eugene Poulin, and it brought a torrent of critical attacks by scholars.

Father Poulin, although he never obtained a college degree, nevertheless had no thought of backing down on his claims. In fact, he was most anxious to take on every scholar who came to battle. He knew he had the proof. It became a very lively combat with several authority figures in theology, scripture, history and archaeology. All of them were ready to duel. They came from numerous museums and universities and from the Vatican. At least one scholar sought the favor of Father Anthony Fiat, the Superior General of the Vincentian Fathers, against the claims of the Vincentian Father

Poulin. Father Fiat did not ask Father Poulin to cease this literary conflict, but he did write, "Even though the matter be true, it should not be for our Congregation [the Vincentian Fathers] to make this question its own affair."[2] With that directive, Father Poulin did not cease writing; he simply published under the pseudonym "Gabrielovich," after his own father, Gabriel.

Sister Marie had done what she could do for Mary's House, up to that point, and she left the rest in the hands of God. This was another act of humility; she accepted it as the will of God. She had received a response, and she was obedient to it. The Community, that is, the Superior General of both the Vincentian Fathers and the Daughters of Charity who had granted to Sister Marie the permission to buy the mountain, never questioned her about the matter, nor did the authorities ever object to her participation in promoting devotion to Mary through *Panaghia-Capouli*. Sister Marie, in her humility, quietly continued putting all her cares, both the spiritual and temporal matters, into her prayers. She also kept supplying funds to carry on the physical needs of Mary's House. All the while that she was doing this, she understood that her temporary owner-ship of Mary's House and all the surrounding area was God's plan alone, prepared long ago through generations of her family for this particular time, and that He had also given her the necessary tools and resources to renovate and refurbish this holy place for the Church and all the people of the world. Remember, too, that this was a tremendously tumultuous time threatened by war in that part of the world, and Sister Marie knew she must act prudently and swiftly, for they never knew if the next day they might be expelled from the country. By placing Mary's House in her name, Sister Marie could tend to the multitude of financial requirements directly, sparing the priests the humiliation of constantly present-ing her with bills and asking her for funds. If conflicts rose up around her regarding the validity of the claims made about *Panaghia-Capouli,* Sister Marie found comfort knowing that Father Fiat had granted his permission to her; in holy obedience to his directive she was at peace.

Chapter Twenty-One

The Vatican Response

*Panaya Kapulu,[1] the name by which Mary's House
and the surrounding area came to be known after World
War II, translates to Doorway to the Virgin. God in His
Divine Providence chose Sister Marie de Mandat-
Grancey to be the humble soul who would give to the
Church and the world the Doorway to the Virgin.*

B EFORE we close out the life of Sister Marie let us look at the
attitude of the Vatican toward Mary's Home both then and
now. Pope Leo XIII, reigning at the time of the discovery of Mary's
House, sent the scholar Father Eschbach on a mission in 1895 to
study the question of the Oriental rites. While on this mission he
met Father Poulin in Smyrna and shared with him his interest in
Panaya. As a result of their discussion Father Eschbach decided to
travel to Ephesus with Father Jung in May of 1895. While there, he
became convinced of the validity of the claims made of Ephesus
and its treasured House of the Virgin Mary. He reported his findings to Pope Leo XIII, who was very interested and quite pleased
to hear about the findings. For the Holy Father, too, the evidence
pointed to Ephesus as the place of residence and Dormition of
Mary, who lived there under the care of Saint John. The following
year, on April 18, 1896, Pope Leo XIII discontinued for all time
indulgences formerly attached to the tomb of Mary in Jerusalem.

Pope Pius X (1904-1914) met with Sister Marie and her companion Sister Fievet on April 20, 1912. He asked Sister Marie if Mary's tomb had been found. Sister Marie replied, "Not yet, Holy Father." Sister Marie continued, "Most Holy Father, I know you believe as did your illustrious predecessor Benedict XIV, that the Blessed Virgin died at Ephesus."[2] The Pope confirmed his agreement with a nod of his head and a smile.

During the World War I years, Pope Benedict XV (1914-1922) delivered lectures on *Panaghia-Capouli* in the Pontifical Roman Seminary. Pope Pius XI (1922-1939) graciously accepted the book on Mary's Home sent to him by Father Eugene Poulin, C.M. Pope Pius XI sent Father Poulin a letter congratulating him on his work and expressing his appreciation for the book.

Favorable attitudes toward Ephesus were greatly strengthened by Pope Pius XII (1939-1958), who defined the dogma of Mary's Assumption on November 1, 1950, omitting questions of Mary's site of Dormition. During his pontificate he also informed the Archbishop of Smyrna, Joseph Descuffi, C.M., that *Panaya Kapulu,* the name applied to Mary's House after World War II, was declared an official sanctuary for pilgrims, giving to priests the privilege of celebrating there the Votive Mass of the Assumption of Mary.

Of all the Popes it was John XXIII (1958-1963) who was the first one to have ever visited *Panaya Kapulu.* He did so when he was Bishop Roncalli, serving as the Apostolic Delegate of Bulgaria as he attended the fifteenth centenary of the Council of Ephesus. Later during his pontificate, on August 18, 1961, he granted a plenary indulgence for all time to all pilgrims to Mary's House.

Next, Pope Paul VI, who was actually the first *as Pope* to visit the Shrine on the Feast of Saint Anne, July 26, 1976, presented to Mary's House a very beautiful gold chalice in honor of its foundress, Sister Marie. Pope John Paul I had too brief a pontificate to pen an encyclical or to travel. He barely had time to deliver a few talks before his sudden death.

It was Pope John Paul II, who, having made so many pilgrimages around the world, especially to various Marian shrines, brought greater attention to *Panaya Kapulu* when he visited and celebrated Holy Mass there before a large crowd on the Feast of Saint Andrew, November 30, 1979. With the greater coverage to the Shrine made by him, the number of visitors increased into the millions. And, of course, Pope John Paul II's Marian Youth found *Panaya Kapulu,* the Doorway to the Virgin, to be a very popular shrine, drawing these Children of Mary in a new and powerful way to the hearth and home of their Mother; into Her Immaculate Heart.

It is the Holy Father chosen by God for these times, Pope Benedict XVI, who has not only visited Mary's House, but has once again opened the door, this time with a new focus and some loving instructions.

Left: Pope Leo XIII took a great interest in the recovery of the House of Mary. *Right:* Pope Pius X also took an interest in Mary's House in Ephesus and met with Sr. Marie in1912. He indicated that he believed the tomb of Mary would be found there.

The seal of Pope Paul VI on the bottom of the chalice *(pictured below)* which he gave to the House of Mary when he visited on July 26, 1976. Pope Paul VI gave the challice in honor of Sr. Marie d Mandat-Grancey, DC, recognizing her as the Fondress of Mary's House while he was visiting the House on July 26, 1967.

Chapter Twenty-Two
Muslim Relations

"Remember when the Angels say, 'O Mary, Allah announces to you the tidings of a Word from Him whose name is Messiah, Issa [Jesus], son of Mary, renowned in this world and in the next, and one that leads to the throne of God.' "[1]

IN OUR day, there was great speculation as to where Pope Benedict XVI, a man who seems to have been chosen for this time in history, would make his first official visit outside Italy. It was to Turkey! And it was to visit Mary's Home, seeking her intercession for the fulfillment of his duties as Vicar of her Son.

He was doing what Sister Marie would have hoped for him to do. He was going into the Muslim country. This scholarly Pope was well aware of the devotion the Muslims paid to Mary. Their Koran mentions Mary thirty-five times. He was also aware of the fact that some local Muslims had, over the centuries in an annual pilgrimage in honor of her Dormition (the Assumption, on August 15) devoutly trudged up the mountain to kneel in prayer around the rubble that was once her Home.

Before going to Turkey, Benedict XVI, just a year after his election as Pope, in his talk at Regensburg quoted a passage from another speech made by the Emperor Manuel Paleologus, who claimed that the power of Islam was spread by violence. Immediately a pejorative interpretation was given to the Pope's talk. The reaction provoked an immediate threat to the Pope's safety. Some leading Shiite and Sunni Muslim scholars and other theologians picked apart the Pope's speech and with a five-page critique publicly sought an open dialogue with the Pope and Catholic scholars. It was exactly what Pope Benedict desired. He wanted placed on the agenda the disparate attitudes held by so many, for they had written him, "Upon this sincere and frank dialogue, we hope to continue to build peaceful and friendly relationships based upon mutual respect, justice and what is common in essence in the shared Abrahamic tradition."

Pope Benedict seemed to have secured his goal of opening an ongoing dialogue with the Muslims. He had earlier spoken about the world conditions and said that without dialogue there can be no peace. His visit was a huge success with a promise for continued dialogue, a goal both sides desired. It was important that the Muslims saw Benedict XVI's presence at the same shrine where they gathered together in Mary's House, *Meryem Ana Evi,* as the home is called in Turkey. Telecast throughout the whole world, Pope Benedict XVI celebrated Mass on November 29, 2006.

The graces promised by Our Lady to Saint Catherine Labouré continue to be showered upon Mary's Children who were praying for a peace-filled visit from Pope Benedict to her little *Panaya* Home, where all are welcomed. On the side of Mary's House there is a plaque to call attention to the fact that here Muslims and Catholics gather for prayer.[2] As they gather in Mary's House they may also recall that after so many, many centuries, *Panaya Kapulu,* now rebuilt and open to the public, is where all people may come to honor the Immaculate Virgin Mary, Mother of God and our Mother, and to pray where she lived and from where she was assumed into Heaven.

This all began with Sister Marie's making the request of Father

Eugene Poulin for a good book for refectory reading, and then her challenge to him and his confreres to search for Mary's Home. For the rest of her life she devoted herself to repairing and preserving Mary's House and welcoming all who came to visit.

How pleased Sister Marie would have been to hear the Holy Father's call for prayers for peace in this little house so many years later.

> From here in Ephesus, a city blessed by the presence of Mary Most Holy—who we know is loved and venerated also by Muslims—let us lift up to the Lord a special prayer for peace between peoples.[1]

Sr. Marie discusses the Blessed Virgin Mary at the House of Mary, with a Muslim woman.

Chapter Twenty-Three

Who Gets the Credit?

Sister de Grancey circulated among the people who had
come to visit Mary's House. Always simple, she seemed
to be radiating joy: "How Beautiful! How beautiful!" she
cried out. Later she said, "I know well that the Blessed
Virgin does not need this exterior glory, but since we can
provide it for her, isn't it a duty of ours?"

SISTER MARIE was not one who sought thanks or recognition
for her acts of charity, whether they were prayer, personal
service, or financial assistance. Father Poulin believed it was his duty
to publicize her charity. She was always very quiet about her family
background and her spiritual family, the Daughters of Charity. He,
a most righteous person, publicly recalled his opposition to mysticism and the revelations about Mary and her House in Ephesus.
Now he owed her public recognition. He penned his expression of
gratitude, which is now resting in the Vincentian archives in Paris.
His words are the very first testimony on behalf of Sister Marie:

The Lord, who sees and organizes things, had taken care
to put before us a soul in love with beauty and goodness,
who was ready to give herself to everything good. A great
soul, devoted, ardent, pious, and generous; the noble Sister Marie de Mandat-Grancey. She was, God had chosen
her to be, the terrestrial Providence, like *Panaghia*'s

161

Mother! For twelve years she has been charged of this valiant religious enterprise; she has never failed.

Oh! How happy I am to give her all the respect she merits! Also, could these writings make known to posterity, long after us, to whom France and the Catholic Church are in debt for *Panaghia*! The Lord gave me this opportunity to say loudly what I had in my heart for a long time, to acquit what I deemed to be a serious debt. It is done. Praise be to God!

For years Sister Grancey had been thinking about the Virgin's Grave, looking forward to its discovery. As soon as she had been told about the opportunity of buying *Panaghia*, her heart was full of joy . . . "Just the time to find the necessary fund," she answered: "Do let's buy it."[1]

Father Poulin declares that the discovery and the building of the Shrine, as detailed in Anne Catherine Emmerich's revelations, were due to Sister Marie. This, the greatest spiritual and archaeological discovery of modern times, he tells us, all came from her. Without her participation in each and every part of it, they could and would have been reduced to nothing. He knew for certain that any portion of the money from her own personal fortune that was not given to the poor was spent on Mary's House. This, too, he saw and knew: the money did not come simply from her purse. It came from her heart.

Father Poulin told of another recorded fact relative to Sister Marie's modesty. Father Fiat, Superior General, wrote a prayer in 1910 that was sent to Father Poulin, in which he stated that the House was purchased "for the Sisters of Charity." Sister Marie complained to him that that was never her intention; the prayer seemed to exclude the Lazarists, and it was they who Sister Marie exclaimed had done everything! Father Fiat then changed it to read, "for the Family of St. Vincent."[2]

In his prayer we hear again the blessed possibilities of the graces flowing from Mary's House for the Church and for the world of which Sister Marie was keenly aware and for which she labored for the last two decades of her life.

> O Mary, conceived without sin, who deigned to entrust the Miraculous Medal to the Family of St. Vincent, who themselves, have prepared the Catholic world for the definition of the dogma of the Immaculate Conception, we beg of you a new favor. The place, which according to all probability possesses your tomb had been providentially discovered by the children of St. Vincent and purchased for the Family of Saint Vincent. We beseech you to return this glorious tomb finally and to delight the entire Church, thus preparing for the definition of your glorious Assumption.

As Father Poulin attests in his journal, Sister Marie's intention always was that Mary's House remain with the Children of Saint Vincent. "Sister Grancey who had been feeling that she was getting old for two or three years, wished to leave the property by will in order that it would remain with the Children of St. Vincent."[3] She took every precaution to protect this intention of a direct transfer by will of the property and keep all the many other interested parties, especially the government, out of that transfer.

Those men who worked on the recovery project of Mary's Home wanted for a long time to give her more than mere words of gratitude for her role in it. When they retrieved some of the first-century stone-work, they shouted for joy. As they spoke about it, someone suggested, and the rest quickly agreed, that the stones from the first century from Mary's Home should go to Sister Marie. They spoke about how it would unite her with the early Apostolic Church. When she accepted this gift, in her accustomed manner, she knew exactly what she had to do with it. After she purchased a decorative glass container, she placed the stones within it and presented it to her family, because, as she told them, "Without you, we would have never found Mary's Home." Again, she looked for no recognition or praise for herself but, in this instance, only for her birth family. The trophy now rests in a very prominent place in the private chapel of the de Mandat-Grancey Castle.

Father Joseph Euzet, C.M., who battled with lengthy legal and political obstacles to come into ownership of Mary's House almost thirty years after Father Poulin's death, wrote the famed *Historique de la Maison de la Sainte Vierge pres D'Ephese (1891-1961)*. In his history of Mary's House he points to the person whom he describes as deserving the "highest mention" and as the "greatest worker." In this excerpt we not only get a new glimpse into Sister Marie's great charity, but we also find a sense of her deep humility as Father Euzet tells that she always saw her contributions as "a small thing."

> And now, after this rapid enumeration of the workers of *Panaghia* how shall we not give the highest mention as is necessary to name the greatest worker, Sister Marie de Mandat-Grancey. Her noble family connections allowed her to make known the Cause among the chosen groups of France, Belgium, and elsewhere. But it had been indeed a small thing [to her]. Thus it is necessary to point out again, as one knows it already, that it was she who took the initiative on everything and that, everything that the other workers did would have fallen into

nothingness [without her]. All from her personal fortune that did not go into the hands of the poor (and how large her own hand) was given for *Panaghia-Capouli.*"[4]

During the last few years of her life, Sister Marie had placed a heavy toll upon her health. She strove to avoid giving a semblance of real care for her heart, even though she was a nurse. Her priorities always in order, Sister Marie's time and energy were spent first on the hospital and school, her assigned works by the Community, and then to the Shrine of Mary's Home.

Even in her last years, while in very poor health, Sister Marie's emphasis with the children in her care was always on their personal sanctity. She would dutifully climb the many stairs to the sewing room, where she knew young girl's hearts and souls still needed formation. As the best of mothers she nurtured them and strove as always to lead the Children of Mary to Heaven. While she was on her sick bed, the young Children of Mary composed notes of love and thanksgiving to be delivered to her along with their promises to persevere in her teachings. One such note contained these words:

> We promise, O good Mother, to strive to acquire this spirit of faith that you wanted to inculcate in us and that your entire demeanor reflected. Thank you, O Mother, for all the good that you have done for us and the joys, so pure, that we have enjoyed close to you.[5]

In those final years Sister Marie would spend hours climbing up and down the mountain. She spent the rest of the daylight hours beautifying the Shrine inside and out. She regarded it as a valuable Church project. She was slowing down. Her intellectual acumen told her that, as a missionary, she had done what she could. It was time to act dutifully. Five years before her death, she made a legal transfer of Mary's Home and its property to Father Poulin, Superior of the local Congregation of the Mission in Smyrna, dated May 11, 1910. Although her personal fortune was shrinking, she would continue paying all the expenses of this holy project until her death.

Chapter Twenty-Four
The Final Gift

IN THE records of the later years of her life, it has been noted that Sister Marie had the privilege of having an audience with Pope Saint Pius X at the Vatican on April 20, 1912, accompanied by Sister Fievet. Sister Marie knew he had a favorable attitude toward *Panaghia-Capouli* because in 1906 he had sent a letter to the workers on the Home, along with his Apostolic Blessing and his promise to keep them all in prayer. In the papal audience the Pope asked of her, "Has the tomb been found?" She replied with utmost simplicity, "Not yet, Holy Father." To the surprise, or even to the shock, of some who were present, she added with what they considered boldness, "I know you believe, as did your illustrious predecessor, Benedict XIV, that Mary died in Ephesus." He looked up, and although said nothing, did smile and nodded agreeably. Pope St. Pius X truly had a favorable view of *Panaghia-Capouli,* as evidenced by his granting a plenary indulgence to those making a pilgrimage that year.[1]

It is claimed that Pope Saint Pius X planned to give indulgences for all future visitors to Mary's Home, but the political health of Europe and the physical health of the Pope prevented it. On June 28, 1914, Archduke Ferdinand was assassinated; on July 28, World War I was declared; and, on August 20, Pope Saint Pius X died. Before the winter set in, the war had spread beyond the borders of

Europe into Asia. Everything in *Panaghia-Capouli* was then shut down because of the war and would remain so until the end of 1923. For Sister Marie it was a real heartbreak, but she strove to continue her work at the hospital and the school.

Early in 1915, Sister Marie contracted a severe cold but did nothing for it. She was moving more slowly. The Vincentian Community, the school, and the Children of Mary all showed great concern for her. She agreed to some rest, and the month went on. The students had vacation in February, and she feared for their young souls that she could not guide them while they were away from her. She seemed to be deteriorating rather noticeably when using the stairs. She frequently paused and took deep breaths. She pleaded it was due to her cold. In mid-April she was confined to bed. She finally asked another Sister to play the harmonium in her place for the singing of hymns during May. She claimed the music was helping to restore her strength, and she began writing notes to the students, thanking them for their kindness, just as she had done in the early days of her teaching.

She made a trip to the sewing room and the girls cheered her, asking for her blessing. Her reply was, "I am not a priest, and so I cannot bless you. But all that the heart of a mother can ask of God for her children, that I ask of Him for you and I shall never cease to ask Him." On Monday, May 17, everyone was alarmed. She had suffered a heart attack. She asked for the Sacrament of Extreme Unction. She had some relief after two days and then took a turn for the worse. On Pentecost, May 23, she asked the Sisters to say the prayers for the dying and to continue praying for her until the end. During the week she alternated between improvement and relapses. On Sunday, May 29, she asked her assistant to announce to the Children of Mary, "Be closely united to one another, loyal and devoted to the Association. Always be courageous Christians, devoted within the family, exemplary outside the family, and avoid all that could adversely affect your faith and unity."

Later that day the pain became acute and excruciating. Those who were able to be near her believed that exhaustion would take her. Through it all they said she retained a celestial smile, and they knew they would soon not see her again.

On Holy Trinity Sunday, May 30, she again asked that the prayers for the dying be offered, and she received the plenary indulgence. At the conclusion of the Exposition of the Eucharist that evening, the Children were warned that she was very near death. They were told that Mass in the morning would be offered for her. Seventy Children of Mary and many of their parents offered their Mass and Communion for her.

It was recorded that on Monday, May 31, 1915, while this very Mass was being celebrated, Sister Marie de Mandat-Grancey, without agony, without fear, as Monsignor Zuchetti Archbishop of Smyrna would say the following day, could confidently smile at death. Sister Marie de Mandat-Grancey breathed her last and threw herself into the arms of God.

The funeral of Sister Marie took place on June 1, with much pomp and ceremony. Three hundred girls from the Children of Mary, along with the schoolchildren, as well as the members of the sewing classes, led the funeral cortege. The French Community in Smyrna was well represented, as were the members of the parish. A great number of local civic and political leaders, plus the French legation, the American Consul, the Daughters of Charity, and the Vincentian Community followed in procession.

The Vatican official in Smyrna, the Archbishop Monsignor Zucchetti, had offered the Mass, and afterward, just before the final obsequies, delivered a very personal address to the Daughters of Charity on the virtues of Sister Marie de Mandat-Grancey.

Allocution Pronounced on June 1, 1915
By Monsignor Zucchetti, Archbishop of Smyrna
At the Funeral of Sister Marie de Mandat-Grancey

My Dear Daughters of Charity,

In His adorable provisions, it so pleases God to take from us, one after the other, those souls most dear to our love and our veneration.

It is only a filial complaint directed to His fatherly kindness, by us, who are so saddened by the departure from this world of so many people, whose presence in our midst was a token of His blessings, an appeal to His love and a comforting example of supernatural life.

These departures, for some time now, are succeeding one another quickly in Smyrna: men and women servants of God, priests, as well as religious, are saying "goodbye" to us after such a great and long service rendered to the Church, to young people, as well as to the ministry of souls and to suffering humanity.

Today, it is the turn of the one that, by your tears, you would like to make live again, in order to see her again in her capacity as the superior of the French Hospital, of her school and of her model sewing workshop—active, energetic, generous, giving of herself and not sparing herself to help everybody, but especially the indigent and the miserable. An abundantly provided soul with natural and supernatural talents, combining with the nobility of a great French family, the enthusiasm and resources of an inexhaustible heart, the admirable Sister Adele Louise Marie de Mandat-Grancey, during a stay in Smyrna that lasted 30 years, has been among us the type of strong woman depicted in Scripture, the true daughter of charity, providence of the poor, consolation of the afflicted, support of socially outcast and uncomplaining poor families, refuge and savior of young people exposed to worldly danger and seductions.

Full of good works, her long earthly career has been remarkable, above all as she was nearing her death, because of such an outstanding dignity of life, which imposes respect, inspires confidence and maintains affection. "The dignity of life," wrote Monsignor Gay, "that is, the loyalty, the candor, sincerity, the manner grave and sweet, the carriage, without stiffness, the nobility without arrogance, authority without being demanding, urbanity without affectation." The motive of such a constant virtue was, in her, the spirit of, the taste for and the practice of sacrifice.

It is to Sister de Grancey that we owe, among many other benefits, the purchase of *Panaghia-Capouli,* the hill of the Virgin, the goal of pious pilgrimages and one of the religious glories of our city.

Such a life of detachment, of dedication, of virile virtues, of a kindness that was always ready to give generously and untiringly—by what kind of death was she to be crowned? St. Vincent de Paul promised to his daughters that the love of the poor would cause them to smile upon their deaths. To smile at what is most frightening to nature, is that possible? "To smile at death, to salute it, as the angel of deliverance, to see in it only God, who comes, invites, extends His arms, isn't it a gift without price!"

The Holy Spirit, by praising the strong woman, had already given a premonition of this mysterious smile: "the one who has opened her hands to the poor and extended her arms to welcome them, this is the one who will smile on that last day of her life—*et ridebit in die novissimo.*"

Our Sister de Grancey, the strong woman, the charitable woman of our time, could not fail to smile at death, with this kind of smile, which is an award and a prelude: an award for the tears shed and wiped, a prelude of celestial happiness, to which death gives access: *ridebit in die novissimo.*

For these privileged souls, which charity purifies and causes to smile, in view of eternity, which is nearing, is there a purgatory after their death? We may believe that their passage to glory does not tolerate any delay, as the impulses of charity produce in them, in advance, the effects reserved to the expiatory flames of divine justice. There is nothing surprising in that, since charity, which flourishes in physical and spiritual works of Christian mercy, entails, in this very world, the assurances of a beatitude: *Beati misericodres!* said Jesus.

Dear Daughters of Charity, have you understood? Our Lord considers you blessed and reveals to you, from this moment forward, the sentence that He will pass on you, at the Last Judgement: *Venite benedicti Patris mei, precipite regnum quod vobis paratum est!*

Admirable and consoling prerogative of charity! It beatifies those who have it and practice it. Would not therein lie the intimate reason for the absence, in your congregation, which is so large, of canonized saints? During the passage of three centuries, not one of you has been elevated by the Church to the honor of altars. However, since Saint Vincent de Paul, this priest with a heart as vast as the universe, since Vincent de Paul had launched you into the civilized and barbaric world in search of suffering, in order to alleviate it and make it bearable, in search of abandoned children, in China and elsewhere, in order to transform them into angels in heaven, in search of orphans, in order to become their adoptive mothers, because the grace of your vocation has created in you this marvel: a heart which combines with the charms of virginity, the attraction, the loves, and the tenderness of maternity; since that time, I say, you are like a large army, an army comprised of about 30,000 sisters spread out over the globe and which is in constant renewal. What nation, what beach, what island has not seen your white cornet, symbol of virginal purity and maternal love, the approach of which soothes, delights, and consoles the sick, the wounded, the dying and makes the small child smile, who has not known the caresses of his mother? And in the midst of this innumerable phalanx, this multitude of heroines, not one of them has been given the honors of beatification, not even the great and sublime figure of the venerable Louise de Marillac, your first mother, in whom we enjoy seeing more than one trait of similarity with the venerable Sister de Grancey. Louise de Marillac, neither has she, this great Christian, yet been placed among the blessed that the Church proposes to public veneration. This conduct on the part of the Church's souls surprises us if we were not permitted to see in it a witness given to the sanctifying power of charity. This is because charity, outside official canonization by the Church, through divine prerogative, beatifies and canonizes secretly the souls: *Beati misericordes.* It is in the intimacy of a private conversation that one day I was presenting to the venerable departed this way of envisioning the fact the Daughters of Charity do not yet have any canonized saints. With this penetrating and gentle look, which was usual in her, she was content to limit her response: "Monsignor always has good things to tell us." Beautiful and holy soul! How the evidence of these good things must now make you happy! Repose in the joy, the happiness of Our Beloved Lord!

Smyrna, your second country, will long keep the souvenir of your blessed name, which will tell it how much charity, by its supernaturalizing power, enlarges and lifts still more, already great souls, and assures them of the respect, the recognition and the admiration of the world, as well as the rewards of infinite love, which is God Himself: *Deus caritas est.*

When the funeral cortege had made its way from the Church to the cemetery, it was necessary, because of road construction, to make a detour in front of the Cathedral. All during the time of its passing, the bells tolled in honor of the noble servant of the poor, Sister Marie de Mandat-Grancey. The sorrow of the mourners deepened over the loss they suffered. Sister Marie was buried in the public cemetery within the section where other Daughters of Charity were buried.

The tomb of Sr. Marie in Ephesus. She was buried in the public cemetery within the section where other Daughters of Charity were buried.

Chapter Twenty-Five
The Struggles of Mary's Home

WITH the assassination of Archduke Franz Ferdinand in Sarajevo, Bosnia, on the 28th day of June 1914, the first peal of World War I sounded. War was declared a month later. The rebuilding activity of Mary's House and pilgrimages to her House were shut down and remained so until 1923. For an already weakened Sister Marie, it had to be a real heartbreak coming in the last year of her life. The rest of her workdays were spent in the hospital and school programs. Some said it was fortunate she did not have to see that the buildings she had erected had been ripped apart and burned for fuel by ravenous soldiers. The Stations of the Cross were no longer visible. The grounds, once so beautifully planted with olive trees and shrubbery were left untended, wild, and overgrown with weeds. There was no Blessed Mother statue in front of the damaged House of Mary. Fortunately, a concerned captain in charge of a military installment atop Nightingale Mountain told a priest that his men found the statue down in a ravine, and he ordered them to retrieve it and place it in the Home.

Later, after the new Republic of Turkey was formed, but before the priests were able to enter the area, during an uprising of disgruntled Turks, the statue disappeared again. In 1926, Aziz, the newly hired devout Muslim caretaker, found it and brought it back to the chapel in Mary's Home. It was blackened, and the nose was smashed and the hands broken off. It stands in Mary's House to this day as a reminder that she participated in the sufferings of her Son for our redemption. Legitimacy was finally given to the new Republic of Turkey by the 1922-23 Conference of Lausanne. When a country has a change of government, it usually has to pass through lengthy travails. Turkey was no exception. The political situation had been so bad that no one would have known to whom the taxes should have been paid. Father Poulin, for his own safety, was advised that he should not go near the property, and he observed this mandate. Upon the death of Father Poulin in 1928, the Vincentian Father Joseph Euzet learned that he became inheritor of Father Poulin's estate.

We know that Sister Marie left a Last Will and Testament, dated May 10, 1910, giving her personal funds and the property of *Panaghia-Capouli* to Father Poulin. Father Euzet sent to Father William Slattery, the first Superior General of the Congregation of the Mission after World War I, a lengthy account of the transfer of title to Mary's House from Sister Marie through Father Poulin and then to him.

Father Euzet attempted to pay the back taxes on *Panaya*. The officer asked, "How can I put in the name of J. Euzet property which no longer belongs to E. Poulin?"[1] The property now, by law, belonged to the Treasury, because according to them the owner had apparently abandoned it. Father Euzet's only recourse was to ask for a judicial hearing. He sought help, not of a lawyer, but of a dragoman (an official Muslim interpreter of the law) before submitting the case to a judge. The two of them that night went to *Panaya* to determine two very important points: whether it was a mountain territory and whether the land could be cultivated. If such was the case, then the Treasury, by law, could confiscate the property.

On May 28, they sought to restrain the Treasury from declaring the property abandoned before it was defined as such in court. On July 10, the Treasury contended Father Poulin did not have the right to bequeath the property to Father Euzet, and Father Euzet, therefore, had no right to file a suit against the Treasury. The dragoman asked for time to study the Code; he was granted four hours. Back in court they declared the case of the Treasury an act of illegal confiscation because they were charging him by the old law. Father Poulin's will was dated October 29. The new law took effect October 3. They asked that the case be dropped. Of course, it took time, but the new law prevailed. Father Euzet and the dragoman reflected on this; they believed it was an act of Providence that held Father Poulin from writing and then submitting his will earlier. If he had submitted a handwritten will before October 3, the Vincentian Community would have lost *Panaya*.

Father Euzet also informed Father Slattery of the transfer of the property of *Panaya* that he made to the Vincentian Archbishop Descuffi of Izmir, who had formed a Dernek (a legal organization) composed of both Catholic Turks and foreigners. In accord with the Vincentian Community they would serve under the direction of the Archbishop of the Diocese as legal proprietors of the *Panayan* property and its religious programs. By reason of his vows of poverty and obedience, he secured the right of the Superior General of the Congregation of the Mission to make the legal transfer. In a little ceremony before the legal officer of the register's office he responded three times to the question, "Does this concern a free gift?" Having responded three times, "Yes," the transfer was made.[2]

What a moment! I felt myself to be the moral inheritor, much more than the legal inheritor of Sister de Grancey and of Fr. Poulin. What would they have done in my place? And I felt that I heard them say: "Yes, it's the only way to assure the future of Panaghia."[3]

Like Sister Marie and Father Poulin, Father Euzet realized the crucial imperative of placing Mary's House in *his name*. Within the parameters of Turkish law there was no other way to protect this holy treasure. The letter of Father Euzet goes on to tell of the further developments at Mary's House. No dates were given, but he does note, "Let us look at what has happened since 1952." He then began to list the shelter improvements made at *Panaya:* the residence and a hermitage and roads. Most of all, he notes the great increase in the number of pilgrims and claims of physical cures.

And thus the number of visitors has grown from year to year. They are to be counted in the thousands, coming from all the countries of the world, Christians and Muslims, those who are simply curious, as well as true pilgrims. They bring the sick here. The sick have been healed. *Meryem Ana* has shown herself to be a mother of all.[4]

Where struggles are many, graces abound. In the case of Mary's House the struggles at the outset were carried on the shoulders of Sister Marie. The next persons in succession, Father Poulin, then Father Euzet, to whom the sacred home was passed, shared the unique understanding of Sister Marie's holy struggles and acknowledged her profound contribution, calling her Mother of *Panaya*. Both noted her expressions as their inspiration to continue this struggle to preserve and protect Mary's House and all of *Panaya* "this external glory, which Mary does not need, but that we must procure for her, when we can."[5]

Chapter Twenty-Six
Another Caretaker

IN SEPTEMBER 1931, after Father Euzet and his advisor won the first appeal, they hired a new caretaker. As mentioned earlier, a devout Muslim named Aziz, who had great devotion to Mary, so highly honored (though misunderstood) in his Koran, together with his wife and two young children were hired as caretakers. They had learned that the Shrine would be reopened under the care of the Vincentians, and they dearly desired to do benefit to the Shrine. They led a rather quiet life there and contributed greatly to the spirituality of the program. As the Deep Depression began to slowly lift, total unrest developed in Europe. Hitler invaded Poland in 1939, setting off World War II, which raged and quickly spread throughout the world. Aziz died in May, 1951, and predicted on his deathbed, "At *Panaya* extraordinary things will happen. Although I shall not see them, my children will see them. It will be like Paradise then."[1]

Problems of ownership were not over. Another threat was hurled at *Panaya* by the Turkish government in 1947, declaring that all forests within the country belonged to the State. Mary's intercession was sought by the Church. The courts finally declared that there were no trees on *Panaya* of requisite size to constitute a forest.

Eventually Turkey learned there was profit in tourism, so the State built a modern highway from Izmir (Smyrna) to *Panaya*. For travelers, modern, comfortable housing with dining and recreational facilities were constructed nearby. Vatican interest and involvement in *Panaya,* along with the Church of Mary where the Council of Ephesus was held in 431, St. John's Basilica, and other sites gave the area greatly aided tourist attraction. An inspired American named George B. Quatman, after a pilgrimage to Ephesus in 1955 during which he was appalled to find the sad condition of these three sacred sites, established the American Society of Ephesus to assist in their upkeep and restoration through the hiring of architects, archeologists, and others. An agreement was struck with the Turks to permit this restoration work. The Society continued its work into the 1990s and to this day assists the resident priests and sisters at *Meryem Ana,* and works with local officials on related projects.

Pope Paul VI's visit had sparked tremendous interest in Mary's Shrine. Recently, increased interest in the personal spirituality of Sister Marie de Mandat-Grancey, along with the ever-growing enthusiasm of the Marian Youth, has added to the larger numbers of visitors to *Panaya.*

Here, where Catholics, Orthodox, and Muslims gather together to honor Mary, there is continued hope this common ground between peoples of different creeds and nations can lead to meaningful dialogue and to improved relationships. The prayers of the Catholic pilgrims rise to Heaven as a spiritual perfume to find the throne of God through the intercession of Mary, Mother of God. These millions of prayers offered over the centuries are the fruit of the very first prayers uttered long ago by the simple and humble nun who believed that Mary's House was a hidden and irreplaceable treasure for the Church and for the world that must be found, preserved, and venerated. All who come and pray, walk in her footsteps and join in her prayer. The spirit of Sister Marie is still in *Panaya.*

Sister Marie would have certainly appreciated the prayer of Carlo Cardinal Martini, Archbishop of Milan, who, while making a pilgrimage to *Panaya* in 2002, quoted the prophecy of Louis Massignon, a recognized Orientalist: "Ephesus, before the large gathering in Jerusalem, must become the place of reconciliation for all Christian and Muslim groups in Mary, our Mother, in the expectation that Israel, recognizing Mary as the glory of Zion, joins this unanimity, which is so desired."

Epilogue

"If God asks me for her, I will give her to Him whole-heartedly and that will be a handsome present with her fervor for goodness, her self control and her intelligence she can serve Him gloriously and usefully."[1]

T HE Countess gave her daughter Marie to God. It was a handsome gift. Each phase of Sister Marie's religious life was filled with ardor, and her gifts increased in proportion. She grew with each response she gave to serve Jesus Christ in the poor and indeed in all God's children.

We see the fruit of that today as people show their interest in, respect for, and veneration of Mary's Home. Most people who come to *Panaya,* whether they are Catholic, Orthodox, Protestant, or Muslim, or simply people of good will, are not concerned with the ownership of the Shrine. They are anxious and grateful to spend time to visit and hope for peace in this world, even if it be for a moment, and to thank and ask a favor of Mother Mary (*Meryem*). Many people are surprised to learn that during the centuries, when entrance into the country was forbidden or extremely difficult to obtain, honorable Greek Orthodox groups preserved the tradition of making a pilgrimage to *Panaya* on the Feast of the Assumption as it was observed as early as the first century. In this current century people the world over have learned that Muslim and Catholic clerics and scholars meet in dialogue, hoping to improve their relationships. They also know that, although the scholars and clerics meet in dialogue, common folk can also meet on a holy common ground: Mary's House.

Ways the Reader Can Respond

W E CERTAINLY must thank Sister Marie, as one of the early promoters of the Children of Mary. She would be pleased to see in these times the large numbers of young people who were inspired by Pope John Paul II's motto: *Totus Tuus, Maria!* Totally yours, Mary. The youth embraced this pope, this motto, and this spirituality; the very same spirituality that define the Children of Mary. Sister Marie also knew that this is the way to bring souls to God: *Ad Jesum per Mariam.* To Jesus through Mary. She cherished Mary's House in large part because it was, and continues to be, a truly blessed gift still bringing people to God through Mary for the betterment of the world.

Many are seeking information about the spirituality of Sister Marie. First, pray to her and pray for her beatification. She is known to have given most extraordinary favors. Trust her. She will help you. Listen to her. Just as she served the Children of Mary in their poverties of body, mind, or soul for her whole earthly existence, she continues to come to the aid of these same children even to this day.

In life and in death she has had a special love and concern for youth. If anyone, and especially the young or those assisting them, need more information on Marian Youth Programs, the Internet can easily provide it. Seek help and information from your local diocesan office. Serve and love the youth as Sister Marie did, and know the blessings that come from following this special invitation of our Lord. Sister Marie was most conscious of her responsibility to have Mary's Home presentable for visitation by people of every land and nation. If you have not been able to make a personal visit to her Home, you are invited to take a virtual tour of it by computer. Visit www.sistermarie.com. This virtual tour will open her Home to you. As you make the virtual visit, let the Blessed Mother conduct you on your tour, being sure to pause and pray to her and thank her for Sister Marie. Consider asking her to bless the efforts of all the people who hope and pray for the opening of the Cause of the Beatification of Sister Marie. On the same site, you are invited—in fact you are urged—to sign an online petition for the beatification of Sister Marie. The names of Mary's children from all countries of the world are desired. Let the *Vox Populi* be heard!

If through your prayer to Sister Marie you have received a favor, please write a testimony of how she helped you, how she answered your prayers, big or small. Your testimony will be added to the growing file of testimonies from people around the world who have had their prayers answered through her intercession.

In anticipation of the many people who will want to be informed about Sister Marie and her special mission for peace in these times, we must raise funds. We need your help to promote and acknowledge awareness of Sister Marie. Sister Marie has already begun her work for peace by giving us Mary's House so long ago. Now it is up to us; people from all over the world joining in a common mission for world peace and conversion to Christ under the patronage of Sister Marie. Peace among nations and peoples under the Kingship of Christ is something we all desire. Please prayerfully consider making a tax-deductible donation to support this cause to help Sister Marie be proclaimed a saint and promote world peace for the sake of our children and generations to come. *Your donation is most needed and will be most welcomed and appreciated.* Please send both your testimonies and your charitable contribution to the address below. Thank you.

The Sister Marie De Mandat-Grancey Foundation
P.O. Box 275
Cold Spring Harbor, NY 11724

Prayer cards may be printed from the website
www.sistermarie.com

We thank God for giving us the privilege
of Sister Marie De Mandat-Grancey.
Through her great generosity she acquired
the property at Ephesus, the home of Mary
and Saint John the Evangelist.
We ask God and Sister Marie to continue
to bless the cornerstone given to her.
"Around this cornerstone we build our faith
and the powers of darkness will not prevail."
We pray for God's will to be completely fulfilled
through the intercession of Sister Marie. Amen.

A painting of Sr. Marie by Candace Eaton.

Final Notes

THIS story began with my being asked by Erin von Uffel to write something about Sister Marie. The text of *The Life of Sr. Marie de Mandat-Grancey and Mary's House in Ephesus* emerged and needed total revising. Then along came Lorraine Fusaro with zest to aid in the making of the final copy. For months the text has been finished, awaiting word from the Lord for printing with additions from others who asked that their observations also be considered. I am most grateful for all of them and especially for the untiring efforts given by Erin and Lorraine to press for its printing. Here I add some of these observations which might give further insight into the personality of Sister Marie and her love for Christ Crucified.

HELPING THE CAUSE

The reader has been encouraged to continue the work of Sister Marie. Erin and Lorraine have strengthened their bond with Sister Marie by helping prayer groups already formed or strengthening others with devotion to Sister Marie. Some have placed their prayer group under her patronage. Their concentration has been mainly on the Eastern Coast of the United States. They would like to have other prayer groups similarly established under the patronage of Sister Marie.

Erin and Lorraine speak before such groups about the person of Sister Marie, and they are often asked the same question: "What has been the reaction of the Church?" "What does the Church have to say about Sister Marie?" They carry with them extra copies of "What Do the Popes Say?" A copy of it follows.

WHAT DO THE POPES SAY?

1891—Mary's House Discovered in Ephesus, Turkey
Sister Marie de Mandat-Grancey, D.C., Foundress

Pope Benedict XIV (1740-1758)

- Commentary on Christ's Third Word from the Cross: "[John] had her live with him while he remained in Palestine, and he took her with him when he departed for Ephesus, where the Blessed Mother at length proceeded from this life into heaven." (Deutsch, p. 63)

- Of the main proponent of the Jerusalem tradition, Juvenal, the bishop of Jerusalem, Pope Benedict had only disdain and he openly disagreed, denouncing the truth of any arguments in favor of Jerusalem. He went so far as to call the arguments lies. (Deutsch, pp. 64-65)

Blessed Pope Pius IX (1846-1878)

- Re-established the Patriarchate of Jerusalem in 1847 and in a letter listed the glories of Jerusalem; first council of the apostles, monuments, and the Holy Sepulcher, but mentioned Mary only once to say that she lived in Jerusalem for a while. In connection with Jerusalem he never once mentioned any Marian shrine. (Deutsch, p. 67)

Pope Leo XIII (1878-1903)

- Pope during the discovery of Mary's House. After repeated requests by Sister Marie de Mandat-Grancey, and financed by her benevolence, Father Poulin and Father Jung located Mary's House. News came slowly to Rome and by accidental means.

- 1895: Sent Father Eschbach, Superior of the Pontifical French Seminary in Rome, to the East to study the Oriental Rites. Father Eschbach met Father Poulin in Smyrna and inquired about Mary's House, for which he held great interest. Arrangements were made, and Father Eschbach traveled to Ephesus with Father Jung. (Deutsch, p. 67)

- Father Eschbach reported his positive findings to Pope Leo, handing him pictures. (Deutsch, p. 67)

- April 18, 1896: Removed the plenary indulgence from Mary's tomb in Jerusalem *in Perpetuum*—for all time. (Deutsch, p. 68)

- October 4, 1902: Cardinal di Lai journeyed to Ephesus and became deeply convinced of the truth of Mary's House and her Assumption from that location.

- August 15, 1903, Feast of the Assumption: Restored the following notation in the Diario Romano: "At Ephesus . . . where according to the more probable opinion Mary died."(Deutsch, p. 68)

- October 1903: Cardinal di Lai sent an affirming letter of complete support to Father Poulin. (Deutsch, p. 69)

- Planned to send a pontifical commission to Ephesus in Autumn 1904 but passed away in August 1903.

Pope Saint Pius X (1904-1914)

- April 6, 1906: Sent a letter with his Apostolic Blessing to all who were doing research on Mary's House and included a prayer to Mary that she would help them find her tomb.

- Received Sister Marie de Mandat-Grancey and her companion Sister Fievet on April 20, 1912 and asked, "Has the tomb been found?" Sister Grancey replied, "Not yet, Holy Father," She continued, "Most Holy Father, I know that you believe, as did your illustrious predecessor Benedict XIV, that the Blessed Virgin died at Ephesus." Saint Pius responded with an affirmative nod and a smile. (Deutsch, p. 69)

- Granted the favor of a plenary indulgence to a 1914 pilgrimage to Mary's House. (Deutsch, p. 69)

Pope Benedict XV (1914-1922)

- WWI—The Great War

- Conference held at the Pontifical Roman Major Seminary on February 27, 1921 in Ephesus in Mary's House, attended by numerous Roman Curia. (Deutsch, p. 70)

- Turkey became a Republic in 1923.

Pope Pius XI (1922-1939)

- Wrote a letter to Father Poulin congratulating him on his recent literary piece on the place of Mary's death. (Deutsch, p. 70) 1967

Pope Pius XII (1939-1958)

- Defined Dogma of Mary's Assumption, November 1, 1950, omitting opinions of the location of Mary's death and specific site of the Assumption. (Deutsch, p. 70)

- August 1951: Dedication of the reconstructed Mary's House (Deutsch, p. 70)

- Sent a communication to Rev. Joseph Descuffi, C.M., Archbishop of Smyrna in 1951, declaring Mary's House an official sanctuary for pilgrims of the Catholic religion. (Deutsch, p. 70)

- June 19, 1951: Papal decree granting special privileges to Mary's House and Basilicas of St. John and Mary in Ephesus. Permission was granted for celebration of Votive Mass of the Assumption in Mary's House. (Deutsch, p. 70)

- Referred to the Sacred Penitentiary the question of a plenary indulgence for all pilgrims to Mary's House. (Deutsch, p. 71)

Pope John XXIII (1958-1963)

- Years earlier in 1931, as Papal legate, visited Ephesus for the 50th Centenary of the Council of Ephesus. Later the Pope functioned as delegate of the Holy See in Istanbul. (Deutsch, p. 71)

- August 18, 1961: as pope, granted a plenary indulgence for all Catholic pilgrims for all time. (Deutsch, p. 71)

- From 1960 through the end of his reign Pope John sent a candle to Mary's House on February 2, the Feast of the Presentation. These candles are sent only to the most important Marian shrines in the world. (Deutsch, p. 72)

Pope Paul VI (1963-1978)

- July 26, 1976: First Pope to visit Mary's House. Presented a gold chalice to honor Sister Marie de Mandat-Grancey.

Pope John Paul II (1978-2005)

- November 30, 1979, feast of Saint Andrew: Celebrated Mass at Mary's House. This received the attention of news media.

Pope Benedict XVI (2005-)

- During his first visit outside of Italy, celebrated Mass at Mary's House on November 29, 2006. His visit and Mass were televised throughout the world.

Pope Paul VI offering Mass at Panaghia Capouli. He was the first pope to visit Mary's House.

All facts so noted above were taken from Father Bernard Deutsch's book entitled *Our Lady of Ephesus,* which is, by all accounts, considered a primary resource on all things Ephesus, particularly Mary's House. Each of his facts is cited from original sources in his voluminous, detailed, and exhaustive notes in the back of his book.

—Lorraine Fusaro

PRESIDENT OF TURKEY
VISITS MARY'S HOUSE

Remember that Sister Marie had hired devout Turks to be the first caretakers of *Mereyem Ana Evi* (Mary's Home) after she had gained title to the property. She would have been delighted to read this article which appeared in Hurriyet, a Turkish newspaper:

> On March 4, 2010, the Turkish President, Abdullah Gul and his wife arrived by presidential plane at Selcuk, outside Izmir. From there they were driven in motorcade to *Meryem Ana Evi* (Mary's Home). This was their first stop of the day.[1]

Zaman, the Muslim paper supporting the ruling party, said that, after visiting the Home, they went to the sacred fountain and, according to custom, took some of the water to sprinkle on their bodies, and the President said after drinking from the flowing water, "God gave us health, forgiveness, and goodness."[2]

This is believed to be the first visit to Mary's Home by a President of Turkey and his wife. We pray it will open the way to bring the grace of conversion and a better relationship between the Turks and all visitors to Mary's House from other countries, knowing that the Mother of God desires all people to be saved by her Son and to be members of Mary's Family.

Above: Archbishop G. Bernardini and Erin von Uffel present His Holiness Benedict XVI with the film, *Sr. Marie de Mandat-Grancey, DC, True Daughter of Charity* on April 19, 2007. *Right:* Pope Benedict XVI's visit to Panaghia Capouli. This was his first official visit outside of Italy.

Author's Note

YOU HAVE read one of the more compelling accounts of God's action in the transference of property to bring together Catholics, Orthodox, and Muslim worshipers. Sister Marie had been chosen and dutifully and beautifully fulfilled the heavy burden of bringing together people of different religious persuasions. Sister Marie knew how to handle the situation. These people were asking her permission to come and pray in Mary's Home. She gratefully hired a Muslim family to care for the Home, and they lovingly began to beautify it. Then the discontent among the nations arose and stopped access to the Home.

Unfortunately we had to have two World Wars, and people wondered what would happen to Mary's House. In the following account by Father Joseph Euzet, C.M., *History of the House of the Blessed Virgin Near Ephesus (1891-1961)*, read about the discovery of Mary's Home. Find, too, the Approbatory Letter by Joseph Descuffi, C.M., then Archbishop of Smyrna. We can see the hand of Mary involved in this. God, it seems, has sent Mary to bring people to Himself. Our Father in Heaven sets a pattern in the activity restarted by Father Euzet's decision to cede the property to the Archbishop of Smyrna.

* * *

The story of Sister Marie as unfolded here is as far as I can take it. In time, others may add to it, for which I would be most grateful.

199

I owe deep gratitude to Sister Marie for inviting me to write this little narrative of her. I say invite because the plea came through Erin von Uffel and was enforced by Lorraine Fusaro. The three of us learned much and we prayed more. I thank you both. I regret that we now bring the matter to a close. I beg the both of you to join me in praying for the Capuchin Order who has taken full charge of Mary's Home. I know they will be great hosts to the worldwide family of God coming to pray together in Mary's Home. What a blessed gift Sister Marie prepared for them.

Appendix A

History of the
House of the Blessed Virgin
Near Ephesus
(1891-1961)

JOSEPH EUZET

HISTORIQUE

DE LA

MAISON DE LA SAINTE VIERGE

PRES

D'EPHESE

(1891-1961)

NOTRE-DAME D'EPHESE
Cami Sokak, 29 - Yedikule
ISTANBUL

The original cover of the book.

Dedicated to the Venerable Memory of
Sister Marie de Mandat-Grancey (+1915)
Daughter of Charity
and of
Eugene Poulin, C.M. (+1928)

Approbatory Letter
Catholic Archdiocese of Smyrna
Izmir, March 19, 1961

To Rev. Joseph Euzet, Izmir.

I congratulate you on your excellent idea to bring together all
the articles that you had put forward up to now in the Review of
Our Lady of Ephesus concerning the history of the discovery and
establishment of the sanctuary of *Panaya*. The book that you have
created from them has the merit of having been written by a con-
temporary of the events, who deepened his personal knowledge by
a direct study of the archives and the writings left by the unforget-
table Mr. Poulin. He was your superior for more than thirty years,
and you were his faithful and devoted heir. You attended his scholarly jousts against those who held positions that were passed down
but without rigorous evidence, remaining closed to the cause of
Ephesus. He deserved a better welcome. But with the legal inheritance of the House of the Blessed Virgin, he also left you the duty
to defend his memory and to continue the work of persuasion that
he began. You complete it fortuitously, with much discretion and
charity, but also with the competence and the maturity assured by
your respectable age and your conscientious work.

You do not break your lance in combat, like your master, who
was a spirited fighter because of his love of the truth. You are more

insinuating, but no less prompt to the parry than to the merited riposte. You let people and facts speak. Their voice is eloquent; may it, reinforced by your serious chronicle, shake off ignorance, indifference and held positions, and also attract the benevolent attention of the religious and intellectual world to the tradition of Ephesus that rests on the historical monuments and serious documents.

It is thus that I wholeheartedly bless your work that it might propagate the cult of Our Lady of Ephesus throughout the world.

Joseph Descuffi
Archbishop of Smyrna

Notice

Until the end of the last century (1896), the site of *Panaya-Kapulu,* since famous, was only known by a few Christian inhabitants of the village of Kirkindjé, located in the mountains west of Ephesus. The most learned travelers were completely ignorant of it. For example, Texier, in his classic work on Asia Minor doesn't even mention it, even as he speaks at length of the little village of Arvalia, two kilometers as the crow flies from *Panaya Kapulu.*

Similarly, in "Our Voyage to Biblical Lands" by Camus and Vigouroux (1890), where they congratulate the Archbishop of Smyrna for resurrecting the tradition of Ephesus in regards to the death of the Virgin and where there are many pages on Ephesus, there is no question of a ruin in the mountain.

On the contrary, in his book on the "Seven Churches of the Apocalypse" (1896), Mgr. Camus, who became the bishop of La Rochelle, speaks at length about the recent discovery, to which he attaches no importance, calling the house of the Virgin "a ruin without any value." However, and one might say in spite of himself, he contributed to making the fact known in the world. Indeed, his handsome volume certainly penetrated in milieus where the pamphlet "*Panaghia Capouli,*" published, as we will see, by Fr. Poulin and Msgr. Timoni, in the same year of 1896, did not reach.

Although the author of these pages was able to follow the history of *Panaya Kapulu* from the beginning, they will not be composed according to a string of personal memories, but very exactly, according to two large notebooks, where Poulin took care, day after day, to note the least details concerning the discovery and all that followed.

Reverend Joseph Euzet

Joseph Descuffi, Archbishop of Smyrna during the years when the *Historique* was written.

First Part
(1891-1914)

Chapter 1

The Discovery of the House of the Virgin

T HE FACT of the discovery of the house of the Blessed Virgin in *Panaghia-Capouli,* near Ephesus, is so much more remarkable in that it occurred twice and by explorers who didn't consult each other.

But before we tell the story, it is absolutely necessary to at least name (we'll speak of her more later) the famous visionary Anne-Catherine Emmerick. Certainly, no partisan of Ephesus would dream of considering the work of this mystic as historical revelations come from Heaven (as revelations are described in the Supplement to the Biblical Dictionary). Yet it remains true that the "Life of the Blessed Virgin" according to these revelations was the occasion, we must even say the cause, of the discovery. How could we pretend to ignore it? It would be to ignore the historical truth.

In 1881, Abbot Gouyet, an unattached priest yet perfectly in line with the diocesan authority of Paris, a great enthusiast of C. Emmerick, went to Palestine to verify on site the exactitude of the descriptions that he had read in the "Life of Our Lord Jesus Christ" by the same visionary. Very satisfied by the results, he had the idea to do the same for Ephesus. He therefore returned by way of

Smyrna where he was the guests of the Vincentians who knew nothing about his project.

But the archbishop Mgr. Timoni encouraged him and gave him for a companion a very young man (who later became a priest). He thus went off to explore the Mountain of Ephesus, only having as a "letter of introduction" a sign written in Greek by Fr. Giampaolo, CM: "Please respect a poor inoffensive traveler without any means."

He had no meeting with thieves. After several days spent in the mountain in difficult conditions, he returned to Smyrna and claimed to have found what he was looking for, but no one, except the archbishop, put any faith in what he said. A letter that he wrote to Rome about it remained unanswered. He had no greater success in Paris.

How did the idea to look come about?

Ten years after (1891), Gouyet was completely forgotten in Smyrna at the Vincentian secondary school, where the personnel had almost entirely changed. But there was then, as the superior, at the French hospital, Sister Marie de Mandat-Grancey, of the best French nobility, who, while being a true daughter of St. Vincent de Paul, was not afraid of mysticism.

She had read in her community the *Life of the Blessed Virgin* according to Catherine Emmerick. When they came to the chapter where the stay and the death of the Virgin in the mountain of Ephesus is recounted, she said to herself, "Ephesus isn't so far away. It would be well worth it to go see!" She said it out loud and repeated it to the Vincentian who said their daily mass, Henri Jung, the man the least likely to hear "such stories" with any sympathy.

Almost at the same time, Eugene Poulin, superior of the school, was brought in a most unusual way to become acquainted with C. Emmerick's book. And imagine his surprise when he learned that the Blessed Virgin had died in Ephesus, when he had always thought she had died in Jerusalem!

The same conversion took place a little later in H. Jung. Not giving up, Sister de Grancey had sent him a copy of the *Life of the Blessed Virgin,* with an urgent request that he would familiarize himself with it. He carried it out, we might say, opening the book and reading it all in one sitting. A Hebrew scholar and very knowledgeable about Judaic customs, what struck him above all was the exactitude of the details that he could check. Naturally, this conversion had a great influence on all the confreres who had almost all been hostile to the idea up to then. "We must go see!" Such was the unanimous cry.

FIRST EXPEDITION:
FRS. JUNG AND VERVAULT'S EXPEDITION

They thus decided on a formal expedition. The caravan was made up of four people: Fr. Jung, CM, chief of the expedition; Fr. Vervault, also a priest of the Mission, missionary in Madagascar but at that time passing through Smyrna, and a former pontifical soldier whom forced hikes didn't scare; a Catholic servant, Thomaso; finally, Mr. Pélécas, former railroad employee of the region, which he knew well. In Ephesus, they added a fifth companion, the brave Mustafa, an African Muslim; they counted on him for his knowledge of the mountain to be able to indicate the best paths. It seems appropriate to us to conserve the names of these humble people who contributed, in their own way, to this memorable expedition.

The departure from Smyrna took place July 27, 1891.

Let us be clear that the two explorers were not hypnotized by the hope of discovering what they were looking for. Quite the contrary. They had no other object than to prove that there was nothing. They simply wanted to finish once and for all with the "girlish imaginings."

Some time earlier a Melchite priest from Aidin (there was at that time a Catholic parish in Aidin served by priests of the Armenian rite) to whom a German lady had sent a sum so that he might search for the house of the Virgin near Ephesus, claimed to have found something. They thought they might be able to benefit from his information. That's why, instead of getting off the train at Ayassolouk (Selçuk), they went on to the Azizié (Tchamlik) station. From there they went toward Deirmen-déré (valley of the windmills), a picturesque site where Charles Texier believed Ortygie was located, according to Strabon.

There was a monastery there with two monks. The received a very warm welcome. They all put their provisions in common, and they got along quite well. H. Jung had the idea to ask the monks where the Blessed Virgin died. "In Jerusalem!" they answered without hesitation. These two monks were well indoctrinated in the purest Byzantine tradition where there's never any question of anything but the tomb of Gethsemane.

In brief, it was a rather agreeable excursion, but one without any result. Deirmen-déré did not correspond at all to the indications of Catherine Emmerick. They pressed on to Scala-Nova (Kouchadassi) to spend the night there. The first investigation had yielded nothing. They had to take another approach.

They left Ayassoluk July 29 and, this time, had compass in hand and the book of the visionary as guide. They read, "Three leagues from Ephesus on the left, when coming from Jerusalem." It was thus necessary to go toward the south, toward Jerusalem, and attack the mountain from the right. They read on: "On a mountain where you arrive by narrow paths . . ." There were, in effect, traces of paths traced some years before in order to access a mine, since abandoned. They went at it valiantly. But how tiring to mount the steep slope, under a July sun, approaching noon!

Toward eleven o'clock our explorers reached a small plateau where they saw a group of women working in a tobacco field. They cried out, "Water!" in their thirst. The Orthodox Christian women said that they didn't have any more, but that it could be found at the monastery, not far away, and they pointed in the direction of a ruined house.

They ran there and soon they could relieve their thirst at a clear fresh stream, forgetting, for the moment, the goal of their expedition.

However, as soon as they were refreshed, they inspected the horizon. That sea that you saw in front of you, this poor house in ruins, those sheer rocks, that mountain behind the house . . . So many characteristic that they recognize for having read about them in the book. They looked at each other, stupefied.

They opened the book. "From the height of the mountain that shelters the house, you can glimpse Ephesus on one side and the sea on the other, closer than Ephesus . . ." "Can you see Ephesus from up there?" they asked. "Yes." Then they forgot their tiredness, climbed up, and arrived at the summit. No more doubt. You could see Ephesus, all the plain and the sea and Samos. They could hardly believe their eyes. They had found it!

However, fearing they might be duped by first impressions, they consecrated two more days to examine everything: the house, orientation, surroundings. They wanted to check if you could see Ephesus and the sea from any other nearby summit. From none, unless you count Aladagh (Solmissos), but that's really too far, in the south, toward Milet.

Book in hand, H. Jung made a cursory inspection. He also examined in the surroundings, the most remarkable stones, and seemed to recognize on some of them Hebrew letters. That wouldn't be surprising if there had been, as indicated in the book, a Jewish colony that later became Christian.

After two days of study, the explorers were convinced. They went back to Smyrna to announce to their friends and enemies (for there were some!) their astonishing discovery.

SECOND EXPEDITION: FRS. JUNG AND POULIN'S EXPEDITION

At first, E. Poulin gave his confrere (H. Jung) a very cold welcome. "He arrived at my door," he wrote, "with the embarrassed look of a fox that had just taken a chicken." "Well," timidly began H. Jung, "I think that we found it." "Oh, joker, don't go looking to make me upset!" "I assure you," Jung responded with a firmer tone, "I think we found it!" And he set to tell the detailed story of the expedition.

Although a little astonished, E. Poulin did not give in right away. He also, in turn, wanted to go see. This resulted in the second expedition, which took place a little while later, in August, the 12th, to be exact.

In order to avoid the difficult climb of the first expedition, they attacked the mountain from the Axixiyé (Tchamlik) side and from there followed the paths leading to the mine, a much less arduous ascent.

E. Poulin wanted to take in everything. "There are the rocks behind the house, the house, the mountain from whose peak you can see the sea, Ephesus and Samos. The terrace that is mentioned, high and nicely planted, we crossed it moments ago" (*Historical Manuscript of Panaghia,* reg. 1, p. 22).

He himself very meticulously inspected the exterior and interior of the house. It was impossible to control all the details, given the little time at his disposal. But that which he was able to see sufficed to inspire in him a strong desire to examine things more closely another time. "August 14 we returned to Smyrna one idea richer and one resolution stronger." This rather enigmatic phrase is clarified by E. Poulin's whole life following that memorable day. The idea was to discover the truth about the mysterious house. The resolution was to obstinately and tirelessly pursue this intriguing research.

THIRD EXPEDITION:
EUGENE POULIN'S EXPEDITION

Thus there was a third expedition August 19-25. It was composed of the leader of the first (H. Jung), E. Poulin and four educated laymen, among them Jules-Ferard Borrel, a man truly remarkable for his varied skills and his knowledge. (He was at the time director of the French postal service in Smyrna.) These gentlemen stayed six days on site, drawing, photographing, measuring, and noting each detail, no matter how important, with the greatest exactitude possible.

Let us say straight off that this long undertaking was in no way done to reveal how the place conformed to the descriptions of C. Emmerick, as the adversaries of Ephesus would have us believe. But because already there was a lively interest in this corner of the earth, they wanted to situate it topographically.

This is why after six days the explorers brought back to Smyrna not only their personal impressions, but also maps, sketches, photographs, etc, and in sum, the very firm conviction that they had found it and that there was no reason to look anywhere else.

Upon his return, H. Jung wrote a long, detailed report, which he sent to Fr. Lobry, the Visitor of the Vincentians in Istanbul. Allow us to cite the most compelling line from the explorers: "If a million investigators came here, all would leave saying: only someone who saw could have written and described in this manner" (J. G. Borrel).

A reflection on this subject. From 1899 the "Civiltà Cattolica" requested that one establish the following thesis: "What is said of *Panaghia* in C. Emmerick could not have been in any previous document nor dictated by an eye witness. This thesis established, the cause of *Panaghia* will not be attackable."

Some claimed, in effect, that C. Brentano could have found the elements of the description in some travel narrative. Has one not noted numerous details that seem to be borrowed from the "Life of Christ" by Fr. Cochen? Yet first of all, why should we be surprised to encounter in a life of Christ, whoever the author, some resemblances with C. Emmerick's Life of Christ? And then there is the description of the *Panaghia-Capouli* site that no adversary of Ephesus has been able to find.

In any case we are not about to argue. We attest. Someone has certainly seen. If you don't want to admit that it was the visionary herself, the fact of the concordance is inexplicable.

THE SITE

But let's not wait any longer to describe the holy house, in the setting that it was at the time, although, sadly, one no longer sees it, for two military occupations (1914 and 1920) could only be disastrous for the vegetation.

"It was framed by eight magnificent plane trees, two on the sea side and two on the south side, linked by a wild vine that, after having climbed to the low branches of the northern plane tree, thrust like a giant boa over the four walls to the southern plane trees and enlaced its powerful branches by its knotty creeping vines. A fifth plane tree in front of the western façade between the door and the left corner; the three others, a little to the side, on a sort of platform. Above these plane trees, a few meters beyond toward the ravine, a trim poplar stood out from the massive plane trees and shot up, like a thin arrow, its elegant and light top.

"The antique chapel appeared beautiful and venerable, with an indescribable sort of discretion and mystery, at the foot of these great rocks of the mountain that shelter and dominate it, under the plane trees that jealously cover it with their protective shade, with the delicate poplar, finally, that climbs so high and seems to regard from afar, as if to signal from a distance an enemy's approach, or, like a flagstaff, destined to rally people and cry out to the pilgrim, Come! It's here!" (Poulin, *Hist. Man. of Panaghia,* reg. 1, p. 30).

From that, how many questions arose! What really was this house, who were the inhabitants of this place? (because one found, on various sides, tombs, old walls and traces of habitation). In an era long ago, surely pagan Greeks. But why not, later, Jews taking refuge, then Christians wanting to live in the very place where the Virgin Mary had died? Simple hypotheses, but realistic enough! We refrain from affirming anything since we are looking not just for realistic, but the truth.

DESCRIPTION OF THE HOUSE OF THE VIRGIN

"The house of the Virgin was made of stone and squared off. Only in the back was it round or octagonal.

"The windows being placed at a considerable height, the house ended with a platform.

"It was divided in two pieces by a foyer in the middle.

"The front part of the house was separated from the other by light wattle screens placed at the right and left of the foyer. When the part of the lodging needed to be transformed into one room, these screens . . . were detached and removed.

"To the right and left and against the foyer there were light doors that led to the other part of the house. It was darker than the other and ended with a semi-circle or an angle . . .

"The back of this section, isolated from the rest by a curtain, made the Virgin's oratory.

"To the right of the oratory, against a niche formed by a wall, was the bedroom of the Blessed Virgin.

"Across the way and to the left of the oratory was another room where she left her linens and her furnishings.

"A large curtain went from one room to the other and closed off the oratory situated between them.

"The back of the bedroom was formed by a wall covered by a tapestry. The right and left parts were covered in woodwork. Finally, the front part had in the middle a light double door opening to the interior.

"The ceiling of the bedroom was also in wattle and formed pieces that came together to make a vault.

"The Virgin's bed against the wall was a sort of hollowed-out box, one and a half feet high and with an ordinary length and width" (from C. Emmerick).

Chapter 2

Formalities

L ET'S recall the events that have taken place up to now. July 29, 1891, discovery of *Panaghia*. August 13, first inspection. August 19-25, detailed and prolonged examination that brought them to the conviction that they had found it and that there was no reason to search anywhere else. They thus began to say to each other, "Wouldn't it be good to own it!" Soon they were saying, "We must have it!" But how could they have it without buying it? And how could they buy it when they were without any resources?

Listen to E. Poulin: "God who sees and prepares far in advance had already taken care to place on our path one of those souls occupied with good, who asks nothing else but to give itself to all that is good, a devout soul, as ardent, as pious and generous, the noble Sister Marie de Mandat-Grancey. It is her that Divine Providence wanted to be earthly providence as the "Mother of *Panaghia*" . . . Ah! How happy I am to render her deserved praise, and may these lines be passed down to posterity (our emphasis) so that all know long after we are gone to whom France and the Catholic Church owe *Panaghia*. Blessed be God to have given me this opportunity to say aloud what I have long held in my heart and to clear myself of a sacred debt I have long felt that I owed. Now it is done. I give you thanks, Lord" (*Hist. Man. of Panaghia,* reg. 1, p. 40). There is no need to add that we adopt Poulin's lines, which honor him as much as Sister de Grancey.

As soon as anything was said to her of the possibility of buying *Panaghia,* she could have certainly answered, "I already thought of it!" Her heart opened itself joyfully. She simply took the time to assure that she would have on the given day the necessary funds, and she answered, "Buy!"

To enter into the details of the laborious negotiations, from January 15 to November 15, 1892, of this purchase would be too long and would interrupt the flow of these notes.

When the moment came to draw up the contract, E. Poulin asked the sister, "In what name should we register the property? In the name of the Superior General, or in the name of the Superior of Smyrna?" "In my name!" she said, simply but firmly.

When one has had the good fortune to know Sister de Grancey and to observe what, in her, under a sort of appearance of noble pride, hid a real and profound humility, this spontaneous cry, "In my name" can't help but astonish a little. Should we suppose that she saw there a means to transport, if we might say it this way, her patrimonial forest of Grancey that were the source of her wealth to be able to enjoy them personally? Certainly not! But she was well allowed to feel a deep satisfaction at the thought of giving her family name to the blessed place where the Blessed Virgin (for her there was never any doubt) was assumed into Heaven.

Moreover, after several years, she herself offered a sacrifice, asking insistently that a transfer take place that would secure, as much as possible, the future of *Panaghia.*

They decided to transfer it to the name of E. Poulin, the Superior of Sacred Heart Church. After a number of difficulties, May 11, 1910, the new title was obtained in such perfect order that Poulin's will permitted his successor to recover the property that had been confiscated during the First World War.

"It is well understood," notes E. Poulin, "that Sister de Grancey remains Lady and mistress of *Panaghia,* as before the transfer, the mentioned transfer having no other aim than to assure the property after her death (1915) and not to rob her of it."

And it is thus that after as before, she continued her inexhaustible generosity, supporting all the costs: developments and repairs of the paths, construction of buildings, landscaping, maintenance of the chapel, trips, digs and research, publications of brochures, etc. "Use and profit while I'm still here!" she would say. "After my death I won't be able to help you any more. Providing and forward-looking, she still assured a capital of 31,000 francs whose use you can easily imagine in the course of a half-century!

OFFICIAL INVESTIGATION

Let's get back to the chain of events. In response to the account that E. Poulin gave of the explorations in the mountain of Ephesus, the archbishop of Smyrna, Mgr. André Timoni, who hadn't completely forgotten Abbot Gouyet, took a great interest. "Oh, I am so happy," he wrote, "I've always thought that the Blessed Virgin came to Ephesus, and even died there." Thus he welcomed enthusiastically the proposition that an official inquiry be made and that he preside over it.

First they went about forming a competent commission: seven ecclesiastics and five professional lay people. December 1, 1892, or just two weeks after the purchase of the land, the twelve designated members left for Ephesus.

It was 9:30 when the group left the Ayassolouk (Seldjouk) station. E. Poulin kept as close as possible to the archbishop. Let's allow him to speak for himself: "Once we arrived at the fountain, we left the route that led to Scala-Nova (Kouchadassi) to take the left paved path. 'Monsignor, what is this path?' 'Oh! I know it well from taking it. It's the old road from Ephesus to Aydin.' 'So it's the old Roman way that went from here to Tralles (Aydin), from Tralles to Apamée, from Apamée to Antioch by the gorges of Taurus and that, there, connects with the route to Jerusalem.' "

A little farther on: "Monsignor, do you see this mountain? On what side is it in relationship to us?" "On our right!" "So to the left for those who would come from Jerusalem. How does it look to you from Ephesus?" "I see it as steep and inaccessible." "Perfect, Monsignor. Listen now." And E. Poulin read (from the book of the visionary): "On a mountain, on the left when you come from Jerusalem. This mountain is very steep on the Ephesus side."

"We arrived at the place where we had to take the footpath. 'Monsignor, listen on, "You encounter to the south narrow paths leading to a mountain with a savage appearance." From what direction did we leave Ephesus?' 'From the right, so the west.' 'We are thus both to the south and east of Ephesus. Listen, Monsignor: "Arriving by the south-east, you see the village against the foot of a mountain." ' "

We decided to cite this dialogue that allows the reader to see for himself the exactitude of the general indications that he could read in "The Life of the Blessed Virgin" by C. Emmerick and "that no traveler would have thought of writing in this way and taking as a point of orientation the route that came from Jerusalem."

After a somewhat difficult assent, they arrived at the summit of Bulbul-Dag. There they could observe next again the exactitude of the seer: "Ephesus, visible from the north, and, to the west, the sea with Samos; *Panaghia,* closer to the sea than to Ephesus. Thin torrents that, traversing the plain in a zigzag, come against the foot of the mountain. . . ." (We leave as it is this bird's eye view that we believe does not minimize the seriousness of the inquiry.)

"One descends by the terrace with pleasure. The building attracts attention by its appearance. The carved blocks 1.5 meters long by .75 meters wide and .5 meter high could not be the remains of a shepherds' cabin. Wouldn't it be the home that the visionary speaks of?"

The inquiry went on for a long time and in minute detail at *Panaghia* itself. The house and its surroundings were the object, book in hand, of an attentive examination, both on the whole and in its details. After that, the commission unanimously recognized a striking correspondence of all C. Emmerick's description. A statement was drawn up to officially establish the result of the inquiry and submitted to the approval of the commission which approved it and signed it eagerly. The original, sealed in impeccable form, is now located at the archdiocesan office in Izmir. It was published in its entirety in the first brochure, "*Panaghia Capouli,*" which we'll talk about later.

Chapter 3
Critical Points of View

STILL in December 1892, two weeks after the official inquiry, there was an authorized attestation of the tradition of the inhabitants of Kirkindjé about the place where the Blessed Virgin died, in *Panaghia*. These Christians were authentic descendents of the Ephesus Christians who took refuge in the mountains to the east of Ephesus and who remained there until the torment of 1922. Living away from society, they had conserved, if not their language (as they speak a sort of Turkish), at least their Christian faith and the traditions of their ancestors.

One can always discuss and even dispute the value of a witness. But it is not permissible to treat as a liar the honest man who interpreted as an untrue manipulation the detailed questioning that you can read in the brochure already mentioned.

There is, also, a fact that preceded the questioning and that has happened since. This is that for a long time (we won't dare write: for all time) the Kirkindjiotes, around the feast of the Assumption, come in pilgrimage to *Panaghia*. And, in what painful conditions! Five hours of walking, on the mountain, on the plain, and again on the mountain! Arrived in *Panaghia,* they set an altar and the priest celebrates the Mass which everyone follows with devotion. How many candles were lit to attest to the love of these simple people for the Most Holy!

It has been said: how could these orthodox people have such a devotion when in their liturgy there is only consideration of Gethsemane and Jerusalem? Obviously this is a little extraordinary. Impossible? Certainly not. The two monks of Déirmen-déré, mentioned earlier, closer to *Panaghia,* were for Jerusalem. But this was only the echo of the Byzantine tradition. On the other hand, the Kirkindjiotes faithfully repeated what they passed on from father to son, never left their refuge and lived cut off from the world.

Waiting that this so important tradition be studied in greater detail, we will read, as an appendix to these notes, a page from E. Poulin.

> While in all the surrounding areas, the Greeks, their neighbors, are for the death of Mary in Jerusalem . . . while all the Orthodox Church, their church, is entirely for Jerusalem, they alone unanimously and firmly are for Ephesus, not just for Ephesus but for *Panaghia-Capouli,* in the region of Ephesus. It's there, they say, that they go each year, with their priests to celebrate her Assumption. According to them, they have done so for centuries. For the Assumption in 1897, almost 200 Kirkindjiotes climbed up to *Panaghia,* and with them, eight of their priests for the Mass and ceremonies.
>
> This tradition, they did not invent it. They just received it, neither from their neighbors nor from the Orthodox Church. From where then? From their ancestors, they answer. And they should know better than anyone.
>
> If Ephesus was in the 7th century, without any tradition like Jerusalem, Ephesus would have followed, no doubt, the apocryphal movement that carried Jerusalem and the Orthodox Church toward the new tradition of

Jerusalem. Ephesus resisted therefore and resisted with invincible force. Why?

THE CONTROVERSIES

Since they were owners of the land in *Panaghia-Capouli,* they could and they should act as owners. First of all, they had to establish a guardian. They didn't have to look far. The head of the family that worked up there, a certain Andréa, a real brigand in his time, who, in his youth, let himself be enlisted by the English to join the artillery in Abyssinia, couldn't be replaced by any other. We learned from him that this name replaced in a way the region's name, as people said, the church of *Panaghia-Capouli,* the *Panaghia-Capouli* fields, the *Panaghia-Capouli* mountain.

It was also necessary to begin as soon as possible the temporary arrangements with which H. Jung was charged, and with whom the new task went well. However, it wasn't possible to get everything done right away.

As for E. Poulin, he put himself on another field of work: the historical problem. Did the Blessed Virgin die in Ephesus or in Jerusalem? The future of *Panaghia-Capouli* depended on the answer to that question.

His first thought was to take the opinion of the best known scholars. Therefore, he addressed himself to the historian L. Duchesne, who was at that time at the height of his fame. Note the date of his first letter: January 22, 1892, that is, hardly six months after the discovery and well before the purchase and the inquiry of December 1892.

E. Poulin was not a man, certainly, to confuse history with mysticism, and his actions are the best proof in that he intended to consult the historian. Yet, presumably thinking he would interest his illustrious correspondent, he recounted to him the discovery of the house of the Virgin with the indications of C. Emmerick.

At the simple mention of the name, L. Duchesne took pen in hand: "The visions of C. Emmerick are nothing more than an abominable imposture. In what measure the supposed visionary and her associate C. Bretano share the merit to have compiled so many apocryphal gospels and untrue legends, it is not up to me to determine, and I think that one could spend one's time better . . . Excuse me for speaking to you in this way, but I am a Breton, and I have the habit of calling a spade a spade. What's more, my religious and moral conscience gives me the duty to protest against the establishment of a sanctuary in such conditions. I wish I had the eloquence of Saint Paul to beg you to go no further and to not expose your community and even the Church to deserved sarcasm that will surely welcome your discovery. I believe that you are more carried along than convinced. For the love of God, resist!" (February 4, 1892).

The next day, L. Duchesne warned Fr. Fiat, superior general of the Congregation of the Mission: "I consider it my duty to call your attention to the recent discovery near Ephesus and to the incredible state in which your confreres there seem to have fallen. In the first place, it seems to me extremely imprudent to use the revelations of C. Emmerick as they do; it's a false path" (February 5, 1892). (The original letters are in the Motherhouse archives of 95, rue de Sèvres.)

The letter to Fr. Fiat reached him without any commentary. There wasn't, thus, from Fr. Fiat, any restriction against continuing research but just a simple warning to do so quietly. E. Poulin therefore resisted, but in a way completely contrary to what L. Duchesne asked of him, that is to say, he went to his studies with all the more ardor. To the good Breton, the good native of Bourgogne, one might say.

Certainly, at that moment E. Poulin was far from being over-
taken by Ephesus. Yet what struck him in the letter from his correspondent was the weakness of his objections.

A second letter astonished him even more. "The correspondence
that strikes you (of the place with the description of C. Emmerick)
does not exist at all." How could he know, he who had not seen
the place? From that time on, the confidence that he had placed in
the famous scholar was completely destroyed. He understood very
well that he couldn't count on others, but that he had to go forward
by himself in the exploration of the first centuries' history, where
we will follow him.

But we should look now at the strange affirmation of L. Duchesne who, after a rapid look at a few maps and photos, claimed to
see better than those who had been there. Was it reasonable to
oppose the witness of the inquiry commission?

However, you might object, there are those who had seen and
affirmed the same thing. Yes, Fr. Barnabé of Alsace wrote: "There
isn't a spectacular relationship, but you find numerous and striking
differences." He claimed to prove this affirmation by mathematical rules (*The Tomb of the Virgin in Jerusalem,* Jerusalem 1903).
That's why he aligns figures and counts, from a bird's eye view on
the map, the length in hours of the distance. A real topographical
chicanery, no more. Who ever claimed that C. Emmerick's description was the equivalent of a Geological Survey map?

Fr. Barnabé objects in the same way by having us look at two com-
positions by a German artist who was inspired by the visionary. It is
quite true that the two images do not much resemble the reality. But
what does that prove? C. Emmerick's description does not give the
exact profile of the mountains that each artist can represent in his
own way. No need to insist. A witness' ability to see was manifestly
falsified by his prejudices, as were those of the historian Duchesne.

There are points on which discussion is permitted. How to explain, for example, the numerous islands, while Samos Island is the only one visible? The play of light differing by time of day and day of the year, are they a sufficient explanation? The sea with its many islands, could it simply be the sea of numerous islands, an epithet that characterizes well the Aegean Sea?

Finally, let us repeat that the official inquiry was done and done well more than sixty years ago. To start over now would give the same results. The essential, in effect, is that on the whole, above all (more than in the details) the description is true. This is why we attach a particular importance to the general indications that we cited above in the company of the Archbishop and E. Poulin.

To the blind witness of L. Duchesne and to the supposedly clairvoyant witness of Fr. Barnabé, we give that of a qualified scholar who seems to us to be worth its weight in gold and worthy of being engraved on a marble plaque:

> Before climbing up to *Panaghia-Capouli* on September 27, 1899, I was convinced, through study of the tradition relative to the tomb of the Blessed Virgin in Gethsemane and especially through study of St. Ephipane, that it was absolutely necessary to look for the Virgin's tomb elsewhere than in or around Jerusalem. This was in no way influenced by C. Emmerick's work. However, September 27 I noted between C. Emmerick's description and the things of *Panaghia-Capouli* such an agreement that only one explanation seemed possible. C. Emmerick had contemplated a vision of the site and the house now called *Capouli-Panaghia*. (Testimony written completely by hand and signed by Paul Joiion, SJ, University of Beirut.)

Let's return to E. Poulin's studies. During this year 1892, he was not content to look in books. He undertook a trip to Palestine that will not be recounted here, but here was the result: "All that I see, all that I've heard, do nothing but strengthen in my spirit the thesis for Ephesus."

While E. Poulin was in Palestine, one of his confreres, G. Dumond, took advantage of a stay in Paris, not to discuss with L. Duchesne, but to transcribe texts of the Church Fathers and of historians concerning the current question. For the documents collected in Paris by G. Dumond, wrote E. Poulin, and those that we have been able to find in Smyrna, reveal clearly five things:

1. No known authentic authority for Jerusalem before the sixth century.

2. The first Fathers who speak of Gethsemane do so in a hesitant manner and support themselves only with apocryphal writings.

3. For Ephesus (and very frankly), the best authors of the 17th and 18th centuries.

4. The more recent historians divide themselves half for Jerusalem and half for Ephesus or simply mention the two options without declaring themselves for either.

5. From this totality, a conclusion comes forth: Ephesus balances with Jerusalem and threatens to overtake it.

Note it well. This result was obtained in 1892, or five years before the brochure "Ephesus or Jerusalem" and 14 years before the monumental work of Johann Niessen (1906). We would only question number 4 on the half and half division of the two opinions, which is in any case impossible to verify, which is not really important, because it's not quantity that makes quality. We have transcribed the result with all the more satisfaction because it perfectly synthesizes the studies that we ourselves have made during many years.

E. Poulin could thus write on March 4, 1893, to one of his confreres in Paris, Amédée Allou: "Don't believe that we threw ourselves blindly into this affair of *Panaghia*. I see with a tranquil eye the obstacles that men and things might try to put in our path to oppose us. The stone has detached from the mountain, and nothing will hinder it from rolling down" (Cited in "Ephesus or Jerusalem," p. 118).

Chapter 4

Panaghia-Capouli and Rome

Fr. Eschbach's trip

"WITH a deliberate purpose," wrote E. Poulin, "we waited four and even five years before putting the discovery before the public and turning it over to the disputes of savants. We wanted first to deepen the question on the very land of the discovery. We wanted then to study it well, know it well from the historical point of view."

It was, however, announced by private letters, by copies of the statement to which was added a notice of several hand-written pages. It was thus until 1895, the providential year.

For months Sister de Grancey had been pressing E. Poulin to announce it directly to the Holy Father. "Oh! Sister," he answered, "the Holy Father has other things to do. Let God work. He will well be able to let the Pope know when the time comes." But the sister, without rebutting him, returned to her charge, receiving the same response each time.

Now, around that time, F. X. Lobry wrote to E. Poulin to tell him that an extraordinary commission was being sent to the East by Leo XIII to study the Oriental Rites. Some time after, E. Poulin read in the newspaper "The Universe" the name of the leader of the commission: R. P. Eschbach, of the Congregation of the Holy Spirit, Superior of the French Pontifical Seminary, Via Santa

Chiaria, in Rome. It was a name to remember.
Three months had passed when, one fine morning, May 18, 1895, E. Poulin was called to the parlor. The stranger made himself known by presenting a letter of introduction from Fr. Fontaine, the procurer of the Congregation of the Mission at the Holy See.— The enemy! Poulin thought right away while appearing all the more friendly to his guest.

Fr. Eschbach demonstrated a lively interest in the simple maps and photographs concerning *Panaghia-Capouli* that decorated the community room. "I heard about this in Palestine," he said. "I'd love to go see it!" He waited two days in order to be able, on the occasion of a break, to be accompanied by H. Jung, to whom E. Poulin gave this advice: "Above all, no proselytism, no commentaries. Limit yourself to showing him around and answering his questions simply."

So it was done. Leaving early in the morning of May 20, the two travelers returned before nightfall. As soon as he could be alone with H. Jung, he asked how it went. "Father saw everything and is delighted and ecstatic."

A little later, when he was alone with the visiting priest, he asked, "Well, are you content?" "Yes, yes," he answered, but with such a cold air that E. Poulin turned the conversation to another subject right away.

When he saw H. Jung again, he asked, "What did you tell me?" "The truth." The priest was so struck that he couldn't contain his emotion. He said to me, "Fr. Jung, leave me alone. I need silence to better think about what I just saw."

Encouraged by this assurance, E. Poulin came back to the question of *Panaghia* the next day with Fr. Eschbach. This time, he responded not reservedly, but with conviction, "Sir, you found it! I saw in Jerusalem what one calls the tomb of the Blessed Virgin.

That is not it! But in *Panaghia,* everything strikes you, everything
down to the ancient walls, and I know my ancient walls, as a
Roman. You found it!"

Delighted, E. Poulin asked him to kindly write down his impressions. "Willingly, but do you want them as impressions in the heat
of the moment or calm, cool reflections?" "The latter, Father."
"Then I will write you from Athens." Fr. Eschbach left armed with
several images, a copy of the statement, the little hand-written
notice, etc., with the expressed recommendation not to speak of
the discovery except with the greatest reserve and above all not to
name anyone, neither Poulin, nor Jung, nor Vincentians nor sisters.
"It was important to conserve in *Panaghia* the character of an
anonymous work which we have had from the start, and for this, to
relentlessly cast off anything that could seem personal, particular
or in someone's interest" (*Hist. Man. of Panaghia,* reg. 1, p. 108).

Three days later, Fr. Eschbach wrote from Athens: "The strong
impression produced by my visit to *Panaghia* strengthens as I think
about it. I will write from Rome."

In Rome, after having recounted his trip to the Holy Land to the
seminarians, he added: "Sirs, I saved for last the most interesting, but as I was asked to be discreet, I will ask you to do the same
in turn." And he told them what he had seen and the deep emotion that seized him when he found himself in the sanctuary of
Panaghia-Capouli.

Panaghia-Capouli and Leo XIII

He didn't restrain himself to that. After having recounted to the
Pope his mission in the Orient, he added, "Most Holy Father, I
reported to your Holiness a bouquet of these countries, a beautiful,
very beautiful bouquet." And he told him what he had told his stu-

dents. Leo XIII listened to him with a lot of attention, giving signs of the strongest interest. "Do you have any pictures?" he asked. "Here they are!" The Pope examined them at length and, the audience ended, forgot to return them. Fr. Eschbach refrained from asking for them back. It goes without saying that E. Poulin, learning this good news, hurried to send other photographs. "And that is how Leo XIII became aware of our discovery. We had nothing to do with it. Providence once again took care of and arranged everything. Who was happy? Sister de Grancey."

After that, the discretion kept up until then was no longer possible. "Let's go then," E. Poulin said, "bring in the pope, the cardinals, the Roman court." The discovery was thus communicated to the press. *Truth, The Gazette of France, The Universe, The Common Good* of Gand, *The Morning Leader* of London, *Italia,* etc., in hostile or benevolent articles, propagated the news in all directions.

It seems thus opportune and even necessary to publish a brochure that had been prepared from the beginning. But, the instruction had been given from Paris: "Even if the thing is true," wrote Fr. Fiat to E. Poulin, "it would not be for our congregation to make the question our own affair." That's why the Vincentians effaced themselves completely to leave Monsignor Timoni all the responsibility for the brochure *"Panaghia Capouli,"* which appeared in 1896.

Now the moment has come to indicate a fact that has its importance. By a decree on April 18, 1896, Leo XIII transferred the indulgences attached to the Tomb of Gethsemane to the Sanctuary of Notre Dame of France in Jerusalem. Johannes Niessen, in a piece published in 1931, regards this decree as a disavowal of the Tomb. On this subject Fr. A d'Alès, in his account "Religious Sciences Research" of 1932, asks himself: "Did Niessen depart from the texts?" We think we can assure that Niessen relied on E. Poulin, in whom he had complete confidence and who deserved it. But, E. Poulin did not depart from texts but read them closely. In effect, we find in his notes the text in question, whole and in Latin. He only allowed himself to interpret it and in the most intelligent manner. He stresses that the indicated reason (the difficulty of access) of the removal of indulgences is perhaps only a diplomatic formula because the church of Gethsemane is among the easiest to visit. He himself did so in 1892. He further recalls that, exactly in that year (1896), Pope Leo XIII already knew by Fr. Eschbach about the discovery of *Panaghia-Capouli*. We will not say that this interpretation, too simple perhaps, is as true as it is intelligent. For it is quite difficult to admit that the wise and prudent Leo XIII would have had the intention to decide a historical debate by this decree. In any case, the fact is worth being noted.

Another fact that makes evident the progress of the cause in Roman circles was that Fr. Eschbach, with the encouragement and support of His Excellency Cardinal Parrochi, was able to initiate the project of a Roman Commission that would come to study *Panaghia-Capouli*. Already the illustrious archeologist O. Marruchi had accepted to take part, already the necessary funds were ready, and already the date for departure had been fixed for the next autumn, when the death of Leo XIII (1903) stopped everything.

St. Pius X's Opinion

However, the interest that had been shown in Rome for *Panaghia-Capouli* did not diminish. Judge for yourself by this letter of Monsignor Di Lai, later a cardinal, to E. Poulin: "I keep in my heart and I will keep the indelible memory of *Panaghia*. In that tranquil retreat, what natural beauty! What sweet emotion! Few places, it seems to me, could have been better chosen to serve as a refuge to the Most Holy Virgin. How you feel closer to her! God has confided a great mission to your reverence and to the lady de Grancey and, in general, to the distinguished Priests of the Mission, in placing this most holy place in their care. I rejoice to see that this mission had been confided to those who fulfill it so well and with so much enthusiasm" (Letter of October 1903).

There was also, a little later, this official letter from the Cardinal Merry del Val: "It was not without a particular pleasure that the Holy Father (Pius X) received the three works published by your most illustrious lordship, with the goal of shedding, in as much as possible, a new light on the difficult problem of the place of the death and the Assumption of the most holy Virgin. His Holiness noticed with great satisfaction the importance of the research done on this serious subject by your lordship and your confreres. Thus, in addressing to your lordship a very special thanks, His Holiness declares himself most grateful also to the other priests of the Mission of Smyrna, and in granting you, as well as these others, the apostolic blessing, he prays wholeheartedly to God and his august Mother to grant with more and more abundance the celestial light to all those who, with the affection of sons, consecrate their studies to the search for the place where the tomb of Mary was erected" (Rome, April 6, 1906).

An official letter, of course, but one that is not a banal piece of the chancery. Little surprise, after that, about the paternal welcome Pius X gave to Sisters de Grancey and Fiévet on April 20, 1912. "Has the tomb been found?" he asked. "Not yet, Holy Father," answered Sister de Grancey, adding that they were disrupted at this point by the suggestions of another mystic (Rosalie Putt). "It is better to believe the older one (C. Emmerick) than the newer," replied the Holy Father, smiling. "One can suppose that Sister de Grancey very much wanted to know the personal opinion of Pius X. "Most

Holy Father," she cried out with that spontaneous boldness that characterized her so well, "I know that you believe like your illustrious predecessor Benedict XIV that the Blessed Virgin died in Ephesus." The Holy Father limited himself to an affirmative smile" (Letter of Sister Eugènie Fiévet to E. Poulin, May 14, 1912).

PANAGHIA-CAPOULI AND POPE PIUS XI

When, later, in 1922, E. Poulin put forward his last publication ("A last word, etc."), he received from the Secretary of State the following letter with Cardinal Gasparri's signature: "I am happy to let you know that His Holiness warmly welcomed the brochure in which you exposed your opinion on the subject of the final abode of the Blessed Virgin. Acknowledging your work and congratulating you on having thus added your contribution on such a disputed topic, the Sovereign Pontiff thanks you paternally and deigns to send you, as a sign of divine favors, an apostolic blessing. I welcome the occasion that is offered me to assure you of my most devoted sentiments in our Lord" (Vatican, August 13, 1922).

You can see now if the sarcasm so feared by L. Duchesne was universal. Before these facts the most entrenched opponents of Ephesus-*Panaghia* are indeed obliged to recognize at least that the cause was taken into consideration in very high places, by cardinals and Popes themselves.

Chapter 5
Panaghia and Archeology

F. VIGOUROUX (director of the Biblical Dictionary) attached a great importance to archeology. "Couldn't you have the house examined archeologically by the Austrian archeologists? Their judgment would be a great weight on the scales" (Letter to E. Poulin, November 1895).

Similarly, His Eminence Cardinal Gotti wrote to the archbishop of Smyrna, Monsignor Zucchetti: "Archeology has not yet made its pronouncement."

Cardinal Gotti and F. Vigouroux got their wish. Here, in effect, is what you could read in "Ephesus," volume one, published by the Archeological Institute of Vienna. "*Panaghia-Capouli* is a little church of the Middle Ages. It is a variety of the oriental churches with a cupola on the transept recently described by Strzywiski. It cannot be dated back to the fifth century. That the description relating to the form and to the interior disposition of the supposed house (of the Virgin) later transformed into a chapel after the death of Mary *has discrepancies on all the essential points does not need to be proven*" (*Hist. Man. of Panaghia,* reg. 1, p. 83; our emphasis).

You couldn't ask for a more decisive judgment. But look closer. What strikes right off is the strangeness of the formulation. After all, since when are you dispensed from proving what you affirm,

241

especially in a case where the evidence is impossible? What's stranger yet is that, right across from this affirmation, you can see the plan of the house, borrowed from the brochure "*Panaghia-Capouli*" but without the explanatory commentary demonstrating the correspondence with C. Emmerick's description.

We do not dispute the personal of the signatory of the article, Otto Bendorff, reinforced by the esteemed patronage of the Institute of Vienna. But are we required to bow blindly to it? It is not realistic that Otto Bendorff examined everything, book in hand, with as much care as the members of the commission presided by Monsignor Timoni.

Who should be astounded, moreover, if there are contestable points? The description of the house by C. Emmerick is no more an architectural drawing than the description of the environs is a map by the geological society. Let's retain from all this that, according to the Archeological Institute of Vienna, the ruin of *Panaghia-Capouli* could date back to the fourth century. Others are less generous.

Father Wogh, archeology professor in Freiberg (Switzerland) and a Byzantine specialist, spent two full days in *Panaghia* (November 1905). Here is his judgment: "The house could as easily be from the seventh century as from the first and from the first as from the seventh. I dare anyone to prove one rather than the other." As for the foundations, he estimates they are from the first century.

Let us link this statement to that of Fr. Fonck, who visited *Panaghia* twice, in 1897 and 1907. "At least one part of the building dates back to the first century."

Such is not the opinion of Fr. Lagrange. He also visited *Panaghia* twice, in 1892 and 1905, the second time accompanied by his confrere and colleague from the Biblical Institute of Jerusalem, Fr. Vincent. Fr. Lagrange thinks that the current construction is from the seventh century. Fr. Vincent is for the sixth century. "Go for the six and even the seventh century," notes E. Poulin, who was quite amused by the elasticity of archeological estimations.

Already in June 1900, E. Poulin could respond to Fr. De la Broise, who had written him, "Historians, archeologists, theologians have for the most part protested against the supposed discovery" that "I, who am on the lookout to count them, can hardly reach a dozen, counting you." Dare we say that theologians had absolutely nothing to say on the subject? And yet it is certain that not all protested. As for the archeologists, we just read some of their testimonies, and we can add with E. Poulin, "I don't have to count far to oppose to the dozen (adversaries) another dozen people just as learned who are unequivocally for *Panaghia* and have over their adversaries the immense advantage of having seen the place" (*Hist. Man. of Panaghia,* reg. 1, p. 233).

But this tops all. In 1907 Georges Lambakis, man of the trade, gave on (or rather against) *Panaghia* a sensational conference before a numerous audience of Orthodox Christians, both laity and priests. He presented himself, armed from head to toe with archeological titles (you can count a good dozen on the cover of the book he published later on "The Seven Stars of the Apocalypse"). And here was the theme of his lecture. He reviewed succinctly the different eras of religious architecture by indicating the traits that characterized each one, from the first century to 312, from 312 to 527, from 527 to 842, from 842 to 1453. (These mathematical precisions were printed in a booklet published in Athens in 1907, p. 58.) He had to wait until he arrived at the 14th century to finally find some traits that corresponded with the ruin of *Panaghia- Capouli*! That was what he called a scientific demonstration. But who couldn't see that a similar method in archeology, like that of Fr. Barnabé in topography, is as false in reality as rigorous in appearance?

We must add that in the present case, archeology tried to play historian. We are quite sure G. Lambakis was not ignorant of history. How then couldn't he have seen that in the 14th century and even much earlier, there no longer was in Ephesus or in the surrounding area (except in Kirkindjé) a group of Christians capable of building the foundation of the house?

We dare say, then, in conclusion on these thoughts on *Panaghia* and archeology, and aside from the respect we owe to His Eminence Cardinal Gotti and to the erudition of F. Vigouroux, that archeology does not have the last word on this subject. In effect, we give archeologists the honor to believe that, while estimating their specialty at its worth, they realize that it's an exceedingly conjectural science and that it is impossible for them to specify a date unless it is found directly or indirectly inscribed on a plate or engraved in the marble.

PANAGHIA-CAPOULI AND THE BIBLICAL REVIEW

This is the way the *Biblical Review* announced the discovery of *Panaghia:*

> We received word from Smyrna that interesting investigations were undertaken recently around Ephesus with the goal of finding traces of the Blessed Virgin's stay there.
>
> The partisans of the belief that the Blessed Virgin was buried in Ephesus are awaiting a discovery affirming their opinion.
>
> You see all the questions raised from this. Wait! It is not probable that the Mother of the Savior's tomb would be found in Ephesus, but Mary's stay around the city of

Diane *seems today beyond any reasonable doubt.* The Smyrnian explorers' research *promises the most interesting results for the history of Christian origins*" (*Biblical Review* 1892, p. 469; our emphasis).

This benevolent attitude did not continue. As evidence, see these lines signed by Fr. Lagrange, discussing a work by Dr. Zahn: "The author has at least established that the completely artificial opinion of Ephesus is excluded by the evidence of the earliest antiquity" (*Biblical Review,* 1899, p. 599).

An even more strange affirmation that you can read in the same issue is the lines from Fr. Séjourné: "Until the middle of the fifth century, until Juvénal (429-458), there was no question in the Christian world about the death of the Blessed Virgin, nor the sepulcher from the topographic point of view." Where then is the primitive tradition invoked by Fr. Lagrange?

Listen to him explain himself: "In the splendid monument that New Zion represents, the memory of the Holy Spirit is in the first place. The Dormition of Mary, which Arculfe fixed between 638 and 670 (We are quite far from a primitive tradition!) recalling that the Mother of God lived with the apostles, surrounded by their respect . . . and, in an annex, remembrance of St. Etienne. . . . This great dogmatic matter well deserves the uncertain restitutions that try to return the place its primitive appearance. After all, it is more important for us to know the veneration of the primitive Church for Mary, the importance that the Church attached to her last moments and to her death, than to know the exact place of her dormition" (*Biblical Review* 1899, p. 600).

We will not deny the greatness of this dogmatic matter, which consists of grouping on Mount Zion the entire Christian memory. But is it admissible history?

It was undoubtedly inspired by Fr. Lagrange that Fr. Magnen wrote in his account of "Saint John" by Abbot Fouard: "You must have known his preference for the older tradition (Jerusalem) to the sensational discovery of *Panaghia-Capouli* and to the imagination of a modern mystic" (*Biblical Review* 1905, p. 283).

You can read in the papers of Jean Parrang, C.M., this sad note: "I went through the *Biblical Review,* from 1906 to 1915 without finding anything on Niessen's work, which appeared in 1906." Perhaps the *Biblical Review* only reviews works that are sent to it. But it is not question, here, of a simple review. This work that Fr. Adhémar d'Alès called fundamental and that calls into question the tomb of Jerusalem deserves to be refuted and not simply ignored.

However, on the contrary, one would say that, not being able to defend Jerusalem, the editor of the *Review* was constantly on the lookout for whatever could undermine Ephesus. As proof, the following brief article about Le Camus' work, *The Seven Churches of the Apocalypse:* "In passing, the author diverts attention from the Vincentians' belief that they rediscovered the residence of Mary, and his reasons are well-motivated. What is best, he says, is the good fortune of the Turk (who sold the property). There would be no better way to make evident the foolishness of the purchaser."

It's the *Biblical Review* who blew this witticism out of proportion!

However, since people have put so much stake in Le Camus' opinion, it would not be without benefit to indicate the extent to which his opinion was changeable. You can read, for example, in his *Voyage to Biblical Lands,* volume III, page 157, ". . . and the tomb of the Virgin, where was it? The ecumenical Council Fathers supposed in Ephesus, perhaps even in the church where they were assembled, dedicated to the Blessed Virgin. Now, at the time when this church was built, they only erected sanctuaries to great servants of God on their sepulchers or their relics. Why then has this ancient tradition, which I congratulate the archbishop of Smyrna for trying to renew, remained in silence for several centuries?"

It is precisely when we began to make this ancient tradition speak that Le Camus thought he should try to make it return to silence!!!

We must confess that this reversal of opinion bears a strong resemblance to that of the *Biblical Review* because, after having solemnly announced the discovery of *Panaghia-Capouli* and affirmed the Ephesus tradition, it treated it thereafter only with a truly inexplicable disdain.

The only explanation is probably the obstinate fidelity of Fr. Lagrange to the Jerusalem tradition, a heartfelt loyalty that is touching and respectable, but without intellectual conviction.

He had been passing through Alexandria in a house of the Congregation of the Mission when one of Poulin's pamphlets, "Ephesus or Jerusalem," arrived. He leafed through it right away with an annoyed air, saying, "I will respond! I will respond!" He could later inspire this one or that, direct their pen, but from him personally, nothing on the subject.

Chapter 6
Achievements

IN *PANAGHIA* itself, they did not remain inactive. But to act, how many difficulties of which the least wasn't to obtain the necessary authorizations to move the earth and above all to undertake the simple construction of a wall. And then, there were the difficulties of finding the workers, transporting materials such a great distance up the mountain, etc. They made paths to make the access to *Panaghia* less difficult. They established a vegetable garden just below the chapel. They made an irrigation path for the water from the stream to bring it close to the house being built. Finally, the house was constructed, very modest and quite in keeping with the mountain style, but solid, because the four walls that remained after the First World War have resisted the weather for almost a half century.

It took a whole year to obtain the permissions for construction, so that the various projects weren't begun until July-December 1894. It was only in 1903 that they brought there, destined for the sisters, a chalet that, since, served as firewood for the military. The house and the chalet allowed them for several years to offer a provisional shelter to a good number of lay and priestly pilgrims who could spend a night there and in the morning say or hear the holy mass and then examine at their leisure the site and the chapel before going down to the Ayassolouk station.

Naturally the main concern was for the chapel. It was necessary, above all, to protect it against the weather. They therefore constructed a windowed framework that was completely independent of the four walls, which they wanted, at all price, to leave such as they were, according to Fr. Eschbach's wish, whom we will meet later. "For the love of heaven, don't touch the four walls."

The path that led to the residence and to the chapel was planted with olive trees. Towards the middle of the path, a rock formed a sort of natural pedestal on which they placed a statue in a fountain (half-sized) of the Virgin with her arms extended as on the Miraculous Medal. On the sea side, they planted holm oaks (green oaks) that, in 1914, had already grown to a good size, six to seven meters in height.

Inside the chapel, they erected an altar: a marble table supported by two colonnades with an elegant, simply sculpted tabernacle by the architect Raymond Péré. They had to transport all the marble, already carved, on camel-back through zigzagging paths through the mountain.

Alas! After the First World War, only the olive trees survived. The handsome green oaks had been cut. And the statue? During our brief appearance in *Panaghia* in 1920 with our confrere Paul Saint-Germain, the captain stationed there with his artillery told us that his men had found it in the ravine and, on his orders, brought it into the chapel. There is no need to say that he was warmly thanked.

In 1926, the statue was no longer there. Finally, in 1931, when, after recovering the property, the guardian Aziz was stationed in *Panaghia,* he rediscovered the statue and put it back in the place of honor where it still is today (1961). Just the hands were mutilated while the arms retained their gentle gesture of maternal welcome.

Of all the destruction, the least regrettable is certainly that of the glass enclosure. Of an uncontestable utility, it had the misfortune of giving the antique and venerable relic the appearance of a temporary barrack.

But the altar? From 1920 it was in pieces and dispersed. You could scarcely find a fragment of the tabernacle. *Etiam periere ruinae!*

This destruction was so little anticipated that they had decided in 1914 to build a more spacious house to better receive pilgrims. The drawings and the quote were readied and the funds available. Raymond Péré would have begun the work in July, when the war broke out. Man proposes . . .

DIGS AND DISCOVERIES

In order to construct the first habitable house, they had to dig into the ground. The first shovel hit the ground in July 1894. Near the house they exposed four walls forming a rectangle with the inside portion smoothed out, while the exterior blocks were irregular, going beyond squared off corners. Courtyard or basin? A large earthenware jug at the end of where the water channels led, built in the same way, soon gave an answer to that question.

A little later at some distance appeared three archways or arcades, the second already broken, the other two intact. Before these two archways were the remains of colonnades on the wall of the basin. Under the third arch, 80 cm from the keystone was a brick tomb with each brick measuring 68 cm long by 49 cm wide. Under these bricks was a complete skeleton with its head turned toward the chapel. On each side was a funeral lamp and, in the hands still wrapped in cloth, a medal of Justinian II. They gathered another seven medals. It would be impossible to count the fragments of glass, pottery, bricks and tile. We will note as more interesting the traces of paint and of a large mosaic.

From all this it was concluded with certainty that this place had been inhabited from a rather ancient time. Was it a Roman colony, as would suggest the basin, this atrium, these remains of columns, these archways that certainly weren't built for a sepulcher? Were these the remains of a bishop or at least a priest, as the curious discovery of a clay mold for hosts would lead us to believe? One thing was absolutely certain: the presence, in this place, of a rather significant group of Christians, dispersed in the time of the invasions and who, before fleeing, secured their dead under these archways covered with earth?

And here are two more unusual finds that one could certainly dispute, but that shouldn't be passed over in silence because they are facts. First, the discovery behind the chapel at a depth of 1.5 meters of the octagon of which C. Emmerick speaks, who then saw underground? This discovery had been hoped for because of the visionary's guidance.

However, the second one wasn't anticipated at all. It was while clearing away the inside of the chapel to see if, under the packed earth, there might not be paving stones, that the shovel revealed fragments of smoky blackened marble. They saw soon, 50 cm lower, other fragments that seemed positioned above a hole where there was ash coagulated in soot and earth. Suddenly, a thought came to light. Impossible! What? The chimney stones demolished by the apostles when the house was transformed into a chapel and that were buried there, out of respect, in the very place of the chimney, and that in the end the most happy of circumstances allowed us to find so randomly?

There was at that time (August 1898) in *Panaghia,* other than H. Jung, two young priests of the African Missions of Lyon, who came from Samos, Matthieu and Fouquet, and Abbot Gouyet. They were so struck by this discovery that they wanted to draw up a statement.

The next day G. Weber, the Protestant archeologist who was well known in Smyrna, came to *Panaghia.* They showed him the stones in support of what they told him, the blackened stones that they even asked him to smell, and asked him what he thought. He declined to make a judgment.

But the same night he wrote on the register of the hotel in Ayassolouk: "I returned from *Panaghia-Capouli,* where I saw Fr. Jung who has discovered some very interesting things."

Two weeks later Jung, in Smyrna, where he had returned, having met Mr. Weber, pressed him. "Oh," he answered, "stones like that, white on one side and black on another, you find a lot of them in the mountain." "What? Stones with ash and soot?" he responded. Mr. Weber remained silent. He could not deny what he had seen and smelled.

Chapter 7
Pilgrimages

G OING back rather far into the past, recall that Monsignor Spaccapietra, C.M., archbishop of Smyrna (+1879), had already led a group of Catholics to Ephesus in 1872. *Panaghia-Capouli* was, at this date, unknown. But there was the memory of the Council and, in the archbishop's mind, the firm conviction that the Virgin had at least stayed in Ephesus. (He had been a part of a controversy on this subject with Monsignor Baunard in "Catholic Missions" in Lyon in 1973.)

Some years later, his successor Monsignor Timoni imitated him, first in 1884 and a second time in 1889. From that time a decision was made to make a pilgrimage every five years, thus, in 1894.

These pilgrimages stopped in Ephesus. They took place in broad daylight with a lot of fanfare. There was a solemn mass in the Sélim mosque (Isa mosque) that was considered at that time as the basilica of St. John. There was a procession with banners flying in the wind, to the great astonishment of the local people who were for the most part Orthodox Christians living in dire poverty and all the more amazed at the display of magnificence.

All those who took part in these pilgrimages wanted nothing else but to undertake them again and communicated their desire with others. Therefore in 1894, after what was discovered on the mountain, the general desire of the Catholics was even stronger.

The movement was directed more toward *Panaghia-Capouli* than Ephesus.

There was no problem doing what had been done before in Ephesus. But it seemed dangerous to attract attention to the place. In effect, exactly at this time the restoration work for which authorization was so hard to obtain had just begun and risked being stopped. It was thus judged wise to postpone the pilgrimage until the next year.

Man proposes . . . In 1895, the preparations were begun too late, and it couldn't have taken place until the end of May, the time when ordinarily the first major heat sets in. They had to thus renounce it.

So, in 1896, they set to it a long time in advance so that all was ready for the desired time, May 20.

E. Poulin notes on this subject: "Setting in motion the pilgrimage, like those that would follow, was not in any way the work of the Vincentians" (*Hist. Man. of Panaghia,* reg. 1, p. 98). You couldn't say that they were indifferent; quite the contrary, they lent their efforts eagerly, but they left the initiative to the faithful, the clergy and, above all, the archbishop of Smyrna.

Panaghia-Capouli was not accessible like Ephesus was. They were going into uncharted territory. How many people would have the courage and the strength to scale the mountain for hours?

As a result, it was decided that there would be two groups, one remaining in Ephesus with Monsignor Canavo, O.M., to celebrate mass there, as before, in the Sélim mosque (Isa bey), and the other with Monsignor Timoni at its head to press on to *Panaghia.*

Two trains brought 1300-1400 pilgrims from Smyrna to Ephesus. More than half went to the mountain and began climbing.

It was a picturesque and graceful spectacle to see this large crowd snaking up the twisting paths, some on foot, others on a donkey or horse, over here in compact groups, further on in strung-out lines. For all, surely, there was an attraction in the new and un-known. The intrepid ones threw themselves into it, proud to arrive first; most went slowly, stopping to rest and also to look behind them and contemplate the pleasing panorama that revealed itself as they ascended higher and that opened up all at once both on the plain towards Ephesus and the sea towards Samos.

Departing at 5:30 am from Smyrna, at 9:30 all had arrived in *Panaghia.* To find themselves there in the nest of green was already a rest that made them forget their fatigue. Having arrived behind the newly constructed house, the archbishop got off his horse, put on his pontifical vestments and, miter on his head and crosier in hand, he headed in procession to the chapel to celebrate mass there. It goes without saying that the chapel had been carefully decorated inside with plants and wildflowers. Outside, cloths decorated the façade and others, held up like veils, made a sort of tent over the altar.

The chapel was immediately invaded. The rest of the crowd pressed at the door and covered the little esplanade that was at the side, silent and recollected.

Monsignor announced first the plenary indulgence accorded by the Sovereign Pontiff Leo XIII (which he had obtained verbally in an audience with the Holy Father). And mass began. At the offertory, an alarm went up. Rain began to fall, going through the cloths curtains and dampening the corporeal and altar linens. (We, as a simple cleric, held an umbrella over the celebrant's head.) One might fear a forced interruption. Fortunately it was only a passing cloudburst. The mass continued.

"Something beautiful, very beautiful: the pious manner of the whole crowd and the ardor of their prayers. Something even more beautiful: communion. We had counted on 20-30 communicants and nonetheless prepared 120 hosts. It was soon required that we break them to nourish the 144 who presented themselves at the holy table. Although they had risen very early, been tired by the train and especially the long and difficult ascent up the mountain, these valiant ones had fasted to have the happiness of receiving communion in the house of the Blessed Virgin. Not just a dozen, but 144" (*Hist. Man. of Panaghia,* reg. 1, p. 100).

To give more splendor to the pilgrimage, they had arranged for the college's brass band to perform, with the instruments coming up the night before on horse- and mule-back. They could, to the great delight of the pupils, make an echo in the mountains and powerfully sustain the first songs. However, the spring rain soon imposed on them a complete silence. There is no need to mention that the people's piety did not suffer in the least. In the future there was no question of attempting this again.

"Where does the desire for profit not emerge? The Ayassolouk innkeeper, counting on a good clientele, had prepared quite a few meals. He just covered his expenses. Andréa, the guard of *Panaghia,* had also installed a little shop with cakes and refreshments. He also made no profit. It was a good lesson that was understood. The Blessed Virgin didn't want any gain or profit, even an honest one, to be mixed up with the pious work of a pilgrimage" (*Hist. Man. of Panaghia,* reg. 1, p. 102).

After the Mass, they separated off into groups to revive themselves with the provisions they had brought. In the afternoon the majority of the pilgrims went back early to explore the ruins in Ephesus, but the most fervent remained several more hours to make the Way of the Cross under the leadership of a priest of the Mission, a real Peter Hermit, Gabriel Larigaldie.

This first major pilgrimage left such good memories that those who had made it wanted to again, and others wanted to make it in turn. It was thus that in 1898 they had to give in to popular demand and, beginning then, it was each year, with the same enthusiasm.

Around Easter, they began preparing. Large posters announced the day and the hours of the train departures.

Easter Wednesday, later Easter Tuesday, early in the morning while the rest of the city was still sleeping, little groups went through the narrow streets toward the Aidin train station. Once arrived in Ephesus, they crossed the plain to the mountain. Once they had passed the first heights, white banners were unfurled across the vegetation, and the echoes resounded with joyful Ave Marias. How all the mountain was pretty in its spring outfit! It really looked like an immense altar covered with flowers in honor of the Virgin.

It is certain that there was a natural attraction of an excursion mixed in with this, but it is also sure that a sincere piety animated all their hearts.

This day at least, the habitual solitude of the holy ground was populated; the silence was broken by joyous exclamations and sanctified by prayer and the singing of songs. Sister de Grancey circulated among the people who had come to her land. Always simple, she seemed to be radiating joy: "How beautiful! How beautiful!" she cried out. Later she said, "I know well that the Blessed Virgin does not need this exterior glory, but since we can provide it for her, isn't it a duty of ours?"

There was also sometimes on this pilgrimage day the happy surprise of meeting Catholics who had come from farther away. There were the priests of the Assumption who brought a group from Eskisehir. From Aydin they came regularly. We saw once a few who, with the African Missionaries of Lyon at their head, had crossed the bay that separated Samos from the Ionian coast. In brief, if you took into account the homelands of some pilgrims and religious, there really was a representation of the Catholic world. Unfortunately, one of these pilgrimages was saddened by the swift death of a Vincentian, George Deroo, the principal of the school, who in a few short years had gained the sympathy and esteem of all. Despite his tired state, he insisted on climbing on foot. Just a few hundred feet short of the chapel, he fell, never to rise again. No one had the heart to sing: Mass was celebrated with great silence.

This was the only time that there was no speech after the gospel. Sometime it was diocesan priests (Abbot J. Fercken or O. Mirzan) and sometimes the Capuchins; often the Dominicans, Frs. Olivier, Summa, and Le Vigoureux. One time only, as an exception, a Vincentian spoke, F.X. Lobry.

Let's look at a few texts chosen for the opening lines. Fr. Le Vigoureux began with these classic words, slightly modified: "*Veni, vidi, victus sum* . . . (I came, I saw, I was conquered.) I was conquered, that is to say, convinced that the Virgin lived here." The famous Fr. Olivier, seeing the mountains and hills, recalled the words of the psalm: "*Montes exsulaverunt ut arietes* . . . The mountains leapt like rams and the hills bounded like sheep." Finally Fr. Timothy (Capuchin): "*Vadam as montem myrhae*, etc. I will go to the mountain of myrrh and to the hill of incense. Here is the mountain of Death and also of the corporal Assumption of the Virgin." The crowd was thus all at once transported into the spiritual atmosphere of the countryside.

In 1914, notes E. Poulin, we were up to the 18th pilgrimage (because, in addition to the major annual pilgrimage, there were others) and around 20,000 pilgrims when the First World War stopped everything.

FOREIGN PILGRIMS AND TOURISTS

During the interval of relative prosperity (1896-1914) no major pilgrimage ever came from another country. It wasn't so much that there was a real impossibility, as the major pilgrimages to the Holy Land often made a stop in Smyrna, from which a few pilgrims pressed on to Ephesus without ever going any farther. Lack of time? Surely. But there was something else: the strong opposition of Jerusalem. One example: In 1896, the itinerary of the Pilgrimage to the Holy Land included a visit to *Panaghia*. (You began to hear about it in the wider world.) However, the boat, instead of stopping at Smyrna, went straight from Haifa to Constantinople. Some strong complaints were heard on board, and a rich businessman is even said to have needed to be threatened with handcuffs to make him be quiet.

How regrettable is it that these Holy Land pilgrimages, so frequent then, though not regular now for years, yet in 1906 a group of German tourists came. They arrived in Smyrna 374 strong, led by Professor Milner and Fr. Kayser, the former superior of the Assumptionists in Alachéir. Two hundred of them went to Ephesus by charter train and exactly 47, among them ten Protestants, still led by Professor Milner and Fr. Kayser, climbed up to *Panaghia*.

All attended a low Mass celebrated by Adrien Bayol, C.M., who had come to *Panaghia* the previous day to spend several days there. You can imagine the welcome H. Jung gave them, and they were happy to speak their native language together. Under his direction, they examined everything at their leisure. They returned delighted.

Professor Milner wanted to go himself to the school to thank E. Poulin in person. "It's the most beautiful and interesting excursion of the whole trip," he liked to repeat, to the point that the others blamed him for not bringing them with him up the mountain.

Even if no significant group ever came from abroad to *Panaghia,* how many individual tourists came and even stayed several days. The list would be long and tedious. However, we should cite several names without worrying too much about the chronological order while still indicating the exact dates.

Priests and religious from all orders: Dominicans, Jesuits, Benedictines, Capuchins, Assumptionists, etc.

- The famous Fr. Lagrange, twice, in 1892 and 1905, the second time accompanied by Fr. Vincent, Fr. Le Vigoureux, also from the Biblical School of Jerusalem.

- Fr. Coubé, SJ, who enthusiastically described his pilgrimage in the magazine that he edited (*O Salutaris hostia,* August 1903).

- Sr. Fonck, S, in 1892 and 1907, who was immediately an ardent propagator of the cause.

- Fr. Jouon in 1899 who wrote in his own hand such a favorable declaration in the guest book.

- Fr. Grivet, SJ, in 1909: Coming up to *Panaghia* an unbeliever (according to his own confession), he returned entirely changed.

- His Excellency Cardinal Di Lai. Already inclined through his studies for Ephesus, he came purposefully to Smyrna with a nascent faith that his visit to *Panaghia* made overwhelming (1902).

- His Excellency Monsignor Netzhammer, OSB, Archbishop of Bucharest, in 1910. "Once one has seen, one has no other desire than to see *Panaghia* more known and the object of a global pilgrimage." He made a real prophecy.

- Abbot Wogh, archeology professor at Freiberg University and great expert in Byzantium. In 1905 he spent two full days in *Panaghia.* We have already cited above his testimony as an archeologist.

- Four Benedictines from Jerusalem, whose superior, after two days in *Panaghia* (1906) said, "What a beautiful site and what conformity with what C. Emmerick said."

- Finally Fr. Michel Hetzenauer, OMC, Capuchin from Tyrol and professor at the Apollinaire (1910). After ten years he had so little forgotten *Panaghia* that in 1923 he gave an excellent talk on it in Rome with seven cardinals in the audience.

Let us cite several lay people:

- Prince George of Saxony in 1905. "Prince, your impressions, please," E. Poulin requested. Here they are: *"Veni, vidi, credo.* I came, I saw, I believe."

- Mr. Blackler, an English Protestant living in Smyrna, who often visited *Panaghia* and, one time, was accompanied by Mr. Hogarth, the director of the digs at the temple to Diana. He made *Panaghia* known at Oxford through a talk that even had slides.

- Baron Carra de Vaux, professor at the Catholic Institute in Paris. "The conformity of the place with the descriptions contained in C. Emmerick's book is striking" (guest book).

During this long period (1896-1914) each time that a French squadron dropped anchor in Smyrna, a good number of officers and seamen came up to *Panaghia,* and once even led by an admiral (Admiral Anthoine), for whom it was, as for many others, a real pilgrimage of filial piety for the Blessed Virgin.

How can we forget Baron Antonin de Mandat-Grancey, nephew of the mother of *Panaghia*? He came a first time as an ensign on the

"Formidable". He returned in 1910 with his wife and their young children to put them under the protection of Our Lady of *Panaghia*. You can easily imagine how much this visit brought joy to Sister de Grancey's heart. The family castle, whose chapel had a painting representing the Blessed Virgin's death with a view of the sea, thus Ephesus, seemed in a way transported to *Panaghia-Capouli* for a time.

Among all these visitors, the majority expressed their enthusiasm without restraint. Others were more reserved or even reticent. Fr. Lagrange was frank enough to declare himself firmly opposed to Ephesus, but he did not protest against the conformity of the location. The only exception on this point was Fr. Barnabé, of whom we have spoken. We could at the most add in this camp Fr. Arsène du Châtel, Capuchin, Provincial of Istanbul, who signed with his family name (Berger) some very aggressive articles in *The Echoes of the Holy Land*.

It is certainly permissible to find certain appreciations too enthusiastic. But what should we say about the passionate criticisms of Fathers Barnabé and Arsène? The latter went to *Panaghia* alone in 1893 and, as a result of a misunderstanding, in unpleasant conditions that he never forgot. As for Fr. Banabé, he visited *Panaghia* in similar conditions and remained only a few hours. This was in August 1903. Now, in November of the same year a large tome on "The Tomb of Jerusalem, etc." appeared. We can say without slander that he didn't take the time to digest his impressions . . .

In any case, had these two judgments been made after a more attentive examination, they still would not prevail against the cloud of witnesses cited above whose already impressive list it would be easy to add to.

Chapter 8
The Supernatural in *Panaghia*

W E SHOULD not be surprised to learn that the supernatural, which was at the origin of *Panaghia-Capouli*'s discovery, should manifest itself several times there: miraculous cures and even apparitions. We will limit ourselves to pointing them out with reservations. But in the end, their facts are sufficiently controlled that they should have a right to be recorded in this history.

APPARITIONS

First apparition: August 13, 1902, between 5 and 6 in the evening while the sun was still rather high in the sky, a young Greek Orthodox woman who had come to *Panaghia* several days earlier, Helen, the daughter of the caretaker Andréa, was collecting off the bushes the clothes she had washed. She was hurrying because she was tired from her long day's work and it was keeping her from going to rest.

Suddenly on the side of Karatchali in front of and not far from her appeared a woman clothed in black, her arms crossed over her chest, her head bent in an attitude of profound sadness with a long veil that covered her head, hid a part of her face and fell on the right and left to her feet. The women remained immobile with her eyes turned toward the chapel.

To see this suddenly, the young woman was greatly shocked. She didn't feel fear but rather a deep sense of God. She understood that it was the Virgin of *Panaghia* whose apparition she contemplated. It seemed to her that her contemplation lasted a half-hour. "What did you think of during that time? What did you do?" "I didn't think about anything. I looked! I looked! I looked!"

At first the lady in black was visible from head to toe. However, soon a white smoke formed that, beginning at her feet, rose little by little, growing larger and thicker and ending by enveloping the lady up to her knees.

As the lady remained immobile and with the same attitude, the visionary thought about calling a priest who was just a hundred feet or so away, busy decorating the chapel. She thus took a few steps in that direction without taking her eyes off the mysterious lady, yelling to her brother to go quickly to find the priest.

Before her brother had even heard the request, the lady and cloud began to rise slowly and silently up the summit of Karatchali (where they had been searching for her tomb). Reaching the summit at the supposed angle of the position of Calvary, the cloud surrounded the lady entirely and disappeared.

The young woman returned home pale and trembling. She immediately told what she had just seen. Such was the impression of her story on the workers who heard her that all the Catholics among them wanted to go to confession and receive communion the next day. As for the Orthodox, they wanted to go to Mass, which they hadn't done, up to then ("The Ephesus Tomb" by Gabriélovich, pp. 259-61).

They were not satisfied with this first account given to the workers the very day. A few weeks later on September 22, the visionary, who had come to Smyrna, was extensively and minutely questioned in the presence of five witnesses who spoke her language.

"We turned her around, returned her in every direction, mincing the questions, giving her from time to time false answers to try to make her contradict herself. She responded to all this with the same simplicity, repeating several times the same things although we questioned her in different forms and corrected the "errors" that we wanted her to take on."

From this interrogation, the good faith and above all the suspicion that she had any self-interest to say what she said comes out clearly because the vision on Karatchali goes against H. Jung, who placed the tomb elsewhere; finally, the vision was very clear in all its details such as they were recorded above. What's more, note that she never sought to give her vision importance. "If we asked her, she responded with the candor of a child. Outside of that, she held herself off to the side and remained quiet" ("The Ephesus Tomb," p. 261).

You certainly have the right to not blindly believe in the sincerity of the visionary and the effectiveness of the examination. But it is not permissible to turn everything into a source of ridicule and in the most hideous manner. This is, however, what Fr. Barnabé dared do. We hardly dare transcribe the following lines: "Returning from Smyrna we wanted again to get more serious information on this apparition when one of the locals said, 'Come now, the Virgin this good woman saw was none other than such and such a priest (clearly H. Jung) out in the fresh air smoking a pipe.' "—This is what really goes too far—"If it were so, goodbye to the celestial vision! But there was no less an allegorical and prophetic vision of the completely artificial opinion of *Panaghia-Capouli*" ("The Jerusalem Tomb, etc.," p. 276).

"You know well," wrote E. Poulin in his response to Fr. Barnabé, "that the only priest present at that time in *Panaghia* was at the very time of the vision on the exact opposite side, busy arranging the chapel for the great feast the next day. Oh! Father, it is a sin before God and man to speak as you have spoken here. I am not insinuating, I denounce it out of love for justice and truth." It is difficult for us, after more than a half century, to feel the same indignation as E. Poulin. Yet what a feeling of deep sorrow to see the abyss of bad faith into which could fall those who, in order to defend a cause that is dear to them, do not fear having recourse to methods that even Juvénal, the famous Patrician of Jerusalem, would have recoiled at, even he who was very suspicious.

Second apparition: October 15, 1903. "Around eight in the evening at dusk, Sister Guerlin, Visitatrix of the Daughters of Charity in Istanbul, was in *Panaghia* in the little garden attached to the residence, waiting for her companions who had gone to walk in the hills. Suddenly, from the direction of Karatchali, a bright light attracted her attention. It was a rather large light, very bright and really extraordinary, that would stop and then follow the ridge of the hill. There was no road or a path on this side going anywhere over there.

"Very stuck by this light that didn't resemble a lit torch and even less a lamp or lantern, the sister called her companions, four of them, who all saw like her in the same conditions as her this strange light (Ch. Picard writes: "a bright fireball" that he calls *Panaghia phosphoros*) that lasted about ten minutes. When it arrived at the same point where, in as much as they could judge in the dark, the previous year the lady in black had disappeared, the light went toward the south without changing size, paled a little and went out altogether."

These details are given in a letter signed by the sister herself whose good faith one cannot question. We can imagine how Fr. Barnabé would have explained this apparition. Fortunately, it happened at almost the same time as this "Tomb of the Virgin in Jerusalem" came out in November 1903.

If you accept, and we willingly accept it, the reality of these two apparitions, you can't help but notice that the more favored was not the Visitatrix of the Daughters of Charity but rather the humble and uneducated mountain girl. Isn't this, so to speak, the way of the Blessed Virgin to prefer to show herself to the simple: Catherine Labouré at rue du Bac, Melanie at La Salette, Bernadette in Lourdes, etc.?

EXTRAORDINARY CURES

A simple preliminary remark. Even if we were dealing with a well-documented miracle like those that are submitted to the Medical Office in Lourdes, we would not offer them as proofs in favor of *Panaghia* nor in favor of the tradition of Ephesus over Jerusalem. These sorts of graces are accorded principally, if not uniquely, as recompense for the faith of those who pray.

We know that there was, later in 1951, a miracle published by the archbishop after a canonical process carried out according to all the rules. There were no official processes between 1896 and 1914, but E. Poulin studied carefully all the cases of cures that he found out about. He counted them and even pulled out three of the most important, deferring to Rome ("A Last Word, etc.," p. 73) and five of lesser importance. We will only cite one from each category.

FIRST CASE: MOUTLOVO IN MACEDONIA

A poor Catholic woman from the Bulgarian village of Moutlovo arrived at the end of December 1904 at the residence of the Daughters of Charity in Koukouch carrying on her back a ten-year-old boy, a real skeleton and in agony.

The sick boy's cheek, ravaged by cancer, had been putrid and hanging on by a sliver of flesh that the mother herself snipped off with her scissors. The wound was horrible to see and smelled terribly.

After a day of rest, the mother and child went to Salonique to consult the doctor in the hospital administered by the Daughters of Charity. By chance, two other doctors were with him when the little cancer patient was presented to him. All three, having made an examination of the wound, made the same prognosis: incurable cancer, imminent death.

The mother returned to Koukouch, crazy with grief. "Sister, they said that my child will die. Save him!" What could they do confronted with such desolation? Nothing ventured, nothing gained, they thought; leave the doctors and their medicines and try the *Panaghia* ash. They began a novena and lotions with ash dissolved in water. Three times a day, prayer to the Virgin: "O Mary, conceived without sin, etc." and lotions three times a day. The little dying boy did not die. He even seemed to revive as his appearance had a marked improvement.

After ten days the mother remembered another child left at the house. She was eager to return to the child. They gave her a little pack of ash and told her how to continue the lotion and prayers. She returned home with the child on her back.

Each week they heard news of the child through the people at the market. The news was good. In February the progress accelerated. In April, the wound had completely healed.

When the child was completely healed, they went to present him to the doctor who had considered him incurable and condemned him to death. Imagine his astonishment to see the total healing. He did not hesitate, although he was Jewish, to give the following certificate:

I just examined Cotcho, the child with cancer on the lower maxillary and upper and lower lips. I am surprised by his truly miraculous cure. My sincere compliments to Sister Pascaut who has produced a real miracle with her power (Dr. Sciaky, doctor at the Solonica Hospital, May 12, 1905).

SECOND CASE: MR. BLACKLER, BOUDJA, NEAR SMYRNA, 1903

Mr. Blackler, English and Protestant, but a great friend of the Vincentians and the sisters (they had at the time a school in Boudja), wounded his hand so badly that the injury took on frightening proportions despite the assiduous care of two, three and four doctors called upon one after the other. The hand swelled considerably, then the arm was affected and turned black up to the shoulder.

At the end of his resources, the doctors had decided to amputate it when the superior, Sister Eudoxie, who knew the family well, ran to them. "Mrs. Blackler, what are you going to do? Why not try the ash from *Panaghia?*" Mrs. Blackler in her sorrow seized upon the ray of hope presented to her.

She took a little pinch of the ash, dissolving it in a little water. She spread the lotion on the afflicted hand and arm. As far as healing, there was none, but the spread stopped. Then, with care and time, the cure came. The hand, arm and invalid were saved without amputation.

"In this case," writes E. Poulin, "two distinct facts: the stopping of the infection and the cure. Is it reckless to attribute stopping the spread of the infection to the Blessed Virgin? As for the healing, we'll leave it to science and the doctors, all the more because (he adds rather jokingly) when the Blessed Virgin gets involved with healings, it happens more quickly, with less complications, and leaves less scars."

Mr. Blackler is the same one who gave, around the same time at Oxford, a presentation with slides on *Panaghia*. We are not able to nail down the date or even the year so as to be able to know if the presentation preceded the cure or the cure the presentation. In the first case, the cure would be a sort of recompense, and in the second, the conference would be an act of gratitude toward the Virgin of *Panaghia-Capouli*.

Chapter 9
Attempt at a Synthesis

SINCE we do not find in *Panaghia-Capouli* any inscriptions, we will not try to indicate precise dates, but it is permissible, according to the facts known, to make of them a sort of synthesis in which we will, without the possibility of absolute certitude, bring together that which is likely.

There is thus there, in a site eminently favorable to human habitation, sheltered as it is against the north wind and open only toward the sea, equipped with water by a fresh and clear spring, the four walls of a building that is modest, we will admit, yet with solid seating and that is clearly a church. Why would there be a church in this out-of-the-way place in the mountain?

The remains of other constructions that we have indicated, are they not of such a nature as to give us precious information? We can affirm that there was, at a date we would like to be able to be sure of, not only a church, but a number of homes and something like a public monument (the basin with its portico and the arches).

When the arcades were discovered (I was there), there were tombs formed of bricks and, in these tombs, skeletons with medals that go back to the seventh century. But, was it really in the seventh century that the arcades were used as sepulchers? Conjectures, we must admit, are our only resource. It only remains to support them by facts.

In the 13th century, Ephesus was taken by the Sedjoucide Turks. The conquest was only completed in 1426 after Tamerian passed through. It would be unlikely that the invaders came through the mountain right away. However, surely the inhabitants of the mountain didn't live in complete isolation and became aware of the dangerous situation. Was it possible for them to flee right away and to set sail for Samos as we have seen recently (1922)? When, then, did they leave their little homeland, after having secured the remains of their dead? At this point in our conjectures, the obscurity is complete. We will not go on further because it is impossible to guess anything.

Let's return to the more distant past. There was there, and this is beyond any doubt, in this place with the strange name of *Panaghia-Capouli,* a small colony of Christians who lived there for several centuries. What remains obscure is the origin of this colony, when it was formed, and the name of its founders. . .

Still, can't we, at least, recall on this subject, the text of St. Epiphane that cites the mysterious text of Revelations, "on the wings that were given to the Woman to carry her to a solitary place so the demon could not tear her apart" (Rev 12:14). There is also the text of St. Jerome: "John returned to Ephesus where he had a small house and devoted friends" (Migne, P.L. 27, 602).

Finally, why not bring the two texts together, these two other most recent ones, cited by Fr. Fonck, by St. Gregory of Tours (+593): "Ephesus is the place where St. John wrote the gospel. There is also at the summit of the neighboring mountain four walls without a roof. He lived there offering the Lord prayers for the sins of the people." From St. Willibad (+726): "After the visit to the tomb of St. John, they (the pilgrims) climbed up to the heights, and they could not admire enough this place where the holy evangelist was accustomed to speak, whom the rain and the wind respected" (Stimmen aus Maria Lach, 1896, p. 492).

We are under no illusion about the fragility of these similarities. But since they exist, however frail they be, why not use them as guideposts?

Fortunately, above all these uncertainties, there is an uncontestable fact (we already know it) from which a bright light shines on *Panaghia:* the remarkable correspondence of the locale with the descriptions of Catherine Emmerick. If one wanted no matter what to suppose that her secretary Brentano imagined these descriptions, then it would be him whom we should recognize as the visionary. That would be a useless way to avoid the supernatural.

For those who would deny it a priori, there is no other possible natural explanation than the phenomena of something seen from a distance, which is complicated here by the phenomenon of seeing across time, something which is quite rare, if not unique and without any example.

As for those who, while finding it difficult to accept supernatural phenomenon, acknowledge the possibility, there is no other explanation than that given by Monsignor Farges. After having recognized the fact, he wrote: "It is clear that the object of this vision went beyond the enthusiasm of a poor girl from Westphalia without culture and who had never traveled outside her province. Transcendence is well manifested and hallucination considered impossible" (*Mystic Phenomena* by Mgr. Farges, p. 367-68).

Yes, transcendence and vision, contemplation. "Tranquil like a mirror, she (C. Emmerick) said, 'Here is what I saw. Here is what was placed before me, here is what I reflected . . .' " (E. Hello: *Glances and Lights,* p. 105).

It is easy to understand how much this fact that goes beyond history, once accepted (and one must accept it if one does not a priori deny the supernatural) has the ability to strengthen the historical thesis of the death of the Virgin in Ephesus (rather than in

Jerusalem) and that, what's more, it gives an incalculable value to this little corner of the earth that has been ignored by all for centuries and discovered as by miracle in 1891, "this place unique in the world, this inexpressibly holy place of the Dormition of Mary" (Léon Bloy: *The Ancient One of the Mountain,* p. 334).

Chapter 10
Those Who Worked on *Panaghia*

THE FIRST COLLABORATORS

HOW could we not take a moment to remember those who were only manual laborers, an anonymous crowd from whom we should still pull out a few names?

Barba Phot, from Aydin, who after annoying conjugal adventures fled all human society to live alone, clothed as one of the poorest of the poor, always walking barefoot on the stones and rocks: "I know all the paths with my feet," he said once when he was surprised walking the mountain during the night. Able to read a little, he converted to Catholicism after reading *The Lives of the Saints* (translated into Greek by A. Elluin, C.M.). He died in a state of grace in Smyrna at the Little Sisters of the Poor.

One of the sons of the guardian Andréa, Cannello. He had been placed as a young child at the St. Joseph Orphanage to be raised as a Catholic. Having learned some French, he served as a translator when foreigners came to *Panaghia.* It was from his mouth that we heard the phrase so picturesque, seeing the hill that was all yellow with flowering broom plants: "You would say that a piece of the sun fell on the hill." He disappeared, along with his large family, during the First World War.

It is appropriate to also cite the name of someone who was not a manual worker but a skilled negotiator, George Binson, totally devoted to the Vincentians. He was able to bring to a happy conclusion the many and difficult transactions necessary for the purchase of the property and later its transfer. E. Poulin, in his notes, consecrates an emotional and grateful memory to him.

There were, in 1896, three young mountain climbers who, delighted with their excursion to *Panaghia* and grateful to H. Jung for his hospitality, paid him with beautiful nature drawings that graced the first brochure: Pinchon, de la Néziières, and Avelot, from the Fine Arts School in Paris.

Other drawings were signed by P. D'Andria, an engineer, and R. Péré, an architect, both established in Smyrna. Finally, others were by J. G. Borrel, who deserves a special mention.

It was he, one will recall, who, after the third expedition in August 1891, exclaimed, "Should a million controllers come . . ." From that time on he dedicated himself entirely to the cause, not shirking under any fatigue when he had to measure the terrain across the hills and valleys. It's to him that we owe, in addition to a few drawings, the maps and sketches. He was the one who wrote the whole technical part of the brochure *"Panaghia Capouli."*

A sketch of the landscape surrounding the House of Mary.

Even when he was far away, he followed the work closely. His letter of September 20, 1898, witnesses to this as he writes from the island of Crete, to which he had been called to caution his son Eugene against the excessive enthusiasm of Fr. Gouyet.

He was the one who made a large-scale blueprint of the house of the Virgin and wrote on the side, in Indian ink in a perfect script, the corresponding texts from C. Emmerick. J. G. Borrel was ambidextrous. We heard him say that when he wanted to make his work even more perfect, he used his left hand. What did he not do? He made a panorama of the plain of Ephesus as seen from *Panaghia* with its horizon of mountains in the distance, which is enclosed under glass in *Panaghia* and has survived all the relocations.

J.G. Borrel with his wife and daughter.

Finally, as he couldn't remain idle a minute, he profited from his rather frequent stays on the mountain to paint one of the refuge walls with a fresco in three parts: the Virgin making the Stations of the Cross on her knees; then, walking toward the next station where her servant puts down the mat that is referred to by C. Emmerick. It is a real repose for the eyes and the heart. On the facing wall he drew, above the text *et accepit eam in sua,* St. John brings the Virgin into his home. This work was never finished, and, in any case, all has been lost. This is all the more reason to conserve it in memory. J. G. Borrel died in Paris April 9, 1914, at age 64.

What we have said of Fr. Eschbach allows us to count him among the number of great workers of *Panaghia* and among the most active.

Let us also mention a confrere of the Smyrna school, Gaspard Dumond. He did the calligraphy on the first pages of the history of *Panaghia.* He did so much and with such heart! He transcribed the brochures of E. Poulin (Gabriélovich), his reports destined to Marian Congresses, a good number of his letters and those of numerous correspondents. He died in Smyrna in 1906.

Another confrere, residing in Paris, Edouard Mott, worked hard in another way. Being disposed to mysticism, he had no reluctance to accept the supernatural. "These were two days in heaven, spent on the holy mountain." (Letter of August 28, 1903). He exchanged a considerable number of letters with E. Poulin and was an intermediary with diverse correspondents, especially F. Vigouroux, whom he often had reason to see. E. Mott insisted strongly that E. Poulin go in person to the Marian Congress in Rome (1904). As the latter obstinately refused, he offered to read himself the report in question. E. Poulin did not hesitate to ask his services. He learned of the publication of a Coptic version of the acts of the Council of Ephesus, and he asked E. Mott to consult it to see if there was the "famous" text in its entirety. E. Mott ran to the orientalist Revillout. There was nothing new on the text, but this detail proves E. Poulin's obstinacy to look for the truth and the avid zeal of this confrere.

JEAN PARRANG

Jean Parrang lived in Smyrna for almost ten years (1904-1913). From the very beginning, the Cause of *Panaghia-Capouli* took hold of him, if that might be said. In close relationship with the Austrian archeologists whose language he spoke, no archeological detail escaped him. An excellent photographer, he left us a series of beautiful views of the mountains of Ephesus. During his stay in *Panaghia,* he was not content to just photograph; he liked to carefully inspect the site to compare against C. Emmerick's descriptions, and he willingly took up his shovel to dig into the earth . . .

Called first to Rome and then to Paris, he never stopped speaking about it to everyone and accumulating document upon document that unfortunately only helped him. Nevertheless, it was he who supplied Fr. Adhémar d'Alès with precious documents for his very favorable article published in the *Review of the Christian Orient* 1931-1932, pp. 376-389.

He corresponded frequently with Fr. Niessen. Should we be surprised if the two researchers came to the same conclusion? We will read Niessen's testament. Here is that of J. Parrang: "Nothing serious for Jerusalem, but a lot against. A great probability for Ephesus. Will we ever come to the absolute certainty that history wants on this question?" (Annals of the Mission 1942, p. 140).

JEAN-MARIE BOUCHET

In 1907, H. Jung traveled in France during the summer. He had to be replaced in *Panaghia* by one of his confreres. Jean-Marie

Bouchet, who had (and he deserved it) the full confidence of Sister de Grancey, was designated by E. Poulin to direct the ordinary work. The next year H. Jung resumed his position. But from 1910 onward, J-M Bouchet replaced him definitively. Of a little demonstrative yet serious and deep piety, he took his role to heart as a sacred mission. An untiring walker with solid footing and a sure eye, he surveyed the land in every sense, trying all hypotheses to find the tomb. He even thought one day that he had found the real place. It was for him a moment of great emotion, which many others shared with him for some time, including F-X Lobry, the Visitor, and E. Poulin himself.

But they were so cautious of being the victims of some illusion on the subject that they subjected it to expertise upon expertise to come to the conclusion that they had to search elsewhere. It was a great sadness for J-M Bouchet, who seemed to have retained his interior conviction.

Recalled to France for the Mobilization in 1914, he never returned to Smyrna where it would have been quite impossible for him to continue his work on *Panaghia*. He died in 1936 at the Berceau of St. Vincent de Paul (Landes).

MGR. ANDRE TIMONI

Mgr. Timoni didn't do any personal research in books or on the ground. However, he presided attentively over the Commission of Inquiry, and it would be an insult to him to believe that he didn't exercise personal control over the inquiry that was done under his watch. Above all, it was he who took the initiative to present to the public the first brochure, *"Panaghia Capouli."* He was not the author, but he was in agreement with what was written, so he adopted it and signed the brief notice to the reader.

They had not forgotten the Superior General's formal order to publish nothing on the subject. A man of austere discipline and strict obedience, E. Poulin would have never made public a brochure, even anonymously or under a pseudonym (Gabriélovich) as he did later. But the archbishop of Smyrna was not bound by the Superior General. He took everything upon himself, including the sarcasm that L. Duchesne feared and made others fear.

Without this first publication, the others would have never seen the light. One might say that everything that followed was present in the beginning, without which, everything would have stayed in the dark. Thus, the attitude of Mgr. Timoni in this affair was of capital importance, and he merits to be counted among the good workers of *Panaghia-Capouli,* right alongside E. Poulin.

He died in 1904.

ABBÉ GOUYET

As we already know, Abbé Gouyet shares with H. Jung the honor of the discovery. "You were the Christopher Columbus of *Panaghia-Capouli* and we were only the Americo Vespucis!" E. Poulin wrote him in 1896. Later, noting certain of Abbé Gouyet's contradictions, E. Poulin felt he had to deny him the first place. The arguments that he made are very strong, but they are not absolutely proven. In any case, this type of taking back his first statement is certainly not a case of jealousy, but rather love of the truth on the part of Poulin.

Jung and Gouyet, what a contrast between two men! Gouyet was as thin as Jung was solid, as reserved and austere as Jung appeared exuberant, jovial and bon vivant.

We saw him in 1898 during his stay in *Panaghia.* In the early morning after having said Mass, he went out in the mountain, armed with a long stick topped with a handkerchief, in place of a flag, and all day long he searched tirelessly, a real knight marching toward the conquest of the holy tomb, and also a manual worker because he dug in the earth with a shovel and would have willingly dug with his hands.

One night he made what Poulin rightly called an "armed vigil." He remained in prayer, with his arms extended, until morning, asking with faith for the grace to finally find the tomb of the Virgin. But, alas, the result of this expedition did not correspond to his ardent desire.

More and more impassioned, he went so far as to ask Sister de Grancey to cede him the property of the hill in which he had put all his hope in order to be able to search in complete freedom.

Once back in Paris, he dreamed of establishing in *Panaghia* a Community of worshippers and multiplied his efforts to arrive at that end. "He was almost there, the dear abbot," wrote E. Poulin (*Hist. Man. of Panaghia*, reg. 1, p. 211) "when death came March 20, 1899, to close his eyes to the illusions of the earth and to open them wide to the beautiful lights of heaven!"

His large volume, a little confused and watered down, is far from being without value. The text of the Conciliar letter is given in its entirety, and the discussion is lively and ingenious. One should also note the very intelligent comparison that he establishes between the two implicated mystics: A.C. Emmerick and Marie d'Agréda.

ABBÉ NIESSEN

He is often called "doctor" because he has argued numerous theses with success. We may be astonished that this strong advocate of *Panaghia-Capouli* has never set foot there. It's not that he lacks the desire, just the time. His correspondence with E. Poulin reveals that this holy priest dealt with the fatigue of extensive study and was burdened with the duties of pastoral ministry such that he could never find a month of vacation that would have allowed him this pious pilgrimage.

In a letter we received from him dated November 23, 1936, and that is somewhat biographical, he attributes to C. Emmerick the preservation of his youth and of his priestly vocation. At the age of 67, he obtained from his bishop (for reasons of health) the authorization to retire from pastoral ministry in order to devote himself fully to *Panaghia-Capouli* and C. Emmerick.

To this end he withdrew to Aix-la-Chapelle "because of its extensive library and also because of the Louvain library not far away." He added, "During these last years, I have brought together a great quantity of material related to the famous question of *Panaghia-Capouli.*"

Alas, his days were numbered. God granted him the favor of not seeing the famous library destroyed yet again.

We learned from our confrere Léopold Dworschak that Niessen died September 8, 1938. In 1937 L. Dworschak received a long letter from him that was like a testament of the untiring intellectual worker. "The more I advance in the literature on the subject, the more I am aware that there is no serious objection against [it], and the more my conviction that the Dormition of the Virgin and her Assumption were in Ephesus is affirmed" (May 27, 1937).

You will note the wise moderation of this testimony. First, it deals with Ephesus and not *Panaghia,* because history properly speaking says nothing about *Panaghia,* known only by C. Emmerick. Niessen does not mix questions that should be separate. What a contrast with the divisive tone of his adversary! "The question of Ephesus being resolutely thrown out, etc. . . ." How can we not admire the reserved attitude of this great enthusiast who, despite his personal certainty, avoids showing himself as a victor and casting out Jerusalem!

The true mission of H. Jung in *Panaghia,* after the honor of having discovered it, was to be the head of those who worked under his intelligent direction. The laying out of paths in the mountains, excavating, transporting material, digging and studying the land, all this rested on him. E. Poulin was content to show a desire or a will, for example, with the digs in the chapel, whose result was the revelation of the mysterious ash.

H. Jung was not uninterested in historical research, but it was enough for him to record in his memoir the results Poulin obtained, so that their work, while very different, contributed to the same goal.

Some of his characteristics could be shocking: his wearing farmer's clothes (wearing the cassock is not compatible with certain types of work), his cavalier style, his sometimes rude language of a former soldier. He could even scandalize some people (recall the history of the pope, exploited by Fr. Barnabé) and thus hurt the holy cause some, although he loved it with all his heart.

How he loved, with the simplicity of a child, to celebrate the Feast of the Assumption in *Panaghia*! Country decorations, lighting with garlands of Venetian lanterns, etc., nothing was left out. He willingly put himself at the level of the most simple to honor with them the true Mistress of the land.

Here is his meditation from August 26, 1899, 8 p.m.:

I am alone with the simple and humble inhabitants of *Panaghia-Capouli.* The nightingales just sang their evening prayer. Responding to each other from one mountain to another, the crickets recited their psalm chorally. The wind blows. You can hear in the distance the sounds of the sea. The sky is brilliant with the light of stars. I recall the words of scripture: *Stellae dixerut: ad sumus.* (The stars having been called, they said: here we are!) It's a concert by nature, an immense incomparable concert, where millions of voices come to harmonize to sing the glory of God, a concert to which the wild mountain animals come to mix their voices. At times, an absolute silence makes me think of these words from the Holy Book: *Tibi silentium laus!* (Silence is praise in your honor.) How could you not hear this wonderful symphony, how could you not take part or, rather, because such is the role of man in this world, how could you not be the chorister to direct to God this concert of divine works? My soul is penetrated by this other line from Scripture: Works of the Lord, bless the Lord! Praise him and exalt him above all forever. Angels and heavens, sun and stars of the night, rain and dew, storm winds and calm, land, mountains, hills, waters of the ocean, clear streams, great trees, humble grass of the prairies, heat and cold, light and darkness, fish of the sea, birds that sing in the heavens, bless the Lord and praise him above all forever. It is you, Spirit of life, who fills the universe with this divine harmony and gives to all creatures, even the inanimate, the gift of speech in order to sing divine songs . . . And you, O Mother most holy, O Mother of my God who heard in this place these natural harmonies and directed them to your divine Son, bless these workers, these poor ones who have worked without knowing it in search of your tomb, bless the poor guardians of this place, of your dear sanctuary, finally bless the poor priest who, by an assignment whose honor confuses him, works, though unworthily, to find the place where your body, as Benedict XIV said, after a momentary stay (in the tomb) was taken up into heaven. Let others look for rocks; I look for only one, that which the apostles carved with their hands to prepare for your tomb. Let others look for flowers; I would like to see, surrounded by lilies, your last resting place. You engraved on the rocks of the mountains the sufferings of your divine Son; engrave with indelible and eternal letters on the even harder material of my heart the memory of the love that Jesus had for you and that you have for us. O *Panaghia!* O Most Holy, I say to you: good bye! Perhaps adieu! Who knows if we will be here next year? Two workers for *Panaghia,* Abbé Gouyet and Pélécas died this year; Lord, give their souls peace! As for me, O my Mother, allow me to say to you before I leave, as my evening prayer:

> *Vitum praesta puram*
> *Iter para tutum*
> *Ut videntes Jesum*
> *Semper collaetemur.*

What is most touching in this meditation, written all at once without a single erasure, is the strong sense of sympathy for the humble and the poor. How moving this memory given to the recent dead and this thought of his coming death, especially when we know that when he wrote this Jung was only fifty-three. Born December 25, 1846, he was in his prime and in a state to live to one hundred or beyond. He died in Paris January 3, 1929, thirty years after this meditation.

EUGENE POULIN

From all that has proceeded, it is clear that, by the extent and the results of his activity, E. Poulin is not only one of the workers of *Panaghia,* but the greatest without comparison. Only Abbé Niessen, in the field of historical research, could be compared with him. On several points (for the scientific rigor of his method), he is incontestably superior to him. But the latter worked in other domains: theology, patristic studies, mysticism, etc.; E. Poulin confined himself to Ephesus and *Panaghia-Capouli.* One might even be tempted to reproach him for being too embedded in his subject rather than dominating it from the heights of his erudition.

But there, he felt he was master and could, without hesitation or fear, defy the greatest scholars. If he didn't convince them, he at least responded to all their objections. The objections did not frighten him. "The objections of our enemies," he liked to say, "are more useful for us to know the truth than are our friends' compliments." However, it is not only in his pamphlets that he fought, but also in a large number of letters that were an asset for him because they obliged him to examine and reexamine the question from every angle.

E. Poulin was thus a fearless knight beyond reproach for *Panaghia-Capouli.* Not only did he fight well, he also suffered. What a torment for him to hold back his ardor and his impetuousness in order to obey the Superior General! He suffered and, patiently, he waited for God's time (his favorite expression). God's time came when Mgr. Timoni took it upon himself to give the public the first brochure that relieved Fr. Fiat of his first apprehensions.

He later received, on the occasion of the second brochure, the following letter that he excused himself for transcribing but that, for the honor of *Panaghia-Capouli,* he didn't want to remain unknown: "I just read part, and skimmed the rest, of 'Ephesus or Jerusalem,' and I feel the need to express to you my satisfaction concerning this brochure that interests me greatly. It required of you a work of intense research and critical study that gives you honor. I have no trouble agreeing with your opinion and am happy to congratulate you for what you and yours have done to elucidate this question and to provoke a religious movement toward *Panaghia-Capouli.* May Immaculate Mary give you a hundred-fold what you have done for her" (letter of October 1, 1897).

This was a great consolation for E. Poulin. He still had a thorn in his side because, excepting the Superior General, E. Mott and Fr. Pouget, everyone else in the Mother House had completely adopted the disdainful attitude of Louis Duchesne.

E. Poulin was not the only tireless fighter. The cause that he defended he loved with an ardent love, and he tried to discover and follow the mysterious indications of Divine Providence. "I have only one regret, a great regret, in finishing this work (his brochure "Neither Zion nor Gethsemane"), that I still cannot say anything about what I call the interior life of *Panaghia,* seductive for hearts, convincing for spirits, and captivating for souls." Alas, the moment to tell what he had in his heart never came, and he carried to the grave the secret of his pious meditations.

His dream? He described it: to be buried in *Panaghia,* not alone, but with H. Jung and Sister de Grancey: "Wouldn't it be, for the three prospectors, or conductors, of the ancient *Panaghia,* rediscovered and restored, a real consolation to rest after their death in the vestry of the old chapel?" Just an ossuary of each is in the sanctuary: H. Jung, on the right, Gabriélovich (his pseudonym) on the left, and in the middle, Sister de Grancey. No names are written. There is a stone on each ossuary with a cross and the simple inscriptions: *Detector Panaghia* for H. Jung, *Panaghia Mater* for Sister de Grancey and *Panaghia miles* for Gabriélovich.

How much he must have suffered with the destructions of 1915 and 1922. All that he did for *Panaghia* was undone.

However, he conserved until the end the hope of better days that he would not see while alive but that he was sure were real. "Sleep, then, dear *Panaghia,* sleep under your ruins, like Lazarus in the tomb. When the time will come, the Master will say to you as to Lazarus, Come out from your ruins, and then you will take on a new life grander than before. Glory to God! Glory to Mary!" (*Hist. Man. of Panaghia,* reg. 2, p. 193).

E. Poulin died in Smyrna at the age of 85 in 1928.

SISTER MARIE DE MANDAT-GRANCEY

Now, after this rapid enumeration of the workers of *Panaghia,* how could we not give a special mention to the one who must be called the great worker, Sister Marie de Grancey? Her high-placed relatives allowed her to make the cause known in choice milieus in France, Belgium and elsewhere. That alone would have been little. What must be brought to light, even though we know it already, is that she had the initiative for everything and that, without her, all that the others did would have never happened.

Everything from her personal fortune that didn't go into the hands of the poor (and how generous her hand was there!) was spent on *Panaghia-Capouli.* This, too, would have been little. When one has a fortune, it suffices to open one's hand for the money to spill out. But Sister de Grancey, admirable Sister de Grancey, went at it not only from her purse, but from her heart, a noble, great, selfless heart.

In November 1910 Fr. Fiat composed the following prayer, transmitted to E. Poulin by Edward Mott:

O, Mary, conceived without sin, who deigned to confide to the Family of St. Vincent the Miraculous Medal and who thus prepared the Catholic world for the definition of the dogma of the Immaculate Conception, we ask you a new favor.

By the children of St. Vincent was providentially discovered in Ephesus and bought by the Company of the Daughters of Charity the place that, according to all probability, hosts your tomb. We ask you to render this tomb glorious and to give joy to the whole Church, thus preparing the definition of the dogma of your glorious Assumption.

When Sister de Grancey heard this prayer, which must have made her heart happy, read, she immediately protested against the formula, "bought by the Company of the Daughters of Charity." "No, no!" she cried in front of a dozen people, "this was never my intention." The energetic protest was not enough. Despite others' reassurance that this was a formula without importance, she wrote to Fr. Fiat to request that he remove the offending words and replace them with "bought by the family of St. Vincent." "I don't understand," she said, "why we would seem to exclude the Missionaries (Vincentians) when they are the ones who have done everything in *Panaghia*." It was indeed her personal fortune that she used so beautifully, but it is still just to give the honor to the entire noble de Grancey family. E. Poulin himself well understood as, after expressing his desire for a grave at *Panaghia,* concluded with these words: "Later, the de Grancey coat of arms on the doors of the new church!"

A LETTER FROM COUNT CHARLES DE GRANCEY

Count Charles was in 1951 the last surviving nephew of Sister de Grancey. We thought it appropriate to announce to him the resurrection of *Panaghia* and to communicate to him the desire, expressed by E. Poulin, to inscribe the coat of arms on the pediment of the chapel. The aunt and the nephew had the same nobility of soul. Here is his response:

Grancey-le-Chateaeu, Côte d'or, June 10, 1951

Reverend Father,

Your letter filled me with joy. The cause of *Panaghia* had been sleeping, and now the proclamation of the dogma of the Assumption gives it new life.

You ask me for a drawing of the coat of arms of my aunt Marie. Wait a little, if you please. These things are a treasure for history and archeology, but their exhibition does not occur without a percentage of vanity that risks spoiling everything.

What I thank you for with all my heart is your pious perseverance to not let the memory of my aunt Marie die out and to show the important role that she played in the discovery (and not just the acquisition) of *Panaghia.*

Providence is evident in her intervention. From her childhood she firmly believed that the Blessed Virgin died in Ephesus. On this subject I permit myself to send a poor photo of the handsome painting of Gérard David (1460-1523) that she constantly saw in our private chapel. It represents the Assumption . . . and the painter placed the scene before a large sea port.

The de Grancey chapel was dedicated, as if by chance, to the Virgin and St. John. The dedication dates from 1360.

If later you find a means to place there, where appropriate, some inscription recalling my aunt, you will be so kind as to let me know, as I would be glad to contribute to any expense stemming from it.

Please accept, Reverend Father, the expression of my most respectful and devoted wishes.

Count Charles de Grancey

P.S. The chapel in Dijon (which no longer exists), birthplace of the Order of the Golden Fleece and famous the world over, was also dedicated to the Virgin and to St. John following a vow by the Duke of Bourgogne, Hugo III, as he returned from the Holy Land in 1171 when he thought he would die in a storm.

Would it be because of Ephesus? I don't think so, as it would be too perfect.

Ct. Ch.

Chapter 11
And the Tomb?

MUCH more than the site and the house, it was the tomb that preoccupied the explorers. They had to be satisfied with the house. It was already a lot. But during the course of the years that followed, from 1892 to 1914, the tomb continued to be the object of persistent searches, each time begun anew and always without a satisfying result.

The visionary said, "I believe that the tomb still exists and that it will be found some day." She did not say that she saw, but that she believed. It was thus more a pious desire than a prophecy.

On the one hand, in effect, the indications that she gives about the tomb could only be rather vague, and on the other hand, over the past almost twenty centuries, how many transformations must the land have experienced since, in just fifty years, certain areas are almost unrecognizable.

The research was almost entirely conducted on Karatchali, the hill from which you can see Ephesus, where a station was found that was believed to be Calvary. The tomb couldn't be far away.

While studying, not on site, but on the map of the mountains of *Panaghia-Capouli,* published in the pamphlet with that name, the priest Brierre–Narbonne, in a February 4, 1934, letter, claims that the search should take place in an entirely different direction, toward the castle. A little later he writes, "We must look for the tomb . . . if we find the tomb, all doubt will fall away" (May 3, 1934).

Such is not our humble opinion. It would not suffice to find the tomb; it would also have to be proven. How? By a miracle? But the miracle would only be a proof for the witnesses. And after that?

Here, we can only cite the demands given in the Supplement to the Biblical Dictionary about the house: "An inscription in Hebrew or Greek, little import which is needed or, lacking that, signs on the walls or in the area attesting clearly and authentically that these walls were built for the Holy Virgin or that they sheltered her."

An authentic inscription in *Panaghia*! Certainly, we would hope for it with all our heart, and we understand the enthusiasm of the first days when they thought they saw Hebrew letters on some of the stones. If such inscriptions existed, no trace of them remains. But did they ever exist? It is remarkable that the visionary made no mention of them and nowhere says that there was anything engraved on marble or stone.

This is why we have never shared either the enthusiasm or the confidence of the obstinate researchers, even when we were among them. Recall what was said above of Gouyet and Bouchet.

It is impossible to reach a conclusion on this subject. Yet, how could we not see a parallel between the tomb of the Virgin and that of St. John? St. John's tomb is on the hill of Seldjouk, within the walls of the Justinian basilica. At what precise spot? It would be quite difficult to say. In any case, it is there, on this hill that over-looks Ephesus.

For those who accept the thesis of Ephesus and recognize the correspondence of the place with C. Emmerick's descriptions, the Virgin's tomb is surely on the mountain, on the side of a hill, at some distance from the house. Where, precisely? We almost dare say (at the risk of scandalizing), what difference does it make? All the more because, for all believers, the holy body was only there as a transitory guest. It's really the whole site with the house where the Virgin lived that we could consider her tomb. This is why we like to call *Panaghia-Capouli* the holy mountain, the Mountain of Mary!

Second Part
(1914-1951)

Chapter 1
Panaghia-Capouli after 1914

THE year 1914 saw the last of the great pilgrimages that had been inaugurated in 1896. From 1915 *Panaghia,* which had, as we have seen, a brilliant entrance into history, suffered a near total eclipse: Lazarus in his tomb, according to Poulin's apt expression. However, guards kept watch over the tomb. They did not lose hope. They even made clear plans for renovations; in a word, they did not lose sight of the Holy Mountain. It is thus that, as soon as it was possible, in July 1920, J. Euzet and P. Saint-Germain were able to visit and observe first-hand the damage.

Then the events of 1922 stopped all the projects. What could we expect of this period when, even after the Treaty of Lausanne, the New Turkey was still being organized? Since 1914, the taxes on *Panaghia,* paid regularly up to then, were not demanded, and we didn't rush out to offer to pay them. In any case, to whom would we have paid them? The policy accepted by E. Poulin (we should write "accepted" because he asked for advice on high levels) was to not make himself seen there. This attitude had its problems because it resembled a complete abandonment of the property.

Thus, as soon as there was an opportunity, J. Euzet did not hesitate in the least. He willingly went with a group of sisters: Sister Hanezo (who had known Sister de Grancey), Sister Lepicard (later Superioress General), etc. Mass was celebrated, and with what piety. They brought back from this little pilgrimage (November 1926) a strong desire to "do something" as soon as possible.

PROCESS OF RECOVERY

It was necessary, before undertaking anything, to provide for the succession of the property. In effect, the property that was initially registered under the name of Sister de Grancey, transferred later to E. Poulin, would inevitably lack an heir soon. Poulin was pressed to make a will indicating his successor. However, despite having passed his eightieth year, he refused with an inexplicable obstinacy. We will see later that he was right. Finally, he accepted. October 23, 1926, he wrote a valid will.

After his death (1928), how many steps had to be taken to get to the end! It was only in May 1931 that, all the formalities fulfilled, J. Euzet took the Ephesus-Kouchadassi road to have *Panaghia-Capouli* registered in his name in fulfillment of Poulin's Will.

The day before (May 25) there had been in Ephesus, in the fifteenth centenary of the Council, a pilgrimage of the Children of Mary to Smyrna. "I will return tomorrow," J. Euzet told them, "and I will return carrying *Panaghia-Capouli* (the title to the property) in my pocket." He did not know what awaited him.

When he was pulling the amount required for the back taxes from his wallet, the official consulted his register: "How can I," he said, "register to J. Euzet a property that did not belong to E. Poulin?" It had been registered to the treasury since 1917! Here was the result of this sort of abandonment that had been considered a necessary precaution. An abandoned property belonging to an "enemy," thus returning to the treasury . . .

What to do? To do nothing would be to renounce everything. The only hope was to open a court case. This was decided within the hour. Yet before going to find a judge, the lawyer wanted to see for himself if the property was "djebel" (mountainous) or "tarla" (cultivatable), as it was a significant point. Thus there was an excursion through the mountains to *Panaghia,* just enough time to see and to return to Kouchadassi in the dark of night. It was thus only the 28th when the case was opened and that they asked the judge to tell the treasury to not alienate the property until the definitive judgment was given.

The case lasted until September 24. The plaintiff, not having a real lawyer but just a clerk, had to attend personally all the sessions, which required travel to and from Izmir and Kouchadassi and sometimes, when for example the next session was postponed to the next day, rather prolonged stays in the little town. You can imagine this was not done without a considerable expense. But God provides.

During the session of July 10, there was strong emotion. The government lawyer claimed that, according to the law that he cited, E. Poulin did not have the right to pass down the property in question and that, as a consequence, J Euzet did not have the right to contest the treasury.

What could the clerk respond to this? He asked for several hours to study the law and reflect. The judge accepted and granted a session that evening.

In the interval Jacques Aboualafia dug up the code. Suddenly: "What was the date of E. Poulin's will?" he asked. October 23, 1926. Good, now they needed to find out when the Swiss code went into effect in Turkey. The article invoked by the Treasury wasn't found there. They researched some more. The Swiss code went into effect in Turkey October 3, 1926. Thus, if the will had been done before that date, it was under the prior code. However, it should be under the new law. We thus see that E. Poulin was right (without knowing it) to not be hurried.

The greatest obstacle was overcome. It remained to prove that the property had not been abandoned. They presumed this would be a little difficult since they hadn't been there at all during many years.

They thus needed to go to the site. The judge, his secretary, two experts chosen by the city and three witnesses chosen by us, went to *Panaghia* and undertook the formalities. It lasted a day and was conducted with great care. The conclusion was that the property had not been abandoned because trees had been planted there. As witness, the magnificent olive trees (that were 33 years old) were cited. As for the apparent abandonment, it was only due to the war that did not permit the owner to go there.

This was September 15. How could we not think, on this day and in this place, of the Way of the Cross that Mary made, of which C. Emmerick spoke?

The court reconvened September 23 with a particularly important session. There were closing arguments by the Treasury's lawyer, and a plea by the clerk and recess until the next day so the judge could prepare his decision.

The September 24 session was impressive. There was no discussion, just a simple reading of the decision. Glory to God! Our Lady of Mercy bought back her house! The decision was so well defined that it would have been very hard to appeal it.

It was January 9, 1932, before the plaintiff was called to appeals court. The session was very short. The Treasury lawyer made a brief argument, to which our clerk briefly responded. After fifteen minutes of deliberation, we were called back into court to hear these simple words: the decision of the Kouchadassi court is just. However, all was not finished. We had to wait until October 23 to bring to Kouchadassi a property deed according to form (in J. Euzet's name) that was uncontestable, which allowed him in 1952 to give *Panaghia* to a group headed by the archbishop. But let's not get ahead of ourselves. We cannot emphasize enough that if the case had not been won and the deed obtained, this gift would have been impossible, and anyone could have bought the land to make a country house or a hunting cabin.

Since that time (and even before, from September 1931), a guardian was established in *Panaghia* as they had to establish their ownership. Fortunately, there was in Kouchasdassi a man in his prime who accepted right away. He came up with his wife and two young children. Other children were born on the mountain. We can easily imagine their hard life in terms of their lodging, food and sustenance on small monthly payments, as we were at the end of our resources.

Aziz, the guardian, who had little education but knew Miriam through the Koran, was well aware that he was guarding a holy place. Having seen the Vincentian's image of the Good Shepherd, he wanted one like it and also requested a picture of the Virgin.

Aziz died in May 1950 at the French Hospital, struck down by an illness. On his death bed (could it be only the effect of delirium?), he said, "In *Panaghia* you will see extraordinary things. Me, I won't see them, but my children will see them. It will be like a paradise."

Note that, at this time, there was no question of the road that the Tourism Department would build, which was only made known in October of that same year.

In 1947, there was a threat of losing the property when all the forests were to belong by right to the state. We had to take steps with the *Orman Idaresi* of Bayindir, and there were experts sent to determine that there were not in *Panaghia* tall forest trees making an official forest. The preservation of the land again hung by a thread, but the Holy Virgin watched over her domain.

Chapter 2
Resumption of Pilgrimages

IF SO many efforts and such great expenses had been made to safeguard the property, it was because it remained the object of most holy desires and that they longed for the day when pilgrimages would be possible.

We have already mentioned the little pilgrimage of Sister Hanezo in 1926, of which a complete account was published in the Annals of the Mission (1927): "It was the first time that a Mass had been celebrated there since 1914! Nothing remains but for us to thank God and the Virgin for our protection, putting off showing our gratitude, by looking for and finding ways to end the state of desolation and abandon that *Panaghia-Capouli* is in now" (p. 351).

Alas! More waiting was required! In 1929 a rapid excursion brought J. Euzet to the House of the Virgin, accompanied by Fr. Grosso, Dominican. They had just enough time to see the Sanctuary paved with cowpats. Oh! There wasn't any profanation there! How can we forget the grotto of Bethlehem and, near the crèche, the donkey and ox? Have there not also been several sanctuaries, for example, Our Lady of Prime-Combe, in France, that had at their origin an ox that obstinately would kneel before a bush where a statue of the Virgin would be discovered?

Still, these pious considerations did not keep us from hoping for more pilgrims for *Panaghia*. In 1931 there was, as already mentioned, a pilgrimage of the Children of Mary from Smyrna to Ephesus, the Council Church, which allowed them to see the mountain with a holy longing.

Yet how could they think of trying the ascent, given the little time they had between two trains?

DISTINGUISHED VISITORS

In June of the same year of 1931, on the occasion of the fifteenth centenary of the Council of Ephesus, Mgr. J. Roncalli, at the time Apostolic Delegate to Bulgaria, accompanied by Mgr. Margotti, Delegate of the Holy See to Turkey, Mgr. Filipucci, Archbishop of Athens, and Mgr. Tonna, archbishop of Izmir, made a rapid excursion to the Basilica of the Council.

PILGRIMAGES REORGANIZED

Finally, in 1932, on April 17, taking advantage of an excursion train that allowed them to spend the whole day in Ephesus, a group of sixty people were gathered. Sisters, Children of Mary and others decided not to stay a minute at Ephesus in order to attack the mountain right away. It was a little frightening. There were at the beginning a few hesitations. But then, forward!

Those who had hesitated a moment wanted to arrive first. It was almost noon, so, exhausted, they had to rest a little and restore themselves by the stream. At two o'clock, they gathered in the House of the Virgin. *Ave Maris Stella,* the rosary, and the Lourdes song were recited. *Ave Maris Stella* hadn't been heard for nearly a quarter century (1914)!

The group also consisted of two Capuchin priests of St. Polycarpe, Fathers Constant and Théotime, and two Christian Brothers.

This very day it was noted, "What can be said about this delicious day? The temperature was mild, the sky was veiled with clouds with a few bursts of sunlight to allow the magnificent robe of spring that clothed the mountain to shine." They had the impression of being present for the dawn of a renaissance.

April 17, 1933. A train had just been put in place that could be rented for the day for a reasonable sum. We had to take advantage of this. About fifty people, including some of the older Children of Mary and some of the students from the sisters' school gathered. They couldn't arrive in *Panaghia* before eleven o'clock. They sang *Salve Regina* and rested, which was necessary after the long and difficult ascent.

At two o'clock they met in the House of the Virgin. They said the rosary and sang the twenty verses of the Lourdes hymn (adapted to Ephesus-*Panaghia*). Finally, they sang the *Regina Coeli* to say goodbye to the Virgin during this Easter time. Then they descended the mountain without stopping at the ruins of Ephesus because they had to be at the train at six o'clock. They returned to Smyrna at eight o'clock. "The weakest were valiant. No accidents. Everyone was enchanted." You will note that each time it's almost the same thing.

May 21, 1934. Again, they go by charter train with about the same number as the previous year. There are three Religious of Zion with a dozen of their students, four Sisters of St. Joseph with ten of their students, and a few others.

At ten o'clock, everything was ready for Mass. The altar was formed by a portable chapel which was placed out in the open against the little terrace wall leading up to the house of the Virgin. They were grouped in a circle a little distance away. "*Introibo ad altare Dei . . . ad montem sanctum tuum.*" Yes, Lord, it's your light and your truth that brought us to your mountain! Distractions were inevitable. "In effect, a gust of wind carried off four consecrated hosts that took flight like butterflies. Three were recovered immediately, but there was no trace of the fourth. Still, they had to continue the sacrifice. Suddenly I saw it at my feet. I was peaceful now!" After the Mass, they rested a little and then regained their strength. Clearly, the fountain was very popular.

At two o'clock, we gathered in the chapel for a rosary, litanies and a reflection. The *Ave Maria* of Lourdes was repeated twenty times. In short, it was a real pilgrimage because there was a Mass with communion.

They returned by the same route. With manageable paths, the descent would have been enchanting because the plain of Ephesus was constantly before their eyes. However, more often our eyes had to be on our feet to avoid falling.

A sister was overheard saying, "It's curious; in the past there was a blanket of daisies!" "Sister, before pilgrimages were made in April. The daisy season has passed. That's all! Nothing has changed."

In effect, except the first pilgrimage in 1896 made on May 20, all the others were made in April during Easter week when there were three holidays at our disposal.

April 23, 1936. Sixty-five places were taken on the train from Arvalia. Around ten o'clock Mass was held with about a dozen people receiving communion. Everyone was enchanted. However, a few expressed a regret not to have been able to visit the Ephesus ruins.

Another regret (that no one thought of) was more significant: descending by the same path to Arvalia. Yes, it's really an aberration to keep the pilgrims from knowing the exact position of Panaghia according to C. Emmerick's information. From the Arvalia side, both going and coming, you are always in a sort of crater without any other horizon than the close hills that just barely allow you to see the sea, and most of them didn't even glimpse it. However, the bus was waiting for us in Arvalia.

Since 1936 until August 1949, no other pilgrimage was documented. Probably these little groups we've mentioned, composed of almost the same people, began to be tired of coming under almost the same conditions.

Certainly, the Second World War didn't make things any easier. We were just able to keep in contact with the guardian of *Panaghia* who came down once a month with his wife to collect his payment and make a few purchases.

Things eventually calmed down, such that in 1949 a group of Children of Mary from Istanbul came to Smyrna with the intention to make the pilgrimage. The Children of Mary in Smyrna and others wanted to join them. We filled two buses, one hundred seats. Since 1914 *Panaghia* hadn't seen so many people. What gave this even more a resemblance with the pilgrimages of old was that the Archbishop, Mgr. Descuffi, celebrated the Mass, with songs, speeches, and numerous communions. As the Mass was celebrated in a chapel without a roof, the four winds made several hosts take flight, which were only found with difficulty.

It is notable that the occupants of the second bus, those from Istanbul, not having seen the first, which had parked a little off to the side, continued to Kouchadassi. This resulted in a considerable delay, and Mass couldn't be celebrated until almost eleven o'clock. As a consequence, all were extra tired.

But at the end of the day, returning to Smyrna, the two buses safe and sound (for the roads were not then what they have since become), everyone was delighted. All the more so because, despite the delay, they were able to make a brief stop at the ruins of Ephesus to pray a moment at the place of the Council Church.

Canon Karl Gschwind

Here we are in 1950, the year of the solemn definition of the dogma of the Assumption. Dr. K. Gschwind, canon of Bâle, whom the war of 1939 had detained in Istanbul while on route to Jerusalem, had profited from his forced stay there to study on location the Christian antiquities of Asia Minor. A great friend of *Panaghia,* he came up at least twice, alone, to celebrate Mass here. What's more, he had frequented the offices of the leaders of the press and tourism.

In October 1950 he came up with the idea to lead a pilgrimage the very day of the definition of the dogma of the Assumption (November 1). The pilgrimage was announced in the Turkish press as a major event. The Tourism Bureau fervently set itself to a project for a road that would allow taxis and buses to go up to Panaghia. "A fire built of straw," said some, to whom one could reply, without being a prophet, "Yes, surely, but if it has a favorable location, it can easily set a great fire." The fire continued, that is, the promises in the newspapers, and, in a few months, a mountain road, a little improvised, to be sure, made it possible for dozens of taxis and a dozen buses on August 19.

The 1950 pilgrimage, announced with such fanfare, was in reality quite modest, hardly thirty people, thus much fewer than that of 1949 by the numbers. However, in terms of its consequences, it deserves to be considered as the starting point for a new period in the history of *Panaghia-Capouli,* 1950-1951, just at the beginning of the second half of the century.

Chapter 3

Panaghia and
Other Countries

IT WAS not only in Smyrna that *Panaghia* was defended. There were in Rome itself, in Germany, France and Switzerland those who had always been loyal and those who were conquered and gained to the cause.

On February 21, 1921, Fr. Michel Hetsenauer, professor of the Roman College, gave a conference with slides on the House of the Virgin in *Panaghia-Capouli* near Ephesus in the college's great hall in the presence of seven cardinals, including Cardinal Gasquet. This talk must have had a considerable impact. It was published in its entirety in "Le Conferenze al Laterano" of May 1921, and the author gave a "Libera retractatio" in "Verbum Domini," published August 1922.

Even the title is significant: "The house of the Virgin" and even more so its Latin title: *"De peregratione BMV in P-C prope Ephesum."* In effect, as much as Fr. Hetsenauer showed himself in favor of recognizing the Virgin's stay in Ephesus, just as much he stays reserved on the subject of her death. Here is his conclusion: "We believe that it is absolutely necessary to separate the question: Did the Holy Virgin live in Ephesus? From this one: Where did the Blessed Virgin die, be buried and be assumed into heaven?"

This is also the opinion of Abbot Brierre-Narbonne who titled his study, "Habitation of the Blessed Virgin in Ephesus" and explained, "It is better not to mix the two questions." It should be noted that this double method was not a part of the controversies that filled the period from 1896 to 1914 although it seems at first glance to be a simple means to bring the adversaries together. With a little reflection, we soon perceive the contrary. If the advocates for Jerusalem accept that the Virgin lived some time in Ephesus, how could they make her come back, since the first voyage already seems unlikely to them. For the proponents of Ephesus the situation is a little better because the Virgin simply spending some period of time there would suffice to make it a place of pilgrimage.

REVEREND FATHERS HOFFMANN AND BENNO GUT

They should be aware of the conference of the two priests who came from Rome on pilgrimage to *Panaghia-Capouli,* Fr. Hoffmann first in 1934 and Fr. Benno Gut in 1935.

Fr. Hoffmann, a Jesuit, professor at the Oriental Institute, made his pilgrimage in the best possible conditions then, accompanied by Fr. Saint-Germain, C.M., a talented photographer, and a great friend of the Vincentians, Remo Missir. He spent the night in the dilapidated shelter, slept on the boards of a closet, and celebrated Mass in the house of the Virgin. He was able to see everything at his leisure and also visit the Ephesus ruins, bringing back with him beautiful photos of Ephesus and *Panaghia.*

Fr. Benno Gut, OSB, had a more difficult pilgrimage. Arriving on a Saturday, he couldn't leave Sunday morning. Trains only left in the evening. He arrived in Ephesus at six in the evening, as night was falling. It was October 13. Without the guardian Aziz it would have been impossible to attempt the climb. However, with him and the moon that soon rose in a calm sky, they could try. Fortunately Fr. Benno had good mountain footing, being Swiss from the Abby of Our Lady of Hermits in Einsiedeln.

We spent the night like Fr. Hoffmann had and, as soon as dawn broke, went to the chapel to celebrate our Masses. A cloud of unwelcome insects swarmed around us and attacked without pity his somewhat bald head without troubling in the least his profound recollection. We were able to descend rather early to visit unhurriedly the Ephesus ruins. Fr. Benno, without fatigue, was delighted. Noted the following day: "On the return train Father couldn't look away from Ephesus and, when the mountain disappeared, he couldn't retain a sigh of regret" (Journal du Sup. Cah. III, p. 125).

Fr. Hoffman and Fr. Benno Gut wrote in the guest book their pious impressions. It appears certain that both had the impression of having visited a holy place. What an admission by Fr. Benno: "Truly, the beloved apostle could not have chosen for himself and the Virgin a more favorable location in terms of its isolation, solitude and the beauty of the countryside."

ABBÉ NIESSEN

Now it is time to indicate other friends who didn't have the good fortune to make a pilgrimage.

First there was Abbé Niessen, whom we already know. During the war, correspondence with E. Poulin was completely interrupted. However, as soon as it was possible, this correspondence between Niessen and Poulin was resumed, and with what eagerness, to request news about *Panaghia* that was, alas, as we know, quite sad. Yet, he did not grow discouraged; he hoped for better days and continued to serve the cause of *Panaghia*.

It was thus that, in his booklet on the occasion of the fifteenth centenary of the Council, he returned to his favorite subject, profiting from the occasion to make the House of the Virgin known. He indicated in a note, that, his large volume from 1906 being out of print, he was preparing an improved edition. Alas! Certainly he wasn't able to realize this project, because he would have written of it in his last letters written a little before his death. We must bow deeply to this relentless champion who was never able to see *Panaghia* and who, nevertheless, died fighting for the defense of the Famous Cause, as he called it.

ABBÉ BRIERRE-NARBONNE

At the very moment when Niessen published his last pages, *Panaghia* made a great conquest in France in the person of Abbé Brierre-Narbonne. He had already read C. Emmerick without much enthusiasm. When he learned, in the course of a conversation with Charles Sauvé, the celebrated author of *Intimate Jesus,* of the discovery of the House of the Virgin according to her indications, he wanted at any cost to learn about it. He inquired in Smyrna, which sent him Poulin's brochures, even the first, with a little hesitation because it had become so hard to find. The request was so pressing, however, and, faced with such good will, that they couldn't hold back. The brochure couldn't have found a better home, as the result proves.

In effect, some months later a well-bound volume containing typed pages of a study on "The Habitation of the Virgin in Ephesus" arrived in Smyrna. It was a knowledgeable study, very detailed and adorned with magnificent watercolors reproducing in the same dimensions the ink drawings from the brochures that had been sent.

Brierre-Narbonne was already the author of scholarly studies on the Messianic prophecies in the Talmud, etc. In his volume on St. Madeline, he did not fail to insert a chapter on the Virgin's stay in Ephesus. The separation of the question that he practiced, on the subject of the *stay* and the *death* of the Blessed Virgin in Ephesus, in no way diminished his conviction about the existence of the Tomb in the Ephesus Mountain because he wrote indications on the place to look and that he desired with all his heart to be able to come himself, *sure to find it.*

We must notice a similarity between Brierre and Gouyet. They have the same mystic tendencies and the same enthusiasm for searching for the tomb. Yet Gouyet had seen, he had found the house, at least he thought so. He returned and spent two weeks there!

When one thinks that Brierre always had to remain with his desire unfulfilled, it seems to us that his enthusiasm for the Cause is just as worthy and admirable. It is worthwhile to cite this passage from a letter addressed to E. Bourrel:

> I regret not having accepted Fr. Euzet's generous offer to serve as chaplain at *Panaghia.* It is surely too late now. I would be so happy to end my days in the Virgin's House where St. John, my patron, lived. My older sister would have been happy to go with me, but she died in 1942. If I had been there, I would have done everything to discover the tomb with the information from C. Emmerick and a study of the terrain. But it is too late; my life is over.

This letter is dated August 27, 1953. Since then he has given no signs of life. He thus lived with his regret, having even more suffered than fought for his beloved cause. One can think without reserve that his intimate sufferings did more for the resurrection of *Panaghia* in 1951 than all the written polemics.

ADMIRAL GASTON DE MAUPEOU

Another conquest and by very different means: Admiral Gaston de Maupeou. His professional obligations brought him to Smyrna in 1918 when *Panaghia* was inaccessible in all meanings of the word. However, he made contact with the Vincentians, and what he learned from them, from the mouths of Poulin and Jung, filled him with an enthusiasm that he never lost. At a time when correspondence was impossible, he found a way through intermediaries to ask in Smyrna about any news of *Panaghia* that wasn't even known in Smyrna.

On July 10, 1930, passing through Smyrna, he was the guest of the Vincentians, and he talked to them at length of his conversations with Poulin and Jung and, given the impossibility still of his making the pilgrimage, he wanted to at least have a Mass said in *Panaghia* as soon as possible and said he would assume the costs of the trip. Finally, seeing the Vincentians' mission ruined, he did not leave without making a generous offering.

Since that time, he hasn't missed an occasion to ask information, and in so doing to propagate the Cause. Having, as the Secret Camerier of His Holiness Pius XII, access to the Vatican, he spoke about *Panaghia,* one might say, to anyone he could, to Mr. d'Ormesson, French Ambassador, to Cardinal Tisserant, etc., who listened with a certain interest but without enthusiasm.

As soon as the upcoming proclamation of the dogma of the Assumption was announced, he had the idea of preparing a few pages that he proposed publishing in Daniel-Rops' *Ecclesia.* He accepted. When Admiral de Maupeou opened the August 1951 *Ecclesia,* he was surprised to have been preempted by E. Borrel. It was a happy surprise without any anger or jealousy. Here, in effect, is what he immediately wrote E. Borrel (whom he didn't know at all) through *Ecclesia:*

Marine Command (Boulogne sur mer)

September 2, 1951

Dear Sir,

I had been in correspondence with Daniel-Rops and was readying myself to ask him to publish in *Ecclesia* an article I was writing on the Assumption of the Virgin in Ephesus, when I had the pleasant surprise to read yours that Daniel-Rops had announced to me. *Deo gratias!*

What could we do for *Panaghia-Capouli* in which I see we both believe?

In the hope of meeting you, I ask you to accept, Sir, with my compliments on your article, the assurance of my distinguished wishes.

Gaston de Maupeou

(Ship Captain,

Marine Commander of Boulogne)

Admiral Maupeou greatly rejoiced over *Panaghia*'s resurrection in 1951. Still being active in Boulogne, his dream was, if it had been possible, to send a French Marine battalion to take part in a great pilgrimage.

EUGÈNE BORREL

Finally, a last mention should be made of the first friend of *Panaghia* (which he has known since the year of the discovery), and who remained faithful to it. Gone from Smyrna for more than a half century, Eugène Borrel never interrupted the connection except during the war years. Erudite in all matters (and not only in musicology) and on the lookout for texts about *Panaghia*-Ephesus, he made the effort to copy them in the National Library and to communicate them to the Vincentians. When he learned in the papers some news, he eagerly shared it.

Although absorbed by his work, he ruminated, one might say, for a long time his distant memories and felt the need not to keep them to himself. He thus made contact also with Daniel-Rops, who allowed him to publish his pages. After having waited a rather long time, he began to despair; he also had the surprise to see himself in the August 1951 *Ecclesia*. He experienced, he wrote, a real sense of relief. Finally, he had been able to do something for *Panaghia*!

Since that time, he has become more and more a propagator of the Cause among his circle of acquaintances. He wrote something really prophetic, at a time when nothing suggested the events of 1951. "If the laity gets involved, the thing could go far." We know that lay people got involved and how far things went.

HIS EXCELLENCY MONSIGNOR JOSEPH DESCUFFI,
ARCHBISHOP OF SMYRNA

It is, however, true that the laity would have done nothing without the support of an ecclesiastic, a great friend of *Panaghia* in its worst days, Dr. Gschwind. We know how he had the marvelous idea to interest the Tourism Office in his 1950 pilgrimage.

This is the moment to point out the useful intervention of His Excellency Mgr. Descuffi, Archbishop of Izmir. The Tourism Office naturally addressed him to deal with the affair, and he, with his knowledge of the Turkish language, could enter into direct communication with the competent authorities to bring projects to completion. Since then, his intelligent and unceasing work has made him the animator of the pilgrimage from Notre-Dame of Ephesus that, in several years, made astonishing progress to become truly global.

It will be for others to write the new period of the history of *Panaghia-Capouli.* Our fathers have sown the seeds and we have collected the harvest.

"Nunc dimittis servum tuum Domine!"

Chapter 4

From 1951 to 1961

THE *PANAGHIA* ASSOCIATION RECOGNIZED AND NEW FACILITIES

The great pilgrimage of August 1951 thus opened a third period. That very year Mgr. Descuffi formed a *Panaya-Kapulu* Dernegi Association, recognized by the Turkish government and authorized to collect funds and to do all the work necessary to make the Christian sanctuary important.

Of course, the first years were a little laborious and fumbling, certainly not because the Dernek was inactive, but because there was so much to do. Animated by its zealous president, Pol. Clark, it started work right away. First of all, there was restoration of the walls that had crumbled, then, construction of a shelter for pilgrims, and then a house that was first called the Priest's house, a post office/communications center, and, at the entrance to the property, a police post, necessitated by the remote location, especially when there were hundreds of visitors.

October 26, 1955, was an important date because, up until that time, there hadn't been a priest in residence. On this day the archbishop canonically installed Joseph Bouys, of the Little Brothers of Jesus of Charles de Foucauld. It is thus that since that time we can have a daily record of the visitors to *Panaya* that is summarized monthly in the *Our Lady of Ephesus Review.*

Finally, more recently, they have built (and still on the rock) a little to the side and dominating the landscape, a Fraternity with a private chapel according to the Little Brothers of Jesus' rules. In this way the priest's house has become a little hotel where pilgrims can spend the night, even in winter.

Each August since 1951 there has been a diocesan pilgrimage that has already become tradition.

A miracle that occurred the very day of the first pilgrimage has been the object of a canonical process, which has permitted the archbishop to officially publish it. But how many cures and other favors have been obtained for Muslims and Christians alike! It is rare that the monthly review doesn't indicate a few.

Thus, the number of visitors does not cease to rise steeply. The year 1960 counted 50,000. Tourists? Yes. Those simply curious? Yes, as well. Yet also real pilgrims: priests who celebrate Mass, the faithful who receive communion, and so many others who pray with great fervor!

Before this very full decade, we sometimes asked: "Why doesn't the Blessed Virgin, rather than inviting her children to Lourdes or elsewhere, prefer to invite them to her house?" and we didn't find any other response than this: "The Blessed Virgin, always maternal, doesn't want to invite them somewhere that is inaccessible."

However, when the time came, she right away did the *miracle of the road.* Oh! We well know that the Tourism Office worked. But why? Could one humanly hope that tourists, after having admired the imposing ruins of Ephesus, would make the effort to go up a mountain to an unimportant ruin?

In short, now that her house is accessible, the Virgin invites them, and they come from all over the world.

This last decade has given us results beyond our wildest dreams, which we can suppose are only a beginning and suggest that there will not be an interruption, as there was in 1914. The moment has not come to write the history that will only be able to be written by others. While awaiting that history, we will find its elements six times a year in the *Our Lady of Ephesus Review*.

Permit us to express a desire and to formulate a wish. From 1891, the Vincentians called Bülbüdag the summit whose sea side shelters the holy house, in a corner of grass where the nightingale can sometimes be heard singing. In contrast, the Austrian maps insist (see the last edition of *Ephesos. Ein Fuhrer durch die Ruinen* by Joseph Keil, Wien, 1930-1955) on applying this name on the rocky ridge of Coressos, where the nightingale certainly has never sung.

Here is our desire and wish: that from now on, on the official maps, the highest summit that the traveler coming from Ixmir perceives in the south, and where he makes out the twisting roads of *Meryem Ana* that lead to the holy house, bear the beautiful name of Mary's Mountain (*Meryem-dag*).

END

Above, below, opposite above: Images of the restored House of Mary as it is today.

Below: The interior of the chapel.

Above: The Holy Sacrifice of the Mass being celebrated in Mary's House. *Below:* The restored wing which was Mary's bedroom, on the north side of the House.

Above: An icon of the Dormition of Mary which was found in the House.
Below: An icon of the Dormition of Mary, which used to be in the House of
Mary, but has recently been moved to the Rectory in 2006 before Pope Bene-
dict arrived. It is often associated with Ephesus.

Top: Muslims (and others) write petitions to Our Lady and then tie them onto this wall near Pahaghia Capouli. *Bottom:* This spring was redirected out of Mary's House where it originally flowed right through Our Lady's bedroom (for her own fresh water at all times—indoor plumbing!) and now is believed to be miraculous water. Muslims and Christians both drink this water and take some home with them for blessing.

Above: An icon of Our Lady which currently hangs inside Panaghia Capouli. Notice the House is painted into the icon. *Below*: This memorial plaque to Sr. Marie is located just inside the doorway that opens to the front of the House of Mary.

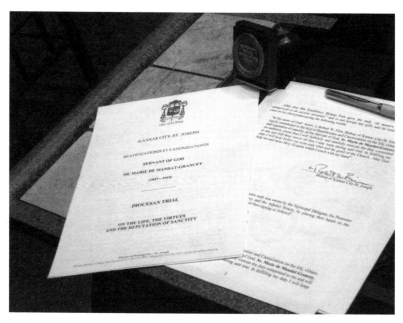

Official Booklet for the Opening of the Cause of Sr. Marie de Mandat-Grancey, D.C.

Appendix B

Sister Marie de Mandat-Grancey, D.C.:

Kansas City-St. Joseph Diocese
Studies Her Life and Work[1]

M ANY times I have said that our goal in this life is to get to Heaven and bring as many others with us as we can. This month of *All Saints* and *All Souls* helps us to focus on the holy and faithful people who have gone before us.

I felt very privileged recently when our Diocese of Kansas City-St. Joseph was asked to participate in a Cause for the Beatification and Canonization of a woman who died almost 100 years ago halfway around the world! It occasionally happens that a diocesan bishop may be expected to participate in the Cause of a holy man or woman who lived or died in the bishop's local diocese. Today I want to tell you about an extraordinary woman who never visited Kansas City, or the United States. Soon she will come to be better known here in Missouri. Her name was Sister Marie de Mandat-Grancey, a Daughter of Charity of St. Vincent DePaul. The Daughters of Charity have been an important part of the history of our diocese in both St. Joseph and Kansas City.

WHO IS SISTER MARIE DE MANDAT-GRANCEY?

Sister Marie was born of nobility in France in 1837. She joined the Daughters of Charity in 1858. She was professed in 1862. She died in Smyrna, Turkey, in 1915. Sister Marie was a devout Religious who gave up her status and wealth to care for the poor. She served as a nurse in France. In 1886, she was assigned to the French Naval Hospital at Smyrna. She became superior of the house and was dedicated to the care of the sick and children. During the time Sister Marie served in Turkey, she was instrumental in identifying and procuring the House of Mary in Ephesus. Mary's Home at Ephesus has become a place of pilgrimage for millions of people every year, the majority of whom are Muslims. Pope's Benedict XVI, John Paul II, and Paul VI have all celebrated Mass there. The process of the cause would attempt to investigate the heroic sanctity of Sister Marie, and present this for consideration by the Church.

WHY IS THIS CAUSE BEING CONSIDERED IN THE DIOCESE OF KANSAS CITY-ST. JOSEPH?

About two years ago I participated in a pilgrimage to *Meryem Ana Evi,* or "Mary's House" in Ephesus, Turkey. I traveled with faithful from Kansas City and various places in the U.S. During that visit I met Mrs. Erin Von Uffel of New York, who had studied the life of Sister Marie and had worked with the Archbishop Emeritus of Smyrna (modern-day Izmir), Most Reverend Giuseppe Bernardini, to research the life and work of Sister Marie.

While I was in Turkey, I met with Erin and the current Archbishop of Izmir, Ruggero Franceschini. In this meeting Erin encouraged the Archbishop to promote Sister Marie's cause. In February of 2010, I was formally petitioned by Archbishop Franceschini to assist with the cause, given the insufficient personnel and other resources of the Archdiocese in Turkey. After a series of discussions and prayerful considerations, I requested, and the Diocese of Kansas City-St. Joseph was granted, jurisdiction by the Congregation for the Causes of Saints for this initiative.

How Will the Process Take Place?

After having received the support of our neighboring bishops in Missouri and Kansas, the Superior General of the Daughters of Charity, the Archbishop of Dijon, France, where Sister Marie was born, and the Presbyteral Council of our Diocese, I nominated a postulator and formally requested permission to "open the cause." Dr. Andrea Ambrosi of Rome is the postulator, the person who will oversee the whole process and bring the case before the Vatican, and has worked on many such causes. He explains that, "a beatification cause involves a years-long process of examination of the candidate's life, virtues, writings, reputation for holiness, and reputation for intercession." When a candidate's cause is opened, that person is called a Servant of God. After the Servant of God's heroic virtue has been proven, he or she is declared "venerable." Then, to be beatified, one miracle must be attributed to the Venerable's intercession. Finally, a second miracle is needed for canonization. Dr. Ambrosi said, "The Church's criteria for accepting a miracle are very rigorous."

When Will the Process Begin?

Although much work has been going on to gather archival materials, and assign responsibilities for the work of the cause, the first step of the process will be the solemn opening. The opening of the cause for Sister Marie is now scheduled for Friday evening, January 21, 2011, at 6:00 p.m. in the Cathedral of the Immaculate

Conception in Kansas City. Everyone is invited to attend this historic event. A number of the family members of Sister Marie have been invited. As the local bishop I will receive the oaths of the postulator, the members of the Tribunal who will gather all the materials, and the Historical and Theological Commissions who will help in evaluating the materials. Sister Marie seems to have been a holy woman who lived her life humbly in God's service. Please pray for God's blessing on our work. A prayer that was written a number of years ago in thanksgiving to God for Sister Marie is provided here.

We thank God for giving us the privilege of
Sister Marie de Mandat-Grancey.
Through her great generosity
she acquired the property at Ephesus,
the home of Mary and Saint John the Evangelist.
We ask God and Sister Marie
to continue to bless the cornerstone given to her.
"Around this cornerstone we build our faith
and the powers of darkness will not prevail."
We pray for God's will to be completely fulfilled
through the intercession of Sister Marie.
Amen.

HOMILY AT VESPERS OF THE BLESSED MOTHER

Ceremonies for the Opening of the Cause
of the Beatification and Canonization of
Servant of God Sister Marie de Mandat-Grancey, D.C.
January 21, 2011
Cathedral of the Immaculate Conception

Most Reverend Robert W. Finn
Bishop of Kansas City-St. Joseph

Your Excellencies,
Brother Priests and Deacons,
Esteemed Religious,
Particularly Members of the Vincentian Congregation
    and Daughters of Charity,
Family Members of Sister Marie,
Friends in Christ all,

The Blessed Anne Catherine Emmerich retold her mystical experiences of the life of the Blessed Virgin, describing in astounding detail the little stone house which overlooked the Bay at Ephesus. These accounts stirred the heart of Sister Marie de Mandat-Grancey, who already loved our Blessed Mother deeply. Sister Marie prevailed over the skepticism of her Vincentian co-workers, persuading the scholarly priests to scour the hot dusty slopes of Nightingale Mountain. Mary herself, it seemed, refreshed the seekers in the cool waters of a spring God had first provided for the Mother of Jesus and St. John the Evangelist.

Fathers Poulin and Jung were compelled by the sincerity and humility of Sister Marie, the holiness they saw in her and which draws us together tonight in this unlikely place to ask God's grace and blessing on a new journey: the study of Sister Marie's life and work.

Adele Louise Marie de Mandat-Grancey, as a young lady, determined to leave the world and the family she loved dearly. She wanted to be among the simple maids she had observed in the streets of Paris, the Daughters of Charity of St. Vincent DePaul. At Rue du Bac, where Our Lady of the Miraculous Medal had appeared to Catherine Laboure, she was formed more fully in the humility and generous faith that was, early on, a hallmark of her life. Near Paris she cared for orphans. She gathered youth in the catechesis of the Children of Mary. When the need was great she went to Turkey, and in time, was pressed into service as Superior.

When God had prepared her, He acquired her will and her heart so that the gift of Meryem Ana Evi, Mary's House, could be revealed to the world. Sister Marie acquired the property with the help of her family, and she and her Vincentian spiritual fathers carried forward the excavations and restorations. They prayed there and walked the path of the Cross which was once traversed by the Lady of Sorrows herself. Today it is visited by Popes, and it is the place of prayer and devotion to millions of children of Mary each year: Christians and Muslims together. They adorn its walkways with their petitions to the Mother of God, *Theotokos,* and to the Lady of the Koran.

In the humility characteristic of her Order, it seems that the foundress of Mary's House, never published a book or signed her name to any teaching, but her spirit of prayer and courageous determination endures nearly a century after her death. After world wars, and cultural and political upheavals in Turkey, admiration for this strong holy woman, Sister Marie, has persisted.

Half a world away, in Kansas City, Missouri, we also have heard her story, and now we seek to fulfill the mandate of the Church and to satisfy the hunger of God's people for saintly models and friends in every age and place.

Our Evening Prayer is a song to God in honor of Mary. In the fullness of time she bore the Savior. At the foot of Jesus' Cross she became our Mother. Under the care of John, she lived her last years on earth in the little stone house near Ephesus. There the Virgin Mother received the Eucharist from the apostle's hands. Her daily devotion was the *Via Crucis* which, according to Anne Catherine Emmerich, she marked on the hill beyond the house. Along that path she would finally be carried by the apostles, laid lovingly in a tomb corresponding to the sepulcher of Jerusalem, only to be assumed body and soul into Heaven and crowned before the Most Holy Trinity.

Three years ago, I too knelt in that holy place and felt I had arrived at our Mother's home. On that same trip I went to nearby Izmir, and visited with His Excellency Archbishop Ruggero Franceschini. I could see his love for Smyrna, and for the ancient Basilicas in Ephesus where more than 1500 years before the bishops of the Church affirmed definitively the profession of the faithful who kept a torchlit vigil in the streets and made the great proclamation of the Council of Ephesus: Holy

Mary Mother of God, *Theotokos!*

Archbishop Franceschini, carrying the cultural challenges and political turmoil part and parcel of his historic See, expressed deep affection for the holy house and admiration for its founder, Sister Marie de Mandat-Grancey. Two years later he would ask me to take the Cause in his stead, a request that was hard to refuse when requested by his good predecessor and envoy, Archbishop Bernardini. Let us offer fervent prayers for Archbishop Franceschini and the Church in Turkey. While I accept this privilege on behalf of the Diocese of Kansas City-St. Joseph, I pledge that if God's will unfolds in accord with our prayer and work—we will, in a sense, give Sister Marie back, not only to France, or to Turkey, or to the United States, but to the world, as a friend and intercessor.

It is a joy and honor for me, and I know also for Archbishop Joseph Naumann of Kansas City, Kansas, and Bishop Raymond Boland, Emeritus of this diocese, to pray in this sanctuary with the Archbishop Emeritus of Izmir, His Excellency Archbishop Giuseppe Bernardini, who himself has done so much to shepherd this effort. *Tante Grazie e Benvenuto,* Monsignore Bernardini!

We also wish to welcome Mrs. Madelaine Kunz, the associate and representative of Dr. Andrea Ambrosi, whose nomination as postulator has been confirmed by the Vatican's Congregation for the Causes of Saints, and whose reputation as a brilliant and dedicated churchman is well established by his work on so many such Processes. Welcome, Madelaine. Please assure Dr. Ambrosi of our prayers and esteem.

Today we are also honored and happy to have among us some of the family of Sister Marie de Mandat-Grancey. Baron and Baroness Jacques and Rosario de Mandat-Grancey, Baron Philippe de Mandat-Grancey, and Sister Elisabeth. *Chère famille de Soeur Marie. Merci d'être venus. Que Dieu vous bénisse, vous et vos familles.*

This week I have received a letter from the head of the de Grancey family. Unable to be with us, Count Adrien de Mandat-Grancey offered his prayerful support in our effort. "Concerning our eldest branch," he writes, "and all those of the family who will not be able to [come] to Kansas City, we will organize a collective prayer and Mass in the Holy Chapel of Rue du Bac, on the very same day you begin the ceremonies in Kansas City! Our joined prayers will be going simultaneously to the Lord from two continents!"

From the homeplace of Sr Marie I have received other messages of support: from His Excellency Roland Minnerath, Archbishop of Dijon; from Sister Evelyne Franc, Superior General of the Daughters of Charity. From France, and from Turkey, and from the heart of the United States we are joined in prayer for this blessed commission.

I also wish to acknowledge and thank one of the many who have worked so hard to spread the story of God's providence through the example of Sister Marie. I welcome Mrs. Erin Von Uffel, who first introduced me to the holy Servant of God. To Erin, and her steady co-worker Lorraine Fusaro, welcome, and we are grateful for your zeal and your faith. I made that first trip with members of the family of George B. Quatman, founder of the

American Society of Ephesus. Bill Quatman and Georgia Quatman Lynch continue to do so much to support and promote the holy sites, and are a great blessing to our Diocese.

It is a joy to greet the Daughters of Charity who have come today. You and our other Religious—there are so many here tonight—have yet another beautiful example in Sister Marie. And I would be remiss if I didn't acknowledge the presence of our Vincentian priests who have long served in our Diocese; particular greetings to Vincentian Fr. Carl Schulte, who is a biographer of Sister Marie. Thank you, Father, for your very important contribution.

In the Ceremony following Vespers, I will call forward and receive the oath of the Tribunal assigned to conduct this Process and the various commission members and assistants who will carry forward this important work. Thank you all, in advance, for your generous service. What you do will bring many significant graces to our Diocese.

Dear friends, the Evening Prayer of the Church echoes the Song of Mary and resonates in every place and time. May God receive our prayer tonight, confirm what we do, and bring it to completion in conformity with His holy will. Holy Mary—Mother of God and our hope: Pray for us!

—Most Rev. Robert W. Finn

Above: (October, 2007), Annual Mass at the Council Church where Mary was declared "Mother of God in 431. (Left to right) Georgia Lynch, Bill Quatman, Fr. Vincenzo Succi, Most Rev. Robert Finn, Archbishop R. Franceschini, Erin von Uffel. *Below:* Kansas City, 1-21-11 Immediately following the Opening Ceremony. *Top:* (left to right) Sr. Elizabeth de Mandat-Grancey, Baron Philippe de Mandat-Grancey, Baron Jacques de Mandat-Grancey, Most Reverend Bishop Robert Finn, Rev. Carl Schulte, CM, Archbishop G. Bernardini, Lorraine Fusaro. *Bottom:* Baroness Rosario de Mandat-Grancey, Erin von Uffel, Ana Banon

Notes

CHAPTER ONE

1. de Mandat-Grancey Family Archives.
2. Pope Gregory XI, "HST 260 DOC 24: Gregory XI, Papal Bull against John Wycliffe 1376." WCCNET.EDU. Fordham University, n.d. Web. 4 Jan 2011. http://courses.wccnet.edu/~jrush/260source24.htm
3. Newman C. Eberhardt, C.M., *A Summary of Catholic History* (New York: B. Herder Book Co., 1961), 756.
4. "He left Avignon on 13 September, 1376, boarded the ship at Marsailles on 2 October, and came by way of Genoa to Corneto on 6 December. Here he remained until arrangements were made in Rome concerning its future government. On 13 January, 1377, he left at Corneto, landed Ostia on the following day, and sailed up the Tiber to the monastery of San Paolo, from where he solemnly made his entrance into Rome on 17 January" (Michael Ott, "Pope Gregory XI," *Catholic Encyclopedia:* http://www.catholicity.com/encyclopedia/g/ gregory_xi,pope.html).

CHAPTER TWO

1. Sister Marie's childhood Catechism notebook; self-composed prayer, 1850.

2. A piece of female headwear especially popular in the 15th to 17th century—a type of wimple consisting of a large starched piece of white cloth folded upwards to create the resemblance of horns (French: *cornes*). It was the head piece of the Daughters of Charity until 1964.

3. Sister Marie's childhood Catechism notebook; self-composed prayer, 1847.

CHAPTER FOUR

1. Sister Marie's childhood Catechism notebook; self-composed prayer, 1847.

2. *Bulletin des Enfants de Marie* (The Bulletin of the Children of Mary) of Smyrna, issues of the months of July, August, and September 1915, pp. 8-9.

CHAPTER FIVE

1. Sister Marie's childhood Catechism notebook; self-composed prayer, 1847.

CHAPTER SIX

1. Conferences of Saint Vincent de Paul to the Daughters of Charity, Conference 11, June 1642, p. 63.

CHAPTER SEVEN

1. *Ephesus: Last Residence of the Virgin Mary, The Revelations, The Excavations, The Ruins, The Pilgrimages.* Countances, Editions Notre-Dame, 1956.

CHAPTER EIGHT

1. Sister Marie's childhood Catechism notebook; self-composed prayer, 1850.

2. *Bulletin des Enfants de Marie,* p. 4.

3. Ibid., 9.

4. Ibid., 6.

5. Ibid., 9.

CHAPTER NINE

1. Sister Marie's childhood Catechism notebook; self-composed prayer, 1847.

2. Eugene P. Poulin, *The Holy Virgin's House; The True Story of Its Discovery* (Istanbul: Arikan Yayinlari Tic. San. Ltd. Sti., 1999), 18.

3. Eugene P. Poulin, *The Holy Virgin's House; The True Story of Its Discovery* (Istanbul: Arikan Yayinlari Tic. San. Ltd. Sti., 1999), p. 12-16.

4. Eugene P. Poulin, The Holy Virgin's House; The True Story of Its Discovery (Istanbul: Arikan Yayinlari Tic. San. Ltd. Sti., 1999), p. 18.

5. The title of the Provincial Superior of the Vincentian Fathers and Brothers is "Visitor" because he has the responsibility to visit each of their houses or missions and give whatever assistance he can to help cultivate among them the charism of Saint Vincent de Paul.

6. Poulin, *The Holy Virgin's House,* 48.

CHAPTER TEN

1. Poulin, *The Holy Virgin's House,* 21.
2. Ibid., 38.
3. This stone given to Father Jung by Andreas, and others from the same place behind Mary's House, are presently on display in Turkey's Museum of Natural History.
4. Poulin, *The Holy Virgin's House,* 41.
5. Ibid., 42.
6. Ibid., 43.
7. Ibid.
8. Ibid., 46.
9. Find the lyrics to this hymn at the introduction to this chapter.
10. "The Mass is ended."

CHAPTER ELEVEN

1. A brimless felt cap with a flat top, usually red and ornamented with a black tassel, worn by men in Egypt and some other countries of the Middle East. It was formerly the national headdress of the Turks.
2. A governor of a town or particular district of country in the Turkish dominions; also, in some places, a prince.

CHAPTER THIRTEEN

1. Poulin, *The Holy Virgin's House,* 19-29.

CHAPTER FOURTEEN

1. p. d. l. m.—priest of the mission, that is, a member of the

Congregation of the Mission, or a Vincentian priest.

2. Rev. Bernard F. Deutsch, *Our Lady of Ephesus* (Milwaukee: Bruce Publishing Company, 1965), 91.

3. Poulin, *The Holy Virgin's House,* 70.

CHAPTER FIFTEEN

1. Constitution 30d: The Daughters of Charity retain their natural rights to inheritance and to legal and testamentary succession, as well as to the ownership and management of personal goods. With the permission of the competent authority, they may use the income accruing for them for what are commonly termed "good work." Without special permission, they may make the necessary expenditures for the preservation of these goods and dispose of them by will. To use personal goods and make and contract loans, they need the permission of the Superior General or of the Provincial Director. The authorization of the Sister Servant suffices for the cases specified at the Provincial level, in agreement with the Visitatrix and the Director.

2. Poulin, *The Holy Virgin's House,* 81.

3. Deutsch, *Our Lady of Ephesus,* 20.

CHAPTER SIXTEEN

1. Poulin, *The Holy Virgin's House,* 81.

2. Ven. Anne Catherine Emmerich, *The Life of the Blessed Virgin Mary* (Charlotte, North Carolina: TAN Books, 1970), 351.

CHAPTER EIGHTEEN

1. J. Euzet, C.M., *Historique de la Maison de la Sainte Vierge*

pres D'Ephese (1891-1961) (Istanbul: Notre-Dame D'Ephese, 1961). See Appendix A.

2. For more detailed accounts of the excavations, including specific events, dates, people, and findings, please refer to Father Poulin's journal, *The Holy Virgin's House; The True Story of Its Discovery* (1999) and Father Deutsch's book, *Our Lady of Ephesus* (1965).

3. Father Lobry was the Provincial Superior of the Vincentian Fathers in Turkey during this period of time.

CHAPTER NINETEEN

1. *Bulletin des Enfants de Marie.*
2. "Meryem" is the Turkish form of Mary.

CHAPTER TWENTY

1. *Ephesus: House of the Most Holy Virgin, Or, Place of the "Dormition,"* Izmir, January 26, 1951, with approval of the Archbishop of Izmir, Monsignor Joseph Descuffi, C.M.
2. Letter from Father Fiat instructing Father Poulin.

CHAPTER TWENTY-ONE

1. The Turkish name for Mary's house.
2. Deutsch, *Our Lady of Ephesus,* 69.

CHAPTER TWENTY-TWO

1. The Koran (Ch. III, 42-63).

2. While Catholics are forbidden from praying in common with non-Catholics because of the risk of indifferentism, Catholics can and should pray for the conversion of non-Catholics. God is also using Mary's House to convert Muslims and other non-Catholics as Catholic pilgrims bear witness to the true Faith.

CHAPTER TWENTY-TWO

1. Pope Benedict XVI, Papal Homily at Mary's House Ephesus, Turkey, November 29, 2006

CHAPTER TWENTY-THREE

1. Poulin, *The Holy Virgin's House,* 71.
2. Euzet, *Historique,* 110. See Appendix A.
3. Poulin, *The Holy Virgin's House,* 81.
4. *Bulletin des Enfants de Marie,* 109.
5. Ibid., 4.

CHAPTER TWENTY-FOUR

1. Euzet, *Historique,* 40-41. See Appendix A.

CHAPTER TWENTY-FIVE

1. Euzet, *Historique,* 123. See Appendix A.
2. Joseph Euzet, C.M.., *Letter: To our very honorable Father William Slattery, Historic Retrospective and Mediation; The Hand of God in the Work of Panaya Kapulu,* Annuls of the Congregation of the Mission, undated.
3. Ibid.

4. Ibid.

5. Ibid.

CHAPTER TWENTY-SIX

1. Deutsch, *Our Lady of Ephesus*, 24.

FINAL NOTES

1. http://arama.hurriyet.com.tr/arsivnews.aspx?id=14241539. President Abdullah Gul spent one day in Izmir remembering his childhood, far from the political atomosphere of Ankara. The President and his wife, Hayrunnisa Gul, first pilgrimaged to Mother Mary's house located in the district of Seljuk. The Gul couple drank water from the fountains found in the house's garden and believed to be sacred. The Presidential couple first tasted water from the "Love" fountain then from the other fountains. Abudullah Gul requested, "God grant us health, forgiveness and goodness." Afterwards, Gul and his wife toured the ancient city of Efes. The Gul couple walked the streets of Kuretler and Mermer hand in hand; they took a sovenir phot in front of the historic Celsus Library. Afterwards, they toured the village of Sirinic. The Gul couple met the thick crowd eager to show their love—and many times they had their pictures taken (translated by Amelia Gallagher).

2. http://www.zaman.com.tr/haber.do?haberno=966571& keyfield=6D657279656D20616E61

At mother Mary's, He Lit a Candle

President Abdullah Gul and his wife Hayrunnisa Gul spent a romantic day in the ancient city of Efes.

Yesterday the Gul couple landed at the airport of Izmir's Selcuk district in a DAP plane. The president and his wife first pilgrimaged to mother Mary's house. Closed off to the press, the president and his wife lit two candles. This is the first time a president of the Republic of Turkey has pilgrimaged to Mother Mary's house. While the president and his wife were leaving, a student wanted to raise the issue of SBS—and the president said he would look into it. Later, the Gul couple toured the ancient city of Efes, hand in hand and arm in arm.

The president and his wife, standing side by side learned about the fountains of health, love and wealth. The president and his wife, drank first from the love fountain, then from the other fountains. Gul stated his hope that "God give everyone health, forgiveness and goodness." Tourists took pictures of President Gul, and he shook their hands and posed smiling.

Touring the Hadrian Tapinak and Kuretler streets in the ancient city of Efes, President Gul and his wife posed in front of the Celsus theater. During their tour, the president and his wife noticed 5 female guards. The Gul couple, after tourning the ancient city of Efes, visited Selcuk's Sirince village, known for its wine and organic produce. There they had lunch at an Inn (translated by Amelia Gallagher).

Epilogue

1. Archives de Mandat-Grancey. The Countess was born Eugenie de Cordoue.

APPENDIX B

1. Robert Finn, "Sr. Marie de Mandat-Grancey: Kansas City-St. Joseph Diocese Studies Her Life and Work." *Catholic Key* (Diocese of Kansas City-St. Joseph) 19 Nov. 2010, Vol. 42, No. 38, p: 4, 5, 21-23.

BIBLIOGRAPHY

Annals of the Congregation of the Mission; Inspiring Letters written by Priests of the Congregation of the Mission and the Daughters of Charity. (Internal Seminary) Paris, 1884.

Bulletin des Enfants de Marie (Bulletin of the Children of Mary) of Smyrna. Excerpts from issues of July, August, and September 1915.

Constitutions and Statutes of the Daughters of Charity of St. Vincent de Paul. (English Translation).—Periodic changes made with each General Assembly of the Daughters of Charity. 1983.

Deutsch, Rev. Bernard F. *Our Lady of Ephesus.* Milwaukee: Bruce Publishing Company, 1965.

De Paul, St. Vincent. *Conferences to the Daughters of Charity.* Private Circulation only. Trans. Joseph Leonard, C.M. London: Burns, Oates, and Washbourne, Ltd., 1938-1940.

De Mandat-Grancey Family Library and Archives, Dijon, France.

Dirvin, Joseph I. *Louise de Marillac.* New York: Doubleday and Company, 1970.

Eberhardt, C.M., Newman. *A Summary of Catholic History.* St. Louis: B. Herder Book Co., 1961.

Emmerich, Anne Catherine. *The Life of the Blessed Virgin Mary: From the Visions of Ven. Anne Catherine Emmerich.* Trans. Sir Michael Palairet. Rockford, IL: TAN Books and Publishers, Inc., 1970.

Ephesus—Last Residence of the Virgin Mary. Coutances: Editions Notre Dame, 1956.

Euzet, C.M., J. *Historique de la Maison de la Sainte Vierge pres D'Ephese* (1891-1961). Istanbul: Notre-Dame D'Ephese, 1961.

Hess, Andrew. "Turkey." *World Book Encylopedia.* Vol. 19. Chicago: World Book, Inc., 1998.

Poulin, Rev. Eugene P., *The Holy Virgin's House: The True Story of Its Discovery.* Comp. Rev. Philibert De la Chaise. Trans. Ivi Richini. Ed. Georgina Ozer. Istanbul, Turkey: Arikan Yayinlari, 1999.

Quatman, George B. *House of Our Lady, "Meryem Ana Evi" The Story of the Virgin Mary's Last Years.* Centennial Edition 1891-1991. Rev. Joseph B. Quatman. Lima, OH: C2, The American Society of Ephesus Inc. 1991.

Quatman, William G. *American Society of Ephesus: Yorghi's Collection.* Marian Library/International Marian Research Institute, University of Dayton, Ohio.

Roman, C.M., Fr. Jose Maria. *St. Vincent de Paul: A Biography.* English Edition first published for the Congregation of the Mission. London: Fox Communications and Publications.

Senior. "Ephesus or Jerusalem, The Temple of the Virgin Mary." *Bulletins of the Children of Mary,* Smyrna: August–September 1915.

Vereb, C.P., Rev. Jerome M. and Erin von Uffel. *Cornerstone: The Story of Sister Marie de Mandat-Grancey,* D.C., A Pilgrim House Production, The House of Mary at Ephesus.

Vincentian Archives, Maison-Mere of the Congregation of the Mission. Paris, France.

"Vincentian Marian Youth History". Vincentian Marian Youth Association. 27 January 2008, http://www.vmy.us/history.htm

Approbation

The Third Order Regular Province of the Most Sacred Heart of Jesus in the United States was honored during the ninety-ninth General Chapter of the Order when a member of the Province, Fr. John Boccella, was elected as the one hundred and third Minister General on July 16, 1947. He was to hold the office of Minister General in the Order for eighteen years. After his tenure he was consecrated bishop on April 17, 1968, and given the Archdiocese of Izmir, Turkey, by Pope Paul VI–the diocese in which Ephesus and the House of Mary are located.

Fr. John had a special devotion to the House of Mary and actively supported its restoration and its position as an important place of worship and pilgrimage. His dedication was recognized by the Holy Father, Pope John Paul II in 1978 when Fr. John retired from active ministry and was given the title of Titular Archbishop of Ephesus.

It is with this history in mind that I read The Life of Sr. Marie de Mandat-Grancey and Mary's House in Ephesus by Rev. Carl G. Schulte, C.M., about the important place that Sr. Marie de Mandat-Grancey played in the discovery of Mary's House in 1891, in its purchase in 1892, and her subsequent work to make it such a wonderful place of pilgrimage until her death in 1915. As Fr. Schulte points out so well, Sr. Marie's love and devotion of the Blessed Mother was so profound and so clearly expressed that she touched the hearts of Orthodox Christians, Roman Catholics, and even Muslims–and all those who honor Mary's important role in salvation history.

In these times, in which the tension between East and West–between Christians and Muslims–seems to be growing ever more intense the witness, example, and intercession of Sr. Marie is so desperately needed. Together let us pray with her in honor of Mary, the Mother of Holy Hope, in sincere hope and longing that the Lord will touch us all with His peace.

Fraternally in Christ, His Holy Mother,
and Saint Francis of Assisi,

(Most Rev.) Michael J. Higgins, TOR
Third Order Regular of Saint Francis of Penance
Minister General

This book, carefully researched and written, is an inspiration. First we hear about the finding and protecting of Our Lady's house in Ephesus, a place that gives hope for the possibility of peace and mutual respect between Christians and Muslims as they honor Mary and pray at this important shrine. We also hear the story of the extraordinary and holy life of Sister Marie de Mandat-Grancey whose humility and single-mindedness will surely give joy to those who come to know of her. Let us pray that Meryem Ana Evi becomes a place of peace and reconciliation.

✠ Reverend Francis Martin,
Founder, The Word Proclaimed ministry.

About the Author

Fr. Carl G. Schulte was born in 1920, five years after the death of Sr. Marie de Mandat-Grancey. He was ordained as a Vincentian priest on May 30, 1948 and was given his first assignment in the China missions. The Communist occupation of his mission in Hokow, Kiangsi forced its closing a few months after his arrival in 1948. From there he was sent to St. John's Seminary and then the new Assumption Seminary, both in San Antonio, Texas. Next, he helped with the opening of St. Vincent de Paul Seminary in Lemont, IL, and then went on to Cardinal Glennon College in St. Louis; St. Vincent's College in Cape Girardeau, MO; and St.

During his last assignment, he began service on the provincial council and became the director of the Vincentian Foreign Mission Society. He was also asked to restart the Vincentian parish missions which had ceded their place some years before to the Miraculous Medal Novena program. In 1981, he was appointed provincial director of the Daughters of Charity for the East Central Province, an office he held for twelve years. He retired in 1993 and acts as something of an unofficial chaplain to the Franciscan Sisters of the Holy Eucharist in Independence, MO, on whose property the Vincentian Parish Mission Center is located. He says Sunday Mass for them and is available for spiritual direction for the sisters, and some clergy and laity.

Describing his priestly life, he says, "As I look back on my years in the priesthood I learned that one assignment led to another—to an assignment I would not have chosen—but in doing it I learned why God had put me in it. That has brought me great satisfaction in my priesthood. I thank God for it." And of His most recent "assignment," that of writing The Life of Sr. Marie de Mandat-Grancey and Mary's House in Ephesus, he says, "I believe that Our Lady had a hand in connecting me with the promoter for the cause of the beatification of Sr. Marie de Mandat-Grancey, a Daughter of Charity [who requested that this book be written] . . . and I have confidence Sr. Marie will be beatified soon."

Rev. Carl G. Schulte, CM

1. **Cut carefully inside the dotted lines.**
2. **Lining up the edges, fold prayercard in the center vertically.**

Or for a printable PDF of this prayercard, visit www.tanbooks.com

July 29, 1891 Mary's House, built by St. John the Apostle, was discovered. Archeologists identified the ruins of a 1st century A.D. house with a Church from the 4th century A.D. having been built over it. On October 21, 1891, Sr. Marie received permission from Fr. Fiat (Superior of Vincentians) to purchase the property in her name which occurred on Nov. 15, 1892. Sr. Marie restored the House making it a place of pilgrimage for all people, especially Christians and Muslims. During restoration three stones from the hearth, built by the Apostles, were found. One of these stones (cornerstone) was given to the de Mandat-Grancey Family Chapel in France to confirm her holy life, work and devotion to God and the Blessed Virgin Mary, uniquely identifying Sr. Marie with this primitive Apostolic community. All of our recent Popes have visited the House. Pope Paul VI on July 26, 1967, Pope John Paul II celebrated Mass Nov. 30,1979 and Pope Benedict XVI celebrated Mass on Nov. 29, 2006. Sr. Marie lived a life of detachment, dedication, virtue, obedience and charity; she died on May 31,1915. Her Cause of Beatification was opened on January 21, 2011.

Carl Schulte, C.M.

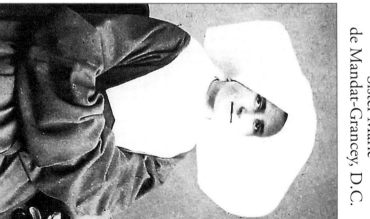

September 13, 1837– May 31, 1915

SERVANT OF GOD

Sister Marie
de Mandat-Grancey, D.C.

MERYEM ANA EVI (DOMUS MARIAE)
Ephesus, Turkey

MARY'S HOME

Sister Marie de Mandat-Grancey, Daughter of Charity of St. Vincent de Paul was born of a noble and holy family in the Diocese of Dijon, France, Sept. 13th, 1837. She desired from a young age to serve God with all her heart and answered her vocation. (Postulant, May 27, 1857, First Vows, Sept. 27, 1862.) At the end of her second assignment in France she was inspired to find the House of Mary in Ephesus, Turkey. At that time Pope Leo XIII requested missionary assistance in Asia Minor. Sr. Marie responded, in 1886 she served at the French Naval Hospital in Smyrna, Turkey, appointed superior in 1890. While in Smyrna she encouraged an expedition to find the House of Mary, Mother of Jesus, headed by Vincentian Priests.

We thank God
for giving us the privilege of
Sister Marie de Mandat-Grancey.

Through her great generosity
She acquired the property at Ephesus,
The home of Mary and
Saint John the Evangelist.

We ask God and Sister Marie
To continue to Bless the cornerstone
given to her, "Around this cornerstone
We build our faith And the powers of
Darkness will not prevail."

We pray for God's will to be
Completely fulfilled through the
Intercession of Sister Marie.
Amen